THE POLITICS OF THE BUDGETARY PROCESS

THE POLITICS OF THE BUDGETARY PROCESS

Fourth Edition

AARON WILDAVSKY

Little, Brown and Company
Boston   Toronto

Library of Congress Cataloging in Publication Data

Wildavsky, Aaron B.
    The politics of the budgetary process.

    Bibliography: p.
    Includes index.
    1. Budget — United States. I. Title.
HJ2051.W485 1984   353.0072′221   83–13588
ISBN 0–316–94041–0

Copyright © 1984 by Aaron Wildavsky

Library of Congress Catalog Card No. 83–13588

ISBN 0-316-94041-0

9 8 7 6 5 4 3 2

HAL

*Published simultaneously in Canada
by Little, Brown & Company (Canada) Limited*

Printed in the United States of America

The author gratefully acknowledges the permission of *New York Affairs* to reproduce portions of his "Policy Analysis Is What Information Systems Are Not," IV *New York Affairs* (Spring 1977) No. 2, copyright 1977. The author also gratefully acknowledges the permission of The American Society for Public Administration to reproduce substantial parts of his "Political Implications of Budgetary Reform," XXI *Public Administration Review* (Autumn 1961) pp. 183–190; "The Political Economy of Efficiency: Cost-Benefit Analysis, Systems Analysis, and Program Budgeting," XXVI *Public Administration Review* (December 1966) pp. 292–310; and "Rescuing Policy Analysis from PPBS," XXIX *Public Administration Review* (March/April 1969) pp. 189–202.

PREFACE TO
THE FOURTH EDITION

No book today, including this one, conveys an adequate understanding of the federal budgetary process. We all lag behind events. But the difficulty goes deeper: because no one can say whither the process is tending, no one can be sure it will not move back to where it used to be. Even as we are celebrating the changes that have taken place, newer changes are proposed that could take us back to our starting point in 1964, when the first edition of *The Politics of the Budgetary Process* came out. If budgeting has been going in circles, it is crucial to try to get our bearings.

It is not that we lack good material on budgeting. On the contrary, there is more and better than ever before. Anyone interested in an up-to-date description of steps in the federal budgetary process can find excellent guides.[1] And talented teachers will help the person who wants to know about new sources of spending or new studies of the process itself.[2] There

[1] Stanley E. Collender, *The Guide to the Federal Budget*, Fiscal 1983 Edition (Washington, D.C.: Northeast-Midwest Institute, 1982). See also *Federal Budget Report*, published by Federal Budget Report, Inc., Stanley E. Collender, Publisher; *Inside O.M.B.*, a biweekly report on the Office of Management and Budget (Washington, D.C.: Inside Washington Publishers); and continuous reporting in the *National Journal* and the *Congressional Quarterly*.

[2] See Dennis Ippolito, *Congressional Spending: A Twentieth Century Fund Report* (Ithaca, N.Y.: Cornell University Press, 1981).

are outstanding studies of the Budget Reform Act of 1974.[3] Tendencies inherent in the budgetary process both before[4] and after 1974 [5] have been analyzed now with greater clarity. A fine beginning has been made on the distribution of expenditures (outlays) among geographic areas.[6] Soon, no doubt, books will appear on loans and loan guarantees, tax expenditures, off-budget expenditures, and the like. The expanded bibliography in this edition gives some sense of how much is being done.

I, too, try to keep up with the times. Old Chapter 7 on the Congress has been thoroughly revised to consider whether the federal budgetary process is biased toward higher spending. In a new Chapter 8, I discuss how discontent with the reformed process has led both to important changes, like "reconciliation" (aggregating taxing and spending items requiring cuts so that they have to be voted on as a whole), and to proposals for radical change — such as making the First Budget Resolution binding, or even amending the Constitution to impose limits on total spending. Consideration of proposals item by item is giving way to fitting programs within prescribed amounts for all spending. Though all this, I hope, is to the good, it can only follow events that proceed at a quicker pace than ours in recording them.

[3] Allen Schick, *Congress and Money: Budgeting, Spending and Taxing* (Washington, D.C.: Urban Institute, 1980); and Joel Haveman, *Congress and the Budget* (Bloomington: Indiana University Press, 1978).

[4] John P. Crecine, David C. Mowery, and Mark S. Kamlet, "Presidential Management of Budgetary and Fiscal Policymaking," xcv *Political Science Quarterly* (Fall 1980) pp. 395–425; Mark S. Kamlet and David C. Mowery, "The Budgetary Base in Federal Resource Allocation," xxiv *American Journal of Political Science* (November 1980) pp. 804–821; Kamlet and Mowery, "Bureaucrats, the President, and the Growth of Government, 1955–1972," Working Paper HBS 82-44 (January 1982).

[5] Lance, LeLoup, *The Fiscal Congress: Legislative Control of the Budget* (Westport, Conn.: Greenwood Press, 1980).

[6] Thomas J. Anton, Jerry P. Cawley, Kevin L. Kramer, *Moving Money: An Empirical Analysis of Federal Expenditure Patterns* (Cambridge, Mass.: Oelgeschlager, Gunn and Hain, 1980).

Even seemingly routine parts of this book reflect the flux in federal budgeting. The first three editions provided charts of the budget process, showing the times at which various steps were to occur. The chart for the congressional process has been omitted because its schedule is in flux, because it depends on the Chief Executive's, which cannot be determined, and because no one knows exactly who reconciliation will involve or when it will take place. I have abandoned charting the executive process, for calls to OMB revealed that it has no charts of its own, because it now keeps to no regular schedule. The Carter Administration did give spending targets for fiscal 1982 (the fiscal year refers to the year ahead) to agencies in July 1980, as the old charts suggest. The Reagan Administration undid all this for the fiscal 1983 budget; OMB did not give agencies targets until September 1981. For fiscal 1984, OMB did not provide written targets at all; instead, agencies were orally advised to use the fiscal '84 estimates that were in the fiscal '83 budget. Get it?

The third edition also had a fairly extensive bibliography. Yet the literature on budgeting has mushroomed (much like the budget), while the new problems of controlling spending totals make new areas of literature — American political culture, comparative studies of public expenditure — relevant. We cannot hope the new bibliography is exhaustive. Literature on health costs alone, though relevant to the policy problem of controlled spending, is extensive. Instead of trying to get it to include everything, we should view the bibliography as an introduction, not a summary.

The crux of the matter is the degree of stability of the foundations on which the post-World War II budgetary process was built; or, if the stones already have crumbled, whether the foundations can (or should) be rebuilt. I plan to help answer these questions by exploring the assumptions underlying the budgetary process described in this book. Changes in behavior may then be ascribed to alterations in the premises of decision on which budgeting is based.

Were I back again in 1962–63 writing *The Politics of the Budgetary Process*, I would look at eighteenth- and nineteenth-century origins of expenditure control. I did not do so then because at the time these norms were so much a part of the budgetary air as to be unnoticeable. It had taken centuries of conflict to institutionalize norms that everyone, by my time, had come to take for granted.[7] No one then imagined budgets that would not last a year or were permanently unbalanced or whose accounts were not comparable. That the budget should be approved annually by the legislature implied that agencies would get what the budget said; that revenues and expenditures would match implied accepted limits on taxing and spending; and that there should be a comprehensive series of accounts implied that revenues went to the Central Treasury, and that an expenditure in one place equaled that of a similar face amount in another. None of this (see "Prologue: The Transformation of Budgetary Norms") is true today.

The decay of the norm of comprehensiveness could hardly be better illustrated than by looking at the Federal Financing Bank (FFB). The ensuing description by Alice M. Rivlin, Director, and Robert W. Hartman, Senior Analyst for Budget Process, both of the Congressional Budget Office, is the clearest I have been able to find:

> The FFB was created in 1974 to reduce the government's borrowing costs in financing the lending activities of federal agencies. Before that time, individual agencies would raise funds in capital markets by issuing their own notes of indebtedness. Now the FFB raises the funds for the agencies but in so doing causes direct loans to disappear from the budget. When credit is advanced as a direct loan, the unified budget records an outlay. A typical arrangement is for the agency to package its direct loans together as backing for

[7] Carolyn Webber and I are nearing completion of our *Expenditure and Taxation in Western History*, in which the genesis of these norms is discussed.

securities (called certificates of beneficial ownership or CBOs) that the agency sells to the FFB. Agency direct loans that are financed by the FFB are thus entirely off-budget and do not contribute to the unified budget deficit.

The FFB also plays a role in federally guaranteed loans. [See Table 1.] The FFB is allowed to lend directly to a private borrower if a federal agency guarantees the loan. In effect, such an arrangement converts a guaranteed loan into a direct loan from the government (FFB), but the loan is not recorded on budget and the Treasury has to borrow on behalf of the FFB.

In short, the existence of the FFB and its treatment in the unified budget means that direct lending can take place without affecting unified budget outlays or the federal deficit, which are the control aggregates for the Congressional budget process.[8]

How can spending be controlled through the budget when the budget does not contain much federal spending?

The latest budgetary reforms propose to do formally (by rewriting Congressional rules, by legislation, by constitutional amendment) what was previously done informally by acceptance of the norms of annualarity, balance, and comprehensiveness. It may be that these classic budgetary norms have collapsed because they no longer conform to the values of citizens or conditions of the welfare state. Should that be so, all efforts at artificial respiration are bound to be futile. Certainly, many who make these proposals, myself included,[9] are properly skeptical of efforts to reform humanity by requiring people to do good.

Were this criticism properly founded, *The Politics of the Budgetary Process* would no longer be descriptive and a whole new book, consonant with quite different assumptions, would

[8] Alice M. Rivlin and Robert W. Hartman, "Control of Federal Credit Under the Congressional Budget Process," Prepared for Toward a Reconstruction of Federal Budgeting, The Conference Board, December 2, 1982, pp. 10–11.

[9] See my *How to Limit Government Spending* (Berkeley: University of California Press, 1980).

TABLE 1

Federal participation in domestic credit markets, 1972–1981
(in billions of dollars)

Funds advanced in U.S. credit markets

| | *Total domestic credit* | *Direct loans* | | *Guaranteed loans* | *Government enterprise loans* | *Total federal credit* | *Federal % of total credit* |
		on-budget	*off-budget*				
1972	151.9	3.0	—	18.9	0.1	22.0	14.5%
1973	198.5	0.9	0.1	16.6	8.5	26.1	13.1%
1974	186.7	3.3	0.8	10.3	11.2	25.5	13.7%
1975	174.4	5.8	7.0	8.6	5.6	27.0	15.5%
1976	241.8	4.2	6.7	11.1	4.9	26.9	11.1%
Transition quarter	65.0	1.1	2.6	−0.1	3.1	6.7	10.3%
1977	310.8	2.6	9.0	13.5	11.7	36.7	11.8%
1978	378.9	8.6	11.2	13.4	25.2	58.4	15.4%
1979	412.9	6.0	13.6	25.2	28.1	72.9	17.7%
1980	342.5	9.5	14.7	31.6	24.1	79.9	23.3%
1981	407.8	5.2	20.9	28.0	32.4	86.5	21.2%

Source: Office of Management and Budget, *Special Analysis F* of The Budget of the United States Government, 1983 (Washington, D.C.: U.S. Government Printing Office, 1982) page 6, Table F-1.

Note: The "Total domestic credit" figure is nonfinancial sectors, excluding equities.

The definition of participation is not necessarily self-evident. For example, this table follows OMB in counting the full principal of a guaranteed loan, rather than the contingent liability. In previous budgets only the contingent liabilities were counted. The difference mainly applies to VA mortgage insurance.

"Funds advanced" is only one way of looking at the federal share of credit. An alternative would be to look at funds borrowed. Federal borrowing is a larger portion of total borrowing, in most years, than is federal lending of total lending. The difference is caused by the budget deficit. Since the deficit fluctuates and is a major source of borrowing, "Funds advanced" provides a better picture of the trend of policy over time.

have to be written. Should some of these reforms take hold, however, thus reestablishing the traditional norms that conveyed a sense of fixed limits, common concern, and yearly predictability, *The Politics* could be revised, without being totally rewritten, because its basic concepts would still ring true. That is why I conclude this fourth edition with a chapter on "Limits."

Looking at this book and reflecting on recent trends, I would say that the sections on calculation are as relevant, if not even more so, than before. As the annual budget becomes less and less predictable, uncertainty grows and with it an even greater need for aids to calculation. As major calculating devices (such as the guardianship role of the House Appropriations Committee) become weaker (so that the Committee becomes just another advocate), the ability of the participants to anticipate each other's behavior declines. With less that can be taken for granted, an agency's calculation of how much to ask for and Congressional calculation of what to give becomes more difficult.

By contrast, the sections on agency strategies for getting funds depend on conditions — trust among participants, ability to anticipate behavior, collective concern for totals, comparability of accounts — that no longer exist. Without limits — that is, much more for one agency or program does not mean much less for others — the feeling of being in the same boat, accepting the same sacrifices, won't last long. Similarly, a sense of "fair shares," essential to a feeling of being equitably treated, is hard to maintain when no one can say how much a loan guarantee or a tax expenditure is worth compared to an open-ended entitlement or just a regular appropriation. If the annual budget no longer is a predictor of events, so that participants cannot count on receiving whatever amount is included for them, they have less reason to moderate their demands for higher spending.

There is no end of irony. So far as I am aware, the substantial changes in the amounts, kinds, and devices of public spending that have taken place in the last two decades have arisen entirely from the cumulative effects of many small moves, no one of which was heralded as extraordinary in relation to the past. Score one for incrementalism. Recent efforts to roll back the rate of increase in spending, while exempting the military and the universal entitlements (such as Social Security and unemployment compensation), have led to cuts in means-tested entitlements (that is, food stamps) and general government. Despite the difficulties caused by these cuts, however, such reductions only nibble at the edges.[10] They do not reduce total spending. They do not do away with or significantly lessen loans or loan guarantees or entitlements, most payments to individuals (see Table 2), or any of the forms of spending outside the appropriations process or the budget.[11] Score two for incrementalism. But the last word is far from being in. To stop spending (in all its forms) from increasing faster than the growth of the economy can support it, radical reforms — such as constitutional spending limits or binding First Budget Resolutions — have received more support than anyone imagined a year or two ago. What, then, has happened to incrementalism? Just this: In order to get back to the golden age of incrementalism (where changes are small, alternatives resemble those of the past, and patterns of relationships among participants remain stable),[12] the budgetary norms that encouraged such behavior — norms of annualarity, balance, and comprehensiveness — have to be

[10] Some individual programs were reduced substantially. A detailed discussion of the effects on individual programs and on the budget as a whole may be found in John W. Ellwood, ed., *Reductions in United States Domestic Spending* (New Brunswick, N.J.: Transaction Books, 1982).

[11] See *Setting National Priorities: The 1983 Budget,* Joseph A. Pechman, ed. (Washington, D.C.: Brookings Institution, 1982).

[12] See M. A. H. Dempster and Aaron Wildavsky, "On Change: Or, There Is No Magic Size for an Increment," XXVII *Political Studies* (September 1979) pp. 371–389.

TABLE 2

Budget receipts and outlays, 1950–1981 (in millions of dollars)

Fiscal year	Budget receipts	Budget outlays	Surplus or deficit (−)	Surplus or deficit as % of outlays	Surplus or deficit % including off-budget outlays*
1950	39,485	42,587	−3,112	7.3%	
1951	51,646	45,546	+6,100	13.4%	
1952	66,204	67,721	−1,517	2.2%	
1953	69,574	76,107	−6,533	8.6%	
1954	69,719	70,890	−1,170	1.7%	
1955	65,469	68,509	−3,041	4.4%	
1956	74,547	70,460	+4,087	5.8%	
1957	79,990	76,741	+3,249	4.2%	
1958	79,636	82,575	−2,939	3.6%	
1959	79,249	92,104	−12,855	14.0%	
1960	92,492	92,223	+269	0.3%	
1961	94,389	97,795	−3,406	3.5%	
1962	99,676	106,813	−7,137	6.7%	
1963	106,560	111,311	−4,751	4.3%	
1964	112,662	118,584	−5,922	5.0%	
1965	116,833	118,430	−1,596	1.3%	
1966	130,856	134,652	−3,796	2.8%	
1967	148,906	157,608	−8,702	5.5%	
1968	152,973	178,134	−25,161	14.1%	
1969	186,882	183,645	+3,236	1.8%	
1970	192,807	195,652	−2,845	1.5%	
1971	187,139	210,172	−23,033	11.0%	
1972	207,309	230,681	−23,373	10.1%	
1973	230,799	245,647	−14,849	6.0%	6.1%
1974	263,224	267,912	−4,688	1.7%	2.3%
1975	279,090	324,245	−45,154	13.9%	16.0%
1976	298,060	364,473	−66,413	18.2%	19.8%
Transition quarter	81,232	94,188	−12,956	13.8%	15.4%
1977	355,559	400,506	−44,948	11.2%	13.1%
1978	399,561	448,368	−48,807	10.9%	12.9%
1979	463,302	490,997	−27,694	5.6%	8.0%
1980	517,112	576,675	−59,563	10.3%	12.5%
1981	599,272	657,204	−57,932	8.8%	11.6%

Source: Office of Management and Budget, *The Budget for Fiscal Year 1983* (Washington, D.C.: U.S. Government Printing Office, 1982) page 9–62, Table 23.

* "Off-budget entities'" outlays, as defined in the source table, are miniscule before 1973. The raw totals since 1973 may be found on the source table.

reinstituted. From where we once were, reinforcement of incrementalism required only more of the same. From where we are today, it turns out, reinstatement of incrementalism calls for radical change.

In any event, whether incremental or radical changes are needed, this is the last edition of the 1964 model of *The Politics of the Budgetary Process*. A few years from now, I expect to write a new book. Whether that volume will be essentially old wine in new bottles, or rather the product of a wholly new vintage, remains to be seen. In the meantime, amidst — or, better, because of — the flux surrounding the subject, budgeting has become more fun than ever, if not for practitioners, then at least for students. As I write, Congress is having difficulty (not so much in agreeing on the budget, which is out of the question, but in) passing a continuing resolution to allow last year's spending levels to continue lest government grind to a halt for lack of money. And it is by no means certain that Congress will be able to agree on a budget resolution — the heart of the reformed process — in 1983. If budgeting appears normless, that may just be because it is.

PROLOGUE
TRANSFORMATION
OF BUDGETARY NORMS

TALK ABOUT horse-and-buggy thinking in a machine age! Though governments in industrial democracies are approaching the twenty-first century, they still depend upon nineteenth-century budgetary norms inapplicable to current circumstances. The legacy of centuries of budgetary reform upon which expenditure control is still based — the norms of annualarity, balance, and comprehensiveness — have been shattered beyond recognition. What is more, the assumptions behind these norms — predictability for a year, accepted limits on taxes and spending, and departmental control of spending — no longer hold.

Budget balance disappeared in most nations by the 1950s and in the United States after the mid-1960s. It was killed off by a vulgarization of Keynesian economics — balance the economy, not the budget — which rationalized the underlying consensus that spending was good. It was not merely that balance fell into disuse, mind you, but that it was replaced by a positive injunction to do good; that is, to spend. Better budgets became those which spent more.

Now the norm of balance evolved to establish an equilibrium between spending and taxing. Strong feelings about the limits of taxation, modified at the margin by raising or lowering tax rates for political purposes, established effective ceilings for government spending. Everyone concerned, consequently, had a pretty good idea of allowable spending for

years to come. Bids by departments to increase their shares
beyond the level of expected increases, if any, would be re-
sisted by others who knew that much more for some departments meant much less for others. Spending was inhibited
at the source; bids to "break the bank" were not put in because everyone knew that also meant breaking social solidar-
ity among departments. The interests entrusted to the care
of these spending departments would expect to suffer. Along
with budget balance, then, went the widely shared assumption that requests for funds would be made in the context
of fairly firm spending limits. Budgets would not merely
bubble up from below but would be shaped by pressure from
above, pressure that affected the perception of departments
about what was reasonable to ask for as well as what they
might get.

The norm of comprehensiveness stipulated the ideal that
all revenues go to the Central Treasury and that all expenditures be made within a comprehensive set of accounts. This
ideal, of course, was never wholly realized; but although there
were some special funds, the ideal was approximated. Today
no one needs to be told that direct loans, loan guarantees, tax
preferences, off-budget corporations, regulations that increase
costs in the private sector, open-ended entitlements, and other
devices have made a hash out of comprehensiveness.

Comprehensive accounting once meant accounting by departments; governmental expenditure, except for a special
fund here and there, meant departmental expenditure. Control departments, the understanding was, and you controlled
expenditure. Now that spending by departments on goods and
services in industrial democracies accounts for only 15 to 30
per cent of spending, the inescapable conclusion is that the
vast bulk of expenditure is not covered by traditional norms.
Most money is spent to affect citizen behavior rather than
on direct government actions. Since most spending is done
by individuals who receive payments or loans and by sub-

national governments, the irrelevance of department control is clear.[1]

Control of spending has declined along with the norm of comprehensiveness because one cannot maximize simultaneously in opposing directions. Varying the level of spending to help modulate swings in the economy, or to redistribute income, or to strengthen family finances is not wholly compatible with a focus on controlling departmental behavior. The more interest a government has in influencing citizen behavior, it appears, the less able is such a government to keep its own house in order. Nor can it be said, following the norm of comprehensiveness, that there is a house of budgeting whose conceptual rooms are comparable. Accounting is in a shambles. Money borrowed one way ends up entirely in the budget; another way, partially; and a third way, not at all. Reallocating resources from loans to tax preferences to entitlements to departmental spending to government corporations is not possible (not, at least, in the sense of being intended) because there is no common budgetary currency.

A phenomenon that used to be confined to poor countries — repetitive budgeting, remaking the budget several times a year[2] — has now become standard practice in relatively rich nations as well. Whether the budget is formally reconfigured or not, its underlying premises, financial assumptions, and actual allocations are subject to rapid change measured in months rather than years. When the volatility of the external environment leads to declines in the rates of spending increases, it imposes such disagreeable choices upon governments that economic uncertainty rapidly becomes political

[1] See the important paper by Allen Schick, "Off-Budget Expenditure: An Economic and Political Framework," Paper prepared for the Organisation for Economic Co-Operation and Development, Paris, August 1981.

[2] Naomi Caiden and Aaron Wildavsky, *Planning and Budgeting in Poor Countries* (New York, 1974). Paperback edition by Transaction, Inc. (New Brunswick, N.J., 1980).

disarray: these hard decisions have to be made not once but several times a year. Hence, annualarity, the one budgetary norm thought to be unassailable (because so simple and so necessary and so uncontroversial) has been gravely weakened.

So what? Does it matter if some old-fashioned norms — derived from an era in which industrialization had hardly begun — have outlived their usefulness and go the way of all things? Not necessarily, a prudent person would reply, providing such norms have been replaced by something better or, at least, not noticeably worse. Or, I would add, even if not replaced at all. For, if one set of norms no longer applies and another is not yet in sight, budgeting is adrift, without rudder or compass. This means that the main governmental process for reconciling differences and setting directions — for consent and for steering — creates problems instead of solutions.

Let us look first at what happens when the traditional norms no longer guide behavior. Annualarity signifies predictability; this norm is not only desirable but feasible; the budget *will* last a year. With this common expectation, agencies are impelled to make accommodation with central controllers, like the Office of Management and Budget (OMB). Though not spelled out, this is the mutual understanding: because the Treasury promises to pay the amount passed in the budget, agencies will exercise restraint in requests and try to stay within the allotted amounts. To break that implied contract is to court a number of consequences. When the Treasury cannot guarantee payment of the allotted amount, agency political activity increases — not merely to get all that it asked for but also to keep it. If the budget sends a signal to "get it if you can," early accommodation is unwise, resulting in delayed decisions and enhanced uncertainty. Agencies that find such uncertainty intolerable will try to escape from prior restraints by making larger demands, and so there will be more left when cuts come. Thus initial bids become ever less reliable as a true gauge of agency expectations. Rather than remain within the appropriations process and absorb the inescapable uncertainty, program advocates seek to escape by making direct drafts on the Treasury (called "back-door spending," or entitlements); by loans or loan guarantees; through shifting functions to "off-budget" entities; through special funds and "earmarked taxes"; and by imposing regulations on private parties, which then must bear the cost even though it does not appear in the agency budget. Inevitably, as funds available to the Central Treasury shrink, representing a lesser proportion of the total; and, without direct control over loan guarantees, entitlements, and the rest, grows less able to calculate how much is being spent — the Treasury tries to impose a harsher regimen on what is left, tempting agencies and program advocates to attempt further escape measures.

We see where we are: the decline of the predictability once based on the norm of annualarity worsens the Treasury's ability to maintain comprehensiveness. Revenues are diverted through increasing use of tax preferences (called tax expenditures by those who dislike them)[3] and special funds. Expenditures are rendered incomparable by the numerous devices just mentioned for getting around the appropriations process. No one can compare an appropriation to a direct loan, to a guarantee, or to any of a number of other spending devices.

The decline of comprehensiveness weakens control. Ignorant of how much is being spent, central budget offices are

---

[3] See John F. Witte, "Tax Philosophy and Income Equality," in *Value Judgment and Income Distribution*, Robert A. Solo and Charles Anderson, editors (New York, 1981) pp. 340–378; and Ronald King, "Tax Expenditures and Systematic Public Policy," Paper prepared for delivery at the Annual Meeting of the American Political Science Association, Denver, Colorado, September 2–5, 1982.

less able to say that any amount (in which account, please?) is too much. Looking good, as opposed to doing well, becomes tempting for guardians as well as advocates. Treasurers, who tend to be judged by the degree of budget imbalance, can improve their position by shifting spending to accounts such as loan guarantees that, except for a small amount for defaults, do not show up in the budget. Or they can (a practice intensified in President Lyndon Johnson's time) trade lower spending outlays in one year for larger authorizations in future years.[4] Without rules that equate all major forms of spending, accounting sleight of hand substitutes for spending control. Naturally, program advocates are more than willing to play this game.

It might be different if there were acknowledged limits on expenditure or taxation or both. Advocates bidding for spending then would be restrained by knowing that much more for them would mean much less for others. And central controllers, besides holding on to an acceptable level of spending, could make the classic argument that understandings about levels of taxation would be violated, thus incurring penalties at the polls. But, as things stand today, without widespread agreement on either taxing or spending, the inner restraint that used to keep the budget battle within tolerable limits has eroded. Anything goes; when ordinary appropriations cannot match insatiable desires, end runs are made to get around even weak restraint. Without the interdependence that resulted from a belief in balance — because the effects of spending here do not necessarily implicate others elsewhere — budget control gives way to a free-for-all.

No longer can spending be controlled by controlling departments; most spending takes place outside of departments. Participants are no longer clear about whether control is de-

---

[4] David C. Mowery, Mark S. Kamlet, and John P. Crecine, "Presidential Management of Budgetary and Fiscal Policymaking," xcv *Political Science Quarterly* (Fall 1980) pp. 395–425.

sirable or feasible. Thus it appears that when one norm degenerates, the others are not far behind.

There is a supportive relationship between the classic budgetary norms, so that a decline in one causes a contraction in being able to apply the others. Diminished predictability encourages advocates to sidestep the appropriations process. The new forms of financing they develop wreak havoc with any notion of a single set of accounts. And, as comprehensiveness withers away, predictability in expenditure declines. It was comprehensiveness across accounts that facilitated predictability, and annualarity that encouraged the fungibility of funds across revenue and expenditure categories. When program budgeting was proposed, its supporters thought that consideration of relationships among programs was thwarted by disinclination to depart from past patterns. Actually, it was the decline of those traditional norms which destroyed the basic conditions for applying the economic criteria — limited resources and a common unit of accounts — on which program budgeting depended.

Instead of an energy-enhancing relationship, there is an energy-depleting tie between budgetary norms: less of one leads to less of the other. Nowhere is this more apparent than in the deleterious effect the decay of budget balance has had upon annualarity and comprehensiveness. Budget balance comprises two kinds of equivalencies: accepted limits on revenue and expenditure, and the desire for these totals to come close together. Such limits fostered a sense of mutual dependence because all faced similar constraints. The balance engendered a sense of self-sacrifice because each of the parts had to sacrifice to achieve a goal outside themselves. Mutual toleration and respect was encouraged by understanding the interactions of all participants. A dual dependence on society was furthered by convergence toward acceptable levels of revenue and expenditure, tested only at the margins, and by knowing that the public saw balance as ensuring that the governmental apparatus was in good working order. In a word, limits enhanced predictability; correspondingly, confidence that the budget contract would be kept rewarded participants for adhering to its provisions. This anticipatory coordination was facilitated by pouring streams of revenue into a single reservoir out of which all (well, most) spending flowed. When comprehensiveness became fragmented, however, no one could be certain of the size of shares, and each participant was encouraged to go his own way.

I hope that readers of *The Politics of the Budgetary Process* recognize the relevance of these abstract formulations to the concrete representations of reality here portrayed. In the book that follows, cuts and increases are based on a philosophy of equal treatment among agencies, called fair shares, which cannot exist without annualarity, departmental responsibility, and fixed totals. There cannot be fairness, for instance, without agreement on the totals from which the shares are derived. Basic to the book is a division of roles between spending advocates and guardians of the Treasury. This separation cannot continue to exist, however, if the budgetary process is geared to expanding rather than limiting spending. When "budgeting by addition" replaces "budgeting by subtraction" from an accepted total, who will take on the role of guardianship? After all, if program advocates can be satisfied by adding the costs of their proposals together, there is no need for anyone to undertake the painful task of cutting by subtraction. Agency officials remain advocates but with a vengeance; the decline of predictability enlarges the ever-present need to play politics; the lack of limits and the inability to constrain spending by controlling departments loosen the ties that bind agencies together. With advocacy less restrained, relationships that rely on trust between agencies and Congressional committees become more variable: either the two sides join to push pet programs or they do not trust each other at all, because common understandings have eroded. Congressional guardianship is gravely weakened because the decline in interdependence among agencies and programs makes it seem less worthwhile. If a rise in certain programs does not imply a fall in others, or if cuts do not make for larger savings, because there are many other additions, why take the heat for turning people down?

Another reason for weakened Congressional control is that the effort to shore up guardianship by imposing budget committees over appropriations (the House Ways and Means, and Senate Finance, committees) has placed subcommittees in the position of advocating programmatic spending to this next level. Thus appropriations subcommittees, like agencies before them, may come in with requests higher than they expect to get so as to allow for cuts by budget committees. Seeing as how everyone has become a strategist for spending, budget committees set their First Resolution high enough to accommodate most demands. The Second Resolution generally includes the overage, and calls it a day. Unless the First Resolution were to be set below demands and made binding — a radical reform — no committee within Congress could be said to act as a guardian of the purse strings.

Yet the Office of Management and Budget (OMB) is hard put to play the role of guardian consistently. For one thing, OMB acts for the President — and not every Chief Executive wants to be known as a nay-sayer. Ronald Reagan, for instance, is intent on rapidly raising the defense budget. Other Presidents may wish to increase spending on social welfare or in some other area of public policy. For another, budget examiners are too few, spending programs too many and too diverse, to permit detailed scrutiny of most agency requests. Only agency people know what is happening, to the extent anyone does; and clearly it is not in their interest (given the lack of protection OMB can afford them) to tell. After all, if OMB is after the heart and muscle of agency operations, it cannot be expected that people identified with these activities will help in their own demise.

Central control makes most sense against a historical background of past agreement, so that only small proportions of the budget are in dispute. Following from the loss of the traditional budgetary norms, however, the erosion of limits, predictability, and collective concern has opened up disputes about the budgetary base: less can be taken for granted in amount or content, because the budget is likely to be redone almost any time; because unwillingness or inability to share sacrifices means that some agencies become especially vulnerable; and because, given the sheer size and diversity of the budget — running well over $700 billion and containing numerous pockets outside of that — it is much more difficult to say whether any particular spending aspiration can or cannot be fulfilled. When drastic changes are commonly considered, or no one is quite sure how large is large, incremental change is in trouble.

Budgeting today does not look like budgeting yesterday because the fundamental norms have been undermined. If budgeting seems shaky, that is because those pillars on which it used to rest — predictability, limits, and collectivity — are trembling.

There are, to be sure, other explanations for the demise of the traditional budgetary process characterized by incrementalism; fair shares; mutual confidence; a division of roles, including legislative guardianship; and the rest of the practices described in this book. The main alternative explanation, in the period from the end of World War II to the present, is economic growth — its presence until the mid-1970s, and its lessening or absence thereafter. It is easy to reach agreements, the growth theory holds, when everyone is getting more, even if some do get more than others. Incrementalism, Schick says, is based on the expectation of continued plenty. Now that prosperity has declined, incrementalism has gone with it.[5]

Doubtless, the decline of expected revenues does make things harder all the way around. The question I wish to raise is whether the change in budgetary behavior is a cause or a consequence of the transformation of norms. Is it economic growth (or its absence) which regulates budgetary behavior, or is it the prevailing norms which determine what happens when growth goes up or down?

Consider the consequences of economic growth. Since it is possible to raise revenue without reducing personal income, budget balance could be easier, not harder, to maintain. Tax rates could remain stable or even decline while spending rose, thus raising budget balance to a higher level. Precisely because there is more to go around, comprehensive accounts could be facilitated. There could be less objection to maintaining the regular appropriations process. Why use backdoor spending when the front door is wide open?

Yet that — the proliferation of spending sources during a time of plenty, from the mid-1960s through the mid-1970s — is exactly what did happen. As I write today, legislators from both parties, with the support of a conservative Republican President, seek substantial increases to support a program of public works to rebuild state and local infrastructure — sewers, bridges, waterworks, tunnels. Why, we may ask, during a time of plenty, was the substructure on which we stand allowed to deteriorate? And why, when economic conditions improve, won't that inattention to essential maintenance recur? To me it seems more reasonable to suppose that a widespread desire to increase spending lies behind the weakening of budgetary norms. Once one believes that govern-

---

[5] Allen Schick, "The Politics of Budgeting: Can Incrementalism Survive in a Decremental Age?" Paper prepared for the 1982 Annual Meeting of the American Political Science Association, Denver, Colorado, September 2–5, 1982.

ment spending is laudatory (the more the better), it follows that balance and comprehensiveness are obstacles, because they restrict opportunity; and annualarity is an impediment, because the money must be voted every year rather than coming in a continuous stream from the Treasury. By contrast, open-ended, "no-year" entitlements, loans, regulations, off-budget entities, and tax expenditures enable government to do good by spending more.

Which comes first, we may well ask, the change in budgetary norms or the change in spending practices? Did the practices change the norms or vice versa? My view is that both change together. The purpose of norms is to justify practices. When there is a strong desire to change behavior, as in the New Deal America of the 1930s about government spending, there is also a search for new norms to rationalize that conduct. It is not only that John Maynard Keynes found America but that influential Americans were actively looking for a theory to justify greater governmental spending.[6] Observation that many new spigots of spending were being opened in the 1960s and 1970s coincides with the civil-rights and environmental movements, seeking enhanced equality and concern for ecology through governmental action. There is a struggle over theory as well as over practice; each influences the other so that one cannot say which came first but only that ideas and actions go together.

The meaning of a practice depends on its operations within the pattern of norms that provide the structure of the budgetary process at a given time. Incremental budgeting is a good example. As portrayed in this book, during the period when budget balance (and, hence, a sense of limits on totals) was the norm, incrementalism referred to small, regular modifications of an agency's accepted level of spending,

[6] Felix Frankfurter, later a Justice of the Supreme Court, played such a role. See H. N. Hirsch, *The Enigma of Felix Frankfurter* (New York, 1981).

a level known as its budgetary base. Increments above and below that base were limited by agreement about rates of taxation and about the desirability of balance between revenue and spending. Spending was also limited by a sense of what the country could afford, tied to observations of economic performance. Alter the norms, however, and the practice that seems the same takes on a different significance. Without agreement on balance, and therefore a sense of limits, spending grows through small but regular increases without regard for corresponding capacities in economic growth or revenue. When continuous increases fall short of aspirations, new sources of spending arise that also grow regularly. The result is that public spending grows faster than the private economy. Thus we see that incrementalism is a neutral concept; it permits both slow or rapid growth of government depending on the structure of budgetary norms within which it is employed.

The importance of these budgetary norms comes out indirectly in new practices and proposals for reform that are meant to make up for what used to be. Take annualarity. There are two ways to go: either learn to live with frequent changes, or extend the budgetary time period to several years. This method of relaxing and enjoying it now is called the "continuing resolution." Rapidly becoming an art form all its own, the continuing resolution is designed to enable all or part of government to continue functioning without passage of appropriations laws. Whether and to what degree inflation is taken into account (should defense and transportation get the same consideration?) is disputed case by case. Congress has become so used to dissensus that it has formalized procedures for what is to happen when the House Appropriations Committee reports out a resolution but the House has not yet acted on it; when the House passes a resolution but the Senate doesn't; and when the two resolutions differ. The basic rule appears to be that, given any Congressional action short of final passage, spending can go on at the lower of the levels passed by either house of Congress. Whether this is a low- or a high-spending rule depends on whether one views it as taking the lower alternative or as permitting high spending to continue without complete Congressional action.

Since Congress so often is so late with appropriations bills,[7] it has been proposed that Congress go on a two-year cycle — one year for regular legislation, and another just for appropriations. Certainly, overworked budget staff would welcome the respite. But it remains to be seen whether a two-year cycle will prove satisfactory when the budget barely lasts a few months. Controversy over what constitutes "current services," or the degree of commitment in continuing resolutions, can only grow.

Lip service to budget balance obscures deep differences. The Reagan Administration, committed to smaller government, for instance, would certainly like to achieve balance, but not at the political price of higher taxes or inflation. When push comes to shove, the Administration would choose a smaller government with a larger deficit (say a $600-billion total, with a $200-billion deficit) over a larger government with a smaller deficit (say a $950-billion total, with a $50-billion deficit). Except when incurred by conservative governments, liberals favor deficits which help achieve employment or which redistribute income. If deficits must be brought down, liberals favor higher taxes, to be paid by people with higher incomes. In the end, it is the size of government, not the balance between revenue and expenditure,

---

[7] This tardiness is due in part to inability to agree, and in part to the complexity of the process. The effects of pushing the fiscal year back appear to have been offset by the extra steps required in the Budget Reform Act of 1974. As historically large deficits exert downward pressure on spending, so that one hears that unaccustomed raspy phrase "cut-back management," meaning how to manage on less, delay is now due more to dissensus than to work load.

which matters most to both liberal and conservative political activists.

Though traditional budgetary norms are, in contemporary terms, conservative as contrasted with liberality in spending, they need not always be so. There is a group — quite possibly speaking for a majority of Americans — who might be called the "party of balance." This party wants balance among social forces as well as among budgets. It is willing to accept much higher levels of spending, providing these are matched by revenues. A national sales tax on different steps in manufacturing, called a "value-added" tax, would suit the party of balance; cuts in income taxes would not. At some stage, however, the party of balance (as opposed to a party of opposition to big government or a party in favor of it) would also want to impose limits.[8] The proposal by Representative David Obey (Democrat, Wisconsin) — to introduce a budget in which all taxing and spending would be voted on simultaneously, rather than to limit spending and taxing — appears designed to show that Congress is behaving responsibly.[9]

The battle over budgetary reform has been joined by the proposed balanced-budget–spending-limit constitutional amendment. In one fell swoop, strict limits would be imposed on federal spending, which could not increase faster than the growth in national income; tax brackets would be indexed, thus limiting allowable increases; balance would, over a period of years, be more closely approximated; and

[8] See my "The Party of Government, The Party of Opposition, and the Party of Balance: An American View of the Consequences of the 1980 Election," in *The American Elections of 1980*, Austin Ranney, editor (Washington, D.C., 1981) pp. 329–350. A shorter version may be found in *The Public Interest*, "The Three-Party System — 1980 and After" (Summer 1981) pp. 47–57.

[9] Richard E. Cohen, "House Braces for Showdown over How It Should Package Its Annual Budget," *National Journal* (November 27, 1982) pp. 2024–2026.

comprehensive accounting would be encouraged. Just as the deterioration of any one norm of budgeting adversely affected the others, so too the strengthening of limits would give added impetus to comprehensiveness. In order to work within spending limits, much more careful records of the rate of spending must be maintained. The definition of spending, called outlays, has to be sharpened. Reserves against a rainy day will have to be kept. Those who wish to make limits work will want to get everything they can within their purview.

The purpose of having budgetary norms in the first place was to restrain spending and taxing. No one deemed it necessary to invent norms for doing what came naturally; that is, more. It was universally thought that reform of budgeting would allow government to do whatever it was doing more efficiently and honestly. No one dreamed of taxes and spending at today's levels.[10] Terms like "entitlement" or "uncontrollable" might have entered into other aspects of government, but they were never conceived as applicable to the budget. The traditional norms are designed to support resource allocation (assuming limits), not resource addition (assuming unlimited resources).

The applicability of the basic concepts in *The Politics of the Budgetary Process* depends on the extent to which its basic presuppositions — the norms of balance, comprehensiveness, and annualarity — hold true. If the budgetary process of the mid-1960s and the 1970s continues into the future, with denigration of predictability, limits, and collective concern, the book will become, at best, a faithful record of a time long since gone. But, if limits are imposed and balance, comprehensiveness, and annualarity become the rule

[10] See Carolyn Webber and Aaron Wildavsky, "Origins of Modern Budgeting: The 19th Century," *Expenditure and Taxation in Western History*, book manuscript, available from authors.

rather than the exception, the politics will really be the same; only the names of the players will be different. Whether *The Politics of the Budgetary Process* becomes epilogue to a bygone era, or prologue to a reassertion of traditional practices, depends not only on what is in it but on what life makes of its subject matter.

CONTENTS

4 REFORMS

5 APPRAISALS

6 PPB AND ZBB 181

7 CONGRESS 222

THE POLITICS OF THE
BUDGETARY PROCESS

"*Oh, it's great here, all right, but I sort of feel uncomfortable in a place with no budget at all.*"

Drawing by D. Reilly; © 1976 The New Yorker Magazine, Inc.

BUDGETS

1

In the most literal sense a budget is a document, containing words and figures, which proposes expenditures for certain items and purposes. The words describe items of expenditure (salaries, equipment, travel) or purposes (preventing war, improving mental health, providing low-income housing), and the figures are attached to each item or purpose. Presumably, those who make a budget intend that there will be a direct connection between what is written in it and future events. Hence we might conceive of a budget as intended behavior, as a prediction. If the requests for funds are granted, and if they are spent in accordance with instructions, and if the actions involved lead to the desired consequences, then the purposes stated in the document will be achieved. The budget thus becomes a link between financial resources and human behavior to accomplish policy objectives. Only through observation, however, is it possible to determine the degree to which the predictions postulated in the budget document turn out to be correct.

In the most general definition, budgeting is concerned with the translation of financial resources into human purposes. A budget, therefore, may be characterized as a series of goals with price tags attached. Since funds are limited and have to be divided in one way or another, the budget becomes a mechanism for making choices among alternative expenditures. When the choices are coordinated so as to achieve desired goals, a budget may be called a plan. Should it include a detailed specification of how its objectives are to be achieved, a budget may serve as a plan of work for those who assume the task of implementing it. If emphasis is placed on achieving the most policy returns for a given sum of money, or on obtaining the desired objectives at the lowest cost, a budget may become an instrument for ensuring efficiency. Yet there may be a wide gap between the intentions of those who make up a budget and their real accomplishments. Although the language of a budget calls for the achievement of certain goals through planned expenditures, investigation may reveal that no funds have been spent for these purposes, that the money has been used for other purposes, that quite different goals have been achieved, or that the same goals have been gained in different ways.

Viewed in another light, a budget may be regarded as a contract. Congress and the President promise to supply funds under specified conditions, and the agencies agree to spend them in ways that have been agreed upon. (When an agency apportions funds to its subunits, it may be said to be making an internal contract.) Whether or not the contract is enforceable, or whether or not the parties actually agree about what the contract purportedly stipulates, is a matter for inquiry. To the extent that a budget is carried out, however, it imposes a set of mutual obligations and controls upon the contracting parties. The word "mutual" should be stressed because it is so easy to assume that control is exercised in a unilateral direction by superiors (Congressmen, department heads, and so on) over those formally subordinate to them. But when an appropriations committee approves some expenditures and not others, when it sets down conditions for the expenditure of funds, the committee is also obligating itself to keep its part of the bargain. A department head (to choose another example) who hopes to control the actions of his subordinates must ordinarily follow through on a promise to support some of their requests or else find them trying to undermine him. A budget thus becomes a web of social as well as of legal relationships in which commitments are made by all the parties, and where sanctions may be invoked (though not necessarily equally) by all.

The proposed budgets that administrative agencies (departments, bureaus, commissions) submit to the Bureau of the Budget may represent their expectations. These are the amounts they expect to see enacted into law and actually spent. It is also possible that agency requests may represent their aspirations. These are the figures they hope to receive and spend for various programs if circumstances are especially favorable, so that they can generate the necessary political support. Since the amounts requested often have an effect on the amounts received, however, budget proposals are often strategies. The total sum of money and its allocation among various activities is designed to have a favorable effect in support of the agencies' budgetary goals. As each participant acts on the budget he receives information on the preferences of others and communicates his own desires through the choices he makes. Here the budget emerges as a network of communications in which information is continuously being generated and fed back to the participants. Once enacted, a budget becomes a precedent; the fact that something has been done once vastly increases the chances that it will be done again. Since only substantial departures from the previous year's budget are normally given intensive scrutiny, an item that remains unchanged will probably be carried along the following year as a matter of course. One cannot, therefore, state unequivocally that an agency budget is an expectation, an aspiration, a strategy, a communications network, or a precedent.

It should now be apparent that the purposes of budgets are as varied as the purposes of men. One budget may be designed to coordinate diverse activities so that they complement one another in the achievement of common goals. Another budget may be put together primarily to discipline subordinate officials within a governmental agency by reducing amounts for their salaries and their pet projects. And a third budget may be directed essentially to mobilizing the support of the clientele groups who benefit by the services that the agency provides. Nothing is gained, therefore, by insisting that a budget is only one of these things when it may be all of them or many other kinds of things as well.[1] One may, however, adopt a particular view of the budget as most useful for the purposes he has in mind. Without claiming to have found the only right perspective, or to have exhausted the subject in any way, I would like to propose a conception that seems useful in talking about the budgetary process as a phenomenon of human behavior in a governmental setting.

Throughout this volume we shall be concerned with budgets as political things. Taken as a whole the federal budget is a representation in monetary terms of governmental activity. If politics is regarded in part as conflict over whose preferences shall prevail in the determination of national policy, then the budget records the outcomes of this struggle. If one asks, "Who gets what the government has to give?" then the answers for a moment in time are recorded in the budget. If one looks at politics as a process by which the government mobilizes resources to meet pressing problems, then the budget is a focus of these efforts.

The size and shape of the budget is a matter of serious

[1] A good discussion of the nature and variety of budgets may be found throughout Jesse Burkhead's *Government Budgeting* (New York, 1956). See also the illuminating comments in Frederick C. Mosher, *Program Budgeting: Theory and Practice, with Particular Reference to the U.S. Department of the Army* (Chicago, 1954) pp. 1-18.

contention in our political life. Presidents, political parties, administrators, Congressmen, interest groups, and interested citizens vie with one another to have their preferences recorded in the budget. The victories and defeats, the compromises and the bargains, the realms of agreement and the spheres of conflict in regard to the role of national government in our society all appear in the budget. In the most integral sense the budget lies at the heart of the political process.

CALCULATIONS
2

PARTICIPANTS IN BUDGETING operate in an environment that imposes severe constraints on what they can do. Neither the opportunities they seize upon nor the disabilities they suffer are wholly, perhaps largely, within their control. Though their perceptions of reality differ somewhat, they are all cognizant of certain elementary facts of life to which they must adjust. Everyone is aware of the structural conditions of political life such as the separation of powers, the division of labor within the appropriations committees, and the customary separation between appropriations and substantive legislative commit- tees. All participants face the usual overt political factors in- volving group pressures, relationships between Congressmen and their constituents, political party conflicts, executive-legis- lative cooperation and rivalry, inter-agency disputes, and the like. Sooner or later the participants go through a process of socialization in the kinds of roles they are expected to play. They come to know the rules of the budgetary game, which specify the kinds of moves that it is and is not permissible for them to make. It would be difficult for them to remain un- aware of the contemporary climate of opinion, of the pressing and recognized needs of the times, as when a rise in defense expenditures becomes obvious to all after an enemy provocation, or growing unemployment requires measures to put people to work. Secular trends in the growth of national welfare programs and increasing federal responsibility for a host of services are unlikely to be reversed. The participants take these environmental conditions as "given" to a considerable extent and so must we if we expect to understand why they act as they do.[1]

In this and the following chapter, budgeting is approached from the standpoint of the participants as they perceive their environment and make the calculations upon which their decisions depend. By "calculation" I mean the series of related factors (manifestly including perceptions of influence relationships) which the participants take into account in determining the choice of competing alternatives. Calculation involves a study of how problems arise, how they are identified as such, how they are broken down into manageable dimensions, how they are related to one another, how determinations are made of what is relevant, and how the actions of others are given consideration. Special attention is paid to the much neglected problem of complexity. For if there is one thing that participants in budgeting share, it is a concern with the extraordinary complexity of the programs and processes with which they deal.

We begin with a statement of the problem of complexity and its "solution" through the use (some would say abuse) of various aids to calculation. Then we deal with problems of calculation as they bear upon three major institutional decisions: deciding how much to ask for (the agencies); deciding

[1] For other approaches see Anthony Downs, "Why the Government Budget Is Too Small in a Democracy," XII *World Politics* (July 1960) pp. 541-563; Fred Riggs, "Prismatic Society and Financial Administration," V *Administrative Science Quarterly* (June 1960) pp. 1-46; Louis R. Pondy, "A Mathematical Model of Budgeting," (Mimeo.) Carnegie Institute of Technology, January 24, 1962.

how much to recommend (the Budget Bureau); and deciding how much to give (the appropriations committee). Discussion of these decisions is prefaced by a description of the roles and perspectives available to the major institutional participants. In this way we are able to reach the goals of the participants. We see how their calculations (and later their strategies) are affected by the roles they adopt and their perceptions of the roles and capacities of others.

COMPLEXITY

The mind of man is an elusive substance. It cannot be directly observed for most purposes and inferences about it are notoriously tricky. No wonder our attention is more readily caught by the clash of wills in the exercise of influence and the confrontation of rival strategies in the pursuit of funds. Yet the ways in which the human mind goes about making calculations in the process of arriving at decisions have a fascination for anyone concerned with how men attempt to solve problems. More important, perhaps, for our purposes, one cannot hope to understand why men behave as they do unless one has some idea about how they make their calculations. And, most important, methods of calculation are not neutral; the ways in which calculations are made affect the outcomes of the political system: the distribution of shares in policy among the participants, the "who gets what and how much" of politics. Different methods of calculation often result in different decisions. Otherwise, it would make no difference what kinds of calculations were made and there would be much less reason to pursue the topic.

Budgeting is complex, largely because of the complexity of modern life. Suppose that you were a Congressman or a Budget Bureau official interested in the leukemia research program and you wondered how the money was being spent. By looking at the National Cancer Institute's budgetary presentation you would discover that $42,012 is being spent on a project studying "factors and mechanisms concerned in hemopoiesis," and that $5,095 is being spent for "a study of the relationship of neutralizing antibodies for the Rous sarcoma virus to resistance and susceptibility for visceral lymphomatosis." Could you tell whether too much money is being spent on hemopoiesis in comparison to lymphomatosis or whether either project is relevant for any useful purpose? You might sympathize with Congressman Laird's plaintive cry, "A lot of things go on in this subcommittee that I cannot understand." It is not surprising, therefore, that one runs across expressions of dismay at the difficulties of understanding technical subjects. Representative Jensen has a granddaughter who is mentioned in hearings more often than most people, and who is reputed by him to have read "all the stuff she can get on nuclear science. She never reads a story book. . . . And she will ask me questions and she just stumps me. I say, 'Jennifer, for Heaven's sake. I can't answer that.' 'Well,' she says, 'You are on the Atomic Energy Commission Committee, Grandpa.' 'Yes,' he replies, 'But I am not schooled in the art.'" A cry goes up for simplification. "I just want this presentation made more simple and easy to grasp," a Representative says to an administrative official. Even those nominally "in the know" may be nonplussed. "That is a budget device," said an agency budget officer, "which is difficult for me to understand, and I have been in this business for over 20 years."

In our personal lives we are used to discovering that things rarely turn out quite as we had expected. Somehow when it comes to political activities we seem to expect a much greater degree of foresight. Yet life is incredibly complicated and there is very little theory that would enable people to predict how programs will turn out if they are at all new. When Representative Preston says "I cannot recall any project of any size that has ever been presented to this committee—that

came out in the end like the witnesses testified it would be at
the outset," the problem is less one of always estimating on
the low side than of not having sufficient knowledge to do
better.

There are cases in which one might do better if one had
endless time, and unlimited ability to calculate. But time is in
terribly short supply, the human mind is drastically limited in
what it can encompass, and the number of budgetary items
may be huge, so that the trite phrase "A man can only do so
much" takes on real meaning. "We might as well be frank,"
Representative Mahan stated, "that no human being regardless of his position and . . . capacity could possibly be completely familiar with all the items of appropriations contained
in this defense bill. . . ." But decisions have to be made.
"There is a saying around the Pentagon," McNeil informs us,
"that . . . there is only one person in the United States who
can force a decision, and that is the Government Printer
[when the budget must go to the press]."[2]

Aside from the complexity of individual budgetary programs, there remains the imposing problem of making comparisons among different programs that have different values
for different people. This involves deciding such questions as
how much highways are worth as compared to recreation facilities, national defense, schools, and so on down the range
of governmental functions. No common denominator among
these functions has been developed. No matter how hard they
try, therefore, officials in places like the Bureau of the Budget
discover that they cannot find any objective method of judging priorities among programs. How, then, do budget officials
go about meeting their staggering burden of calculation?

[2] Subcommittee on National Policy Machinery, Committee on Government Operations, *The Budget and the Policy Process*, U.S. Senate,
87th Congress, First Session, 1961 (hereafter cited as *Jackson Committee
Hearings*) p. 1061.

AIDS TO CALCULATION

Some officials do not deal with complexity at all; they are just overwhelmed and never quite recover. Others work terribly hard at mastering their subjects. "This [House Appropriations] Committee is no place for a man who doesn't work," a member said. "They have to be hardworking. It isn't just a job; it's a way of life."[3] But sheer effort is not enough. It has become necessary to develop mechanisms, however imperfect, for helping men make decisions that are in some sense meaningful in a complicated world.

Budgeting is experiential. One way of dealing with a problem of huge magnitude is to make only the roughest guesses while letting experience accumulate. Then, when the consequences of the various actions become apparent, it is possible to make modifications to avoid the difficulties. This is the rationale implicit in former defense comptroller McNeil's statement justifying the absence of a ceiling on expenditures at the beginning of the Korean War.

> There was no long background in the United States, with 150 years of peak and valley experience, as to what carrying on a high level of defense year in and year out for a long period would cost, or what was involved. I think a very good start was made in listing everything that anyone could think they needed . . . knowing full well, however . . . that if you overbought certain engines or trucks, it could be balanced out the following year. That method was used for a year or two and then sufficient experience had been gained . . . to know that . . . defense would cost in the neighborhood of $35 to $40 billion.[4]

Budgeting is simplified. Another way of handling complexity is to use actions on simpler items as indices of more

[3] Richard F. Fenno, Jr., "The House Appropriations Committee as a Political System: The Problem of Integration," LVI *The American Political Science Review* (June 1962) p. 314.

[4] *Jackson Committee Hearings*, p. 1075.

complicated ones. Instead of dealing directly with the cost of a huge atomic installation, for example, Congressmen may seek to discover how personnel and administrative costs or real estate transactions with which they have some familiarity are handled. If these items are handled properly then they may feel better able to trust the administrators with the larger ones. The reader has probably heard of this practice under some such title as "straining at gnats." And no doubt this is just what it is in many cases; unable to handle the more complex problems the Congressmen abdicate by retreating to the simpler ones. Here I am concerned to point out that this practice may at times have greater validity than appears on the surface if it is used as a testing device, and if there is a reasonable connection between the competence shown in handling simple and complex items.

A related method calls for directing one's observations to the responsible administrative officials rather than to the subject matter, if one is aware that the subject is so difficult and the operations so huge that the people in charge have to be trusted. They are questioned on a point here and there, a difficulty in this and that, in an effort to see whether or not they are competent and reliable. A senior Congressman reported that he followed an administrator's testimony looking for "strain in voice or manner," "covert glances" and other such indications and later followed them up probing for weaknesses.[5]

Budgeting officials "satisfice."   Calculations may be simplified by lowering one's sights. Although they do not use Herbert Simon's vocabulary, budget officials do not try to maximize but, instead, they "satisfice" (satisfy and suffice).[6]

[5] L. Dwaine Marvick, *Congressional Appropriation Politics* (Ph.D. Dissertation, Columbia University, 1952) p. 297.

[6] Herbert Simon, *Models of Man* (New York, 1957); see also Bruner, Goodnow, and Austin, *A Study of Thinking* (New York, 1956), for a fascinating discussion of strategies of concept attainment useful for dealing with the problem of complexity.

Which is to say that they do not try for the best of all possible worlds, whatever that might be, but, in their words, they try to "get by," to "come out all right," to "avoid trouble," to "avoid the worst," and so on. If he can get others to go along, if too many others do not complain too long and too loud, then the official may take the fact of agreement on something as the measure of success. And since the budget comes up every year, and deals largely with piecemeal adjustment, it is possible to correct glaring weaknesses as they arise.

It is against a background of the enormous burden of calculation that the ensuing description of the major aid for calculating budgets—the incremental method—should be understood.

Budgeting is incremental. The largest determining factor of the size and content of this year's budget is last year's budget. Most of the budget is a product of previous decisions. As former Budget Director Stans put it, "There is very little flexibility in the budget because of the tremendous number of commitments that are made years ahead."[7] The budget may be conceived of as an iceberg with by far the largest part below the surface, outside the control of anyone. Many items in the budget are standard and are simply reenacted every year unless there is a special reason to challenge them. Long-range commitments have been made and this year's share is scooped out of the total and included as part of the annual budget. There are mandatory programs such as price supports or veterans' pensions whose expenses must be met. The defense budget accounts for about half of the total and it is rarely decreased. There are programs which appear to be satisfactory and which no one challenges any more. Powerful political support makes the inclusion of other activities inevitable. The convergence of expectations on what must be included is indicated in Representative Flood's comments on the census of

[7] *Jackson Committee Hearings*, p. 1118.

business, which had been in trouble in previous years. "I guess this is a sacred cow, is it not . . . ?" Flood said. "This has been generated by . . . the manufacturing industry community of the nation, for its particular benefit and the general welfare. . . . There is no longer any doubt that this is built right into our system any more. . . ." Agencies are going concerns and a minimum must be spent on housekeeping (though this item is particularly vulnerable to attack because it does not appear to involve program issues). At any one time, after past policies are paid for, a rather small percentage —seldom larger than 30 per cent, often smaller than 5—is within the realm of anybody's (including Congressional and Budget Bureau) discretion as a practical matter.

In order to be more precise, it is desirable to discover the range of variation of the percentage of increase or decrease of appropriations as compared to the previous year. Table 2-1 shows the results for 37 domestic agencies over a 12 year period. Almost exactly one-third of the cases (149 out of 444) fall within the 5 per cent range. A little more than half the cases (233) are in the 10 per cent bracket. Just under three-quarters of the cases (326) occur within 30 per cent. Less than 10 per cent (31) are in the extreme range of 50 per cent or more. And many of these are accounted for by agencies with extreme, built-in cyclical fluctuations, such as those of the Census Bureau.

TABLE 2-1*

Budgeting is incremental.**

0-5%	6-10%	11-20%	21-30%	31-40%	41-50%	51-100%	101+%
149	84	93	51	21	15	24	7

* Figures recalculated from those supplied by Richard Fenno.
** Table shows the number of cases of 37 domestic bureaus over a 12 year period that fall into various percentages of increase over the past year (444 cases in all).

Budgeting is incremental, not comprehensive. The beginning of wisdom about an agency budget is that it is almost never actively reviewed as a whole every year in the sense of reconsidering the value of all existing programs as compared to all possible alternatives. Instead, it is based on last year's budget with special attention given to a narrow range of increases or decreases. Thus the men who make the budget are concerned with relatively small increments to an existing base. Their attention is focused on a small number of items over which the budgetary battle is fought. As Representative Norrel declared in testifying before the House Rules Committee, "If you will read the hearings of the subcommittees you will find that most of our time is spent in talking about the changes in the bill which we will have next year from the one we had this year, the reductions made, and the increases made. That which is not changed has very little, if anything, said about it."[8] Most appropriations committee members, like Senator Hayden in dismissing an item brought up by the Bureau of Indian Affairs, "do not think it is necessary to go into details of the estimate, as the committee has had this appropriation before it for many years." Asked to defend this procedure, a budget officer (or his counterparts in the Budget Bureau and Congress) will say that it is a waste of time to go back to the beginning as if every year was a blank slate. "No need to build the car over again." No one was born yesterday; past experience with these programs is so great that total reconsideration would be superfluous unless there is a special demand in regard to a specific activity on the part of one or more strategically placed Congressmen, a new Administration, interest groups, or the agency itself. Programs are reconsidered but not all together and generally in regard to small

[8] The Committee on Rules, U.S. House of Representatives, *To Create a Joint Committee on the Budget*, 82nd Congress, 2nd Session, 1952, p. 61.

changes. The political realities, budget officials[9] say, restrict their attention to items they can do something about—a few new programs and possible cuts in a few old ones.[10]

Senate practice is undoubtedly incremental. "It has been the policy of our [appropriations] committee," Senator Thomas reported, "to consider only items that are in controversy. When the House has included an item, and no question has been raised about it, the Senate Committee passes it over on the theory that it is satisfactory, and for that reason the hearings as a rule do not include testimony for or against items contained in the House bill."

FAIR SHARE AND BASE

Time and again participants in the budgetary process speak of having arrived at an estimate of what was the "fair share" of the total budget for an agency. "None of this happened suddenly," a man who helps make the budget informed me. "We

---

[9] This term includes all those in government who deal regularly with federal budgetary matters.

[10] Professor James D. Barber of Yale University has conducted a valuable small-group experiment, which suggests that the kinds of aids to calculation described here have general application. Barber arranged for 13 Connecticut Boards of Finance to meet under controlled conditions and (among other things) to solve two hypothetical problems dealing with allocating a reduction in their most recent set of budgetary recommendations. In summarizing this part of his preliminary findings, Barber states that the Boards sought to simplify their tasks by several characteristic ways of thinking. "First, the BF tends to exclude from its consideration items over which it has little or no control. . . . Second, the Board repeatedly refers to the previous level and the magnitude of expenditure. . . . But the primary base line for budget decision-making appears to be the last appropriation. . . . Using the above criteria to isolate categories for special attention . . . the predominant consideration is the effect of a cut on actual services rendered by the department. . . . Very few comments compared expenditures in one department with those in another department: the Board considers the budget 'horizontally' (last year vs. this year) rather than 'vertically' (Department A vs. Department B). Comparisons almost never reached as far as another town."

never go from $500 to $800 million or anything like that. This [the agency's] total is a product of many years of negotiations in order to work out a fair share of the budget for the agency."

At this point it is necessary to distinguish "fair share" from another concept, "the base." The base is the general expectation among the participants that programs will be carried on at close to the going level of expenditures but it does not necessarily include all activities. Having a project included in the agency's base thus means more than just getting it in the budget for a particular year. It means establishing the expectation that the expenditure will continue, that it is accepted as part of what will be done, and, therefore, that it will not normally be subjected to intensive scrutiny. (The word "base," incidentally, is part of the common parlance of officials engaged in budgeting and it would make no sense if their experience led them to expect wide fluctuations from year to year rather than additions to or subtractions from some relatively steady point.) "Fair share" means not only the base an agency has established but also the expectation that it will receive some proportion of funds, if any, which are to be increased over or decreased below the base of the various governmental agencies. "Fair share," then, reflects a convergence of expectations on roughly how much the agency is to receive in comparison to others.

The absence of a base or an agreement upon fair shares makes the calculation of what the agency or program should get much more difficult. That happens when an agency or program is new or when rapid shifts of sentiment toward it take place. A Senate Appropriations Committee report on the United States Information Agency demonstrates the problem. "Unlike the State Department," the report reads, "the USIA does not have a fixed, historic structure which sets a floor or ceiling on the amount of money which should be expended. Furthermore, its role must necessarily vary with the times.

Therefore the issue of how much should be spent is not a matter of fixed obligations but a matter of judgment. . . ."

THE AGENCY: ROLES AND PERSPECTIVES

Agency people are expected to be advocates of increased appropriations. "You may blame the War Department for a great many things," General Douglas MacArthur said in 1935, ". . . but you cannot blame us for not asking for money. That is one fault to which we plead not guilty." A classic statement of this role was made in 1939 by William A. Jump, a celebrated budget officer for the Department of Agriculture, who wrote that in budgeting

> . . . there inevitably are severe differences of judgment as to whether funds should be provided for a given purpose and, if so, in what amount. . . . This simply means that two sets of individuals, starting from opposite angles, even though their final objective may be the same, will find themselves miles—or I should say, "millions"—apart.
>
> It is at this stage that the departmental budget officer becomes an advocate or special pleader of the cause he represents. His position in representing the department then is analogous to that of an attorney for his client. In such circumstances, departmental budget officers put up the strongest and most effective fight of which they are capable, to obtain . . . funds. . . . On these occasions no apologies are offered for a vigorous position, or even an occasional showing of teeth, if circumstances seem to require it. The [national political] system is one of checks and balances, and the Federal machinery for combatting and deflating departmental concepts of what is necessary is so extensive and at times so difficult of persuasion that unless departmental representatives proceed to present their viewpoint in a vigorous and tenacious manner, objectives which are essential . . . to the public welfare might, for the time being at least, be submerged by some purely budgetary objective, or by the budgetary power, rather than served thereby. At this point the departmental budget officer proceeds on the principle that

the government exists to serve the needs of a great people and not primarily for the purpose of creating a model budget system. . . .[11]

It is instructive to note that Jump justifies adoption of the advocate's role partly on the grounds that other participants have counter-roles that necessitate a strong push from the departmental side.

Appropriations committee members tend to view budget officials as people with vested interests in raising appropriations. This position is generally accepted as natural and inevitable for administrators. As Assistant Chief Thayer of the Forest Service put it, "Mr. Chairman, you would not think that it would be proper for me to be in charge of this work and not be enthusiastic about it and not think that I ought to have a lot more money, would you? I have been in it for thirty years, and I believe in it." At times this attitude may lead to cynicism and perhaps annoyance on the part of House Appropriations Committee members: "When you have sat on the Committee, you see that these bureaus are always asking for more money—always up, never down. They want to build up their organization. You reach the point—I have—where it sickens you, where you rebel against it."[12]

It is usually correct to assume that department officials are devoted to increasing their appropriations. Yet this assumption alone will not prove too powerful unless we also consider their perspectives toward other goals, toward time, and toward innovation. If a department head or budget officer is concerned only with maximizing appropriations, that is one thing. But if he also has other goals—strong policy preferences, gain-

---

[11] W. A. Jump, "Budgetary and Financial Administration in an Operating Department of the Federal Government." (Mimeo.) Paper delivered at the conference of the Governmental Research Association, September 8, 1939, p. 5. See also the psychological portrait in Robert Walker, "William A. Jump: The Staff Officer As a Personality," XIV *Public Administration Review* (Autumn 1954) pp. 233-246.

[12] Fenno, *op. cit.*, p. 320.

ing control of his organization, commendation from various reference groups—then a simple maximizing position will not be appropriate. He may decide to try to cut out a program or slap down a bureau chief even though these actions result in a loss of appropriations income. "Sometimes getting more funds increases your troubles," an official declared, in a reference to strengthening certain organizational tendencies to which he was opposed. This same individual pointed out that he could never quite get himself to act in a way that would decrease his total appropriations and that he would seek to offset decreases in some areas with increases in others. Perhaps the most useful axiom would be that agency people seek to secure their other goals so long as this effort does not result in an over-all decrease in income.

Time perspectives are important because the participant who wishes to raise or lower appropriations may not act quite the same way if he wants to secure this goal immediately than if he has a long-run view. The kinds of actions that appear likely to improve one's present position (claiming great things for a program) may have just the opposite effect (disenchanting Congressmen) when the claims prove specious over a period of time. Some agency people try to maintain an "even-keel" approach that will eventually lead to a greater total through gentle increases even though the prospects of a sharp rise at first might seem tempting.

Finally, we want to examine the orientation of the participant who considers the factors affecting his present position as given and seeks to adjust his actions accordingly, versus the participant who perceives at least part of his environment as subject to change. The opportunities that these hypothetical individuals find and create may be radically different. One person acts as if he were hemmed in on all sides and another, referring to much the same conditions, tries to alter the conditions.

Hence two administrators looking at the same circumstances may decide upon different strategies because of differences in perspectives. An agency felt it had a good case for a supplemental appropriation to meet an emergency situation. The agency head was told that it would be unwise to ask for too much and that a small request of $25,000 would stand a better chance than one that would really be sufficient to do the job. He later discovered that the President liked the idea but felt that the sum was too small to justify asking for a "supplemental." The following year the top official (an "innovator") overrode objections from a more cautious colleague (an "adjustor") and came in with a supplemental for $2 million, which was granted.

DECIDING HOW MUCH TO ASK FOR

Agencies do not usually request all the money they feel they could profitably use. Most agencies find that they cannot get funds for all the projects authorized by Congress. They also have projects not yet authorized but which they believe desirable. With appropriations always falling short of authorizations and apparent needs, how much of what they would like to get do agencies ask for from the Budget Bureau and Congress? The simplest approach would be to add up the costs of all worthwhile projects and submit the total. This simple addition is not done very often, partly because everyone knows there would not be enough resources to go around. Largely, however, the reason is strategic. If an agency continually submits requests far above what it actually gets, the Budget Bureau and the appropriations committee lose confidence in it and automatically cut large chunks before looking at the budget in detail. It becomes much more difficult to justify even the items with highest priority because no one will trust an agency that repeatedly comes in too high.

But how high is too high? The difficulties an agency encounters when it guesses wrong come through clearly in the following exchange.

Rep. Rooney: How much did you [the Census Bureau] ask of the Department . . . ?

Moore [of the Census Bureau]: We asked the Department of Commerce for $89,923,564.

Rooney: How much did they cut you?

Moore: $2,735,564.

Rooney: How much did you ask of the Bureau of the Budget?

Moore: $86,500,000.

Rooney: How much did they cut you?

Moore: $16,500,000.

Rooney: So that there are other folks who do not depend as much as you ask us to depend on your estimates?

Yet it might be unrealistic for an administrator not to make some allowance for the cuts others will make.[13]

The word "pad" may be too crass to describe what goes on; administrators realize that in predicting needs there is a reasonable range within which a decision can fall and they just follow ordinary prudence in coming out with an estimate near the top. "If you do not do this," an official told me rather vehemently, "you get cut and you'll soon find that you are up to your ass in alligators." Another way of looking at it is to say

[13] Under different conditions, however, when a Congressman takes on the unusual role of advocate, the same sequence of events is given quite a different interpretation. What follows is the first exchange between the Director of the NIH and Representative John Fogarty:

Fogarty: What did you ask the Department for?

Shannon: $885,314,000.

Fogarty: What did you get from the Bureau of the Budget?

Shannon: $780,000,000.

Fogarty: Between the two, they only cut you $100 million. Did you ask for too much?

Shannon: No, sir.

Fogarty: Do you think you could use that $100 million if Congress voted it . . . ?

Shannon: I think we could use the bulk of it; yes, sir.

that in many cases "padding" consists of programs the agency wants badly but can do without, a matter of priorities.

Budgeting proceeds in an environment of reciprocal expectations that lead to self-fulfilling prophecies as the actions of each participant generate the reactions that fulfill the original expectations. Agencies are expected to pad their requests to guard against cuts. As Representative Jamie Whitten put it, ". . . If you deal with the Department [of Agriculture] long enough and learn that they scale down each time, the bureau or agency can take that into consideration and build up the original figures." The Budget Bureau is expected to cut partly because it has an interest in protecting the President's program and partly because it believes that the agency is likely to pad. The appropriations committees are expected to cut to fulfill their roles and because they believe that the agency has already made allowances for this action. Cuts may be made in the House in the expectation that the Senate will replace them. Congressmen get headlines for suggesting large cuts but they often do not follow through for they know that the amounts will have to be restored by supplemental appropriations. Things may get to the point where members of the appropriations committees talk to agency officials off the record and ask where they can make a cut that will have to be restored later. Whether it was disposed to pad or not, the agency finds that it must take into account the prospect of cuts and the cycle begins again as these prophecies confirm themselves.

William A. Jump, who spoke with the authority of great experience, believed that the internal life of agencies acted to prevent most padding. He observed to a Congressional committee:

> That there is what amounts to a natural law that is working all the time . . . that is more of a guaranty against overstaffing and similar offenses than anything that budget ex-

perts or anybody else might do, and that is that . . . our
program leaders . . . have got so many things that they see
that ought to be done within the range of authorized activity
in their respective fields . . . and that are needed in the
public interest but that they are unable to do at any given
period. . . . People who have this kind of interest in their
program simply do not use 25 employees where 20 would
suffice. . . . To do so makes it impossible to utilize men
and money for another part of the job they have been authorized to do.

Jump believed that there was greater danger of understaffing
as program leaders tried to get in as many projects as possible
without always considering whether adequate personnel was
available.[14] Against this opinion we can place the private statement of a veteran budget officer: "It can be said without con-
tradiction that seldom does the Bureau underestimate anything which it can reasonably see for the future."

We have seen that most of an agency's budget is a product
of past decisions. Beyond this area is one of discretion in
which budget people cannot get all they want but want to get
all they can. Moreover, asking for too much may prejudice
their chances of realizing a lesser amount. It soon becomes
apparent that (to use a phrase of budget officials) ability to
estimate "what will go" is a crucial aspect of budgeting.

Participants seek out and receive signals (indicators) from
the Executive Branch, Congress, clientele groups, and their
own organizations in order to arrive at a composite estimate
of what to ask for in the light of what they can expect to get.
After an Administration has been in office for a while, agency
personnel have scores of actions and informal contacts to tell
them how its various programs are regarded, especially for the
last year. They also pay attention to public announcements

[14] House Appropriations Committee, *Hearings on Agriculture Dept.
Appropriation Bill*, 79th Congress, 2nd Session, January 14, 1946, pp.
78-80.

and private reports on how tough the President is going to be in regard to new expenditures. Formal word comes in the shape of a policy letter from the Budget Bureau, which usually has some statement on how closely this year's budget should resemble the previous year's. This impression may be strengthened or weakened by reports of remarks made in Cabinet meetings or by statements from men high up in the Administration. Such a remark might be akin to one Maurice Stans, Budget Director for three years under President Eisenhower, reported that he made to the Secretary of Defense, "I hope that you can come up with a budget that will not exceed a given amount of money."[15] If the President's Science Advisor speaks favorably of a particular program, his comments may offset tough remarks by the Director of the Budget. And all these impressions are affected by the agency's experience in day-to-day dealings with the Budget Bureau staff. Their attitudes, nuances of behavior, may speak more eloquently than any public statements as to the Administration's intentions.

A major factor that agencies take into consideration is the interest of specialized publics in particular programs. Periodic reports from the field on the demand for services may serve as a general indicator. Top officials may travel and see at first hand just how enthusiastic the field personnel are about new programs. How detailed and concrete are the examples they give of public reaction? Advisory committees provide a source of information on the intentions of the interests concerned. Newspaper clipping services may also be used. The affected interests ordinarily lose no time in beating a path to the agency's door and presenting data about public support. Equally likely, the agency or its supporters in Congress generate this response. When the agency begins to notice connections between the activities of supporting interests and calls from Congressmen, it has a pretty good idea of the effectiveness of the program.

[15] *Jackson Committee Hearings*, p. 1119.

Agency officials are continuously engaged in "feeling the pulse" of Congress. What kind of action they take, however, depends on their attitudes toward Congress. Some feel comfortable in dealing with Congressmen, develop close personal relationships, and ask direct questions about future prospects. Others are fearful of Congressional contacts (though they cannot avoid them) and rely largely on the public record. The usual thing is for agency personnel to avoid blatant inquiries and to rely on other indicators. Since there is much continuity of personnel in agencies and their committees and staffs in Congress, there is a rich history on which to base predictions. The likes and dislikes of influential Congressmen are well charted. Hearings on the preceding year's budget are carefully perused for indications of attitudes on specific programs and particularly on items that may get the agency into trouble. The degree to which a Congressman goes into detail on an item and his expression at the hearings provide clues about the intensity of his feelings. First-hand information is necessary, however, because a detailed grilling may represent a Congressman's attempt to get information to take to the floor in support of the agency as well as possibly indicating hostility or concern. If the committee chairman makes a speech or lets a comment drop to the effect that not enough is being done in a certain area, the agency knows that a program in that area will meet with sympathetic consideration. Should a Congressman inform an agency, in case it did not know, that "We have heard Sam Rayburn and some of the other most distinguished members of Congress, urging us to bring up these 11 authorized watersheds more rapidly . . . ," the agency might well take the hint and ask for more. Over-all Congressional support may be indicated by debates on votes or amendments or new legislation. Finally, continuous contacts with appropriations committee staff may leave agency people with definite feelings about what is likely to go over with the committee.

Literature is now beginning to appear[16] that suggests that there is a great deal of stability with the passage of time in committee attitudes toward agencies, partly as a result of the socializing processes by which members are indoctrinated in committee norms, and partly as a result of years of contact. This finding fits in well with the point just made about agency attempts to take actions on the basis of stability in these attitudes and makes plausible the development of notions like base and fair share.

It would take a real dullard to disregard the indicators in the remarks that follow, taken from the House Appropriations hearings.

Representative O'Brien (1947, Census Bureau): I have just come back from Chicago and . . . the people of this nation are complaining about the spending of the Government's money, and they want to know when we are going to quit. . . . I do not know why you ask for these additional employees. . . . I have never been against anything you wanted. . . . It is now time to stop it. That is all I have to say.

Representative Thomas (1952, Housing and Home Finance Agency): Keep up your research. We want to admonish you to do that. We are not going to give you all of the money you think you ought to have. We are going to keep you going over a period of years because we know that you are going to come up with something that will save John Q. Public many millions of dollars.

Representative Flood (1957, Weather Bureau): Do you need dollars? . . . Can you "crash" weather observation? . . . You told Mr. Thomas that you do not have [the necessary equipment]. . . . The mood of the House is that they do not want to quibble about that [cost of equipment].

[16] See Fenno, *op. cit.*, and Charles O. Jones, "Representation in Congress: The Case of the House Agriculture Committee," LV *The American Political Science Review* (June 1961) pp. 358-367.

O'Brien's comments might be interpreted to signal a "go slow, be careful approach"; Thomas' statements might indicate "be sure to include this in moderately rising amounts"; and Flood's strongly suggests "you can get virtually anything you ask for that is remotely reasonable."

Bureaus seek information on the Department head's policy preferences. His speeches, press releases, and private comments are collected and evaluated. After an initial period of sounding him out the Bureau generally knows where it stands. One important indicator in some Departments is a letter on its budget sent out by the Secretary. Of course, a bureau may decide to disregard an unfavorable position by the Department if other signals are favorable.

The national political situation is also taken into account by agencies in deciding how much to try to get. Are there apparent political reasons for increasing or decreasing spending? Is control over the national government split between the parties with resulting competition for credit for support of particular programs or for holding the line? Do certain elements in Congress want to force Presidential vetoes or will the threat of veto result in program changes more favorable to the President? Has the concept of the balanced budget become a symbol in the political wars so that drastic efforts will be made to achieve it?

From time to time agencies are affected by emergent problems, current events which no one is in a position to predict but which radically alter budgetary prospects for particular programs. A change in missile technology, a drought, a new plant disease, advances in Soviet military capability, developments in the cold war, and similar events may drastically improve the prospects for some programs and possibly lead to restrictions on others. The agency that is able to exploit the recognized needs arising from these events is in an excellent position to expand its budgetary support and it is frequently expected to do so. When the rather sluggish Weather Bureau failed to respond immediately to the opportunities created by a series of climatic disasters in the middle 1950's, Representative Flood, who could not resist the obvious pun, was impelled to comment at an appropriations hearing: "Your Weather Bureau is looked upon by the people and has been for 100 years as a collection of old men on an island some place, and nobody ever heard of you until the last couple of years. Now you have become adults, and everybody is excited. If you do not take advantage of it you are not well advised. . . ."

The Weather Bureau did eventually respond ᵗ to this prodding, but it is clear that the mental set of the listener plays an important part in the interpretation of signals. This is as good a time as any to say that although words like "signal" and "indicator" have their uses, we must not be led into an adding-machine approach to the budgetary process—looking at the process as a matter of adding up a number of signals in a neat total. The participants live in the world as real people and not as calculating machines. Just as Dexter has shown that Congressmen tend to select what they hear from their constituents,[17] so may administrators view their signals with preconceived notions or not view them at all. Nevertheless, one would expect that over the years reality would assert itself and strong and clear signals would be received with a minimum of static.

The indicators are not formally evaluated; rather, it appears that the results flow through the minds of the responsible officials and, through internal processes they are understandably hard put to describe, emerge as conclusions about what will and will not go. These conclusions may be modified or reinforced by conversations with other officials in the agency or with their counterparts in other agencies. The most that participants will claim is to have an informed judgment or an

[17] Lewis A. Dexter, "The Representative and His District," XVI *Human Organization* (Spring 1957) pp. 2-13.

educated guess. They claim to be right most of the time but are occasionally surprised at developments running contrary to their expectations.

One may ask whether the agencies simply add up the costs of the programs for which they can get support to arrive at their total or whether they arrive at the total amount by an independent estimate. The answer seems to be that both processes of calculation go on at the same time. Obviously, the total amount is dependent upon an evaluation of how much can be gotten to support individual projects. And after a certain level has been reached, estimates of whether or not funds can be secured to support individual items depend to some extent on whether or not the total is deemed too large. A bureau official pointed out that it was not difficult to conclude that the most his department could expect to get in additional funds was $100 million. At the outside, therefore, and considering the competition of many other bureaus in the same department, his bureau could get $5 million. This same official also gave a run-down on the individual increased appropriations his bureau could hope to get and the total just turned out to be between $4 and $5 million.

The kinds of conclusions that result from this process of determining expectations may be indicated by citing a few examples. One agency decided that the next year would be tough for its budget and that increases would be particularly hard to get. It decided to try to hold the line. Senator Smith noticed this approach once when she told an administrator, "you are telling us that you are asking for what you can get rather than for what you actually need." Another agency concluded that a new pet program simply would not be approved and decided to wait for a more propitious moment lest antipathy caused by inclusion of this item jeopardize the rest of its budget. Instead, the agency concentrated on a less-expensive new program for which it expected support. A third agency decided that prospects for one program were bleak but not hopeless and that it was worth fighting for as a means of mobilizing support for future attempts. A fourth agency saw events as uniquely favorable for several of its programs and decided to get as much as possible and then try to hold on to it as a base for future years. A fifth agency deliberately disregarded what it considered a favorable opportunity in order to create a record that would enable it to have a slightly rising and stable fund for administrative expenses. The most common conclusion resulted in some range of figures considered to be the most the agency could get; figures, however, which always bore some relationship to the agency's going base plus or minus increments involving a few programs expected to garner support or run into opposition.

DECIDING HOW MUCH TO SPEND

Not only is deciding how much to ask for a problem, it is sometimes difficult for an agency to figure out precisely how much to spend. If an agency has a substantial carryover, the Budget Bureau and especially the appropriations committees may take this as a sign that the agency does not need as much as it received the previous year and may cut off that amount in the future. This practice used to lead to a last-minute flurry of spending in the fourth quarter of the year but it has been somewhat reduced by Budget Bureau apportionment of quarterly allotments. On the other hand, if the agency comes out exactly even, the suspicion is raised that the agency has merely spent up to the limit without considering the need for economy. Coming out even seems just too neat to be true. "It just seems strange," a Representative told the Army, "that you are always able to consume everything you have purchased for that specific period." Should the agency run out of funds, however, it may be accused of using the tactic of the coercive deficiency, of trying to compel Congress to appropriate more funds on the grounds that a vital activity will suffer. (It is also true that deficiencies may serve a useful political function by allowing Congressmen to appear to cut the agency's request when attention is focused on appropriations and to restore the funds in the relatively less visible deficiency hearings.) Most agency budget people try to come out with a little amount in reserve for most programs with an occasional deficit permitted in programs to which they are quite certain the funds will have to be restored. They are acutely aware that the reputation they have built up can help or hinder them greatly in matters of this kind. The agency with a reputation for economy may be praised for turning funds back and not get cut the following year, whereas the agency deemed to be prodigal may get slashed.

One outside limitation on the funds that even an affluent agency finds it useful to spend is the number of competent personnel available, the time it takes to train people for special jobs, and the material resources at hand at a point in time. It may take several years to train expert personnel or to accumulate agricultural products or hospital space without which certain projects are not feasible. An agency may discover that its field officials have put in requests that cannot be fulfilled because they do not realize that they are all competing for the same limited number of experts. The agency need not always be helpless in a situation of this kind. Like the Cancer Institute, it may seek funds for training programs that, in the words of a spokesman, "are designed to increase the supply of manpower in the disciplines needed for cancer research."

DEPARTMENT VERSUS BUREAU

We have used the term "agency" thus far because the considerations apply for the most part with equal force to departments and bureaus. Now it will be useful to make this elementary distinction in discussing the special problems that departments face in deciding how much to try to get for the bureaus under their jurisdiction. Let us assume that the Department Secretary and his staff have managed to work out some notion of what his policy preferences are and would like to implement them. Problems of influence immediately arise.[18] The most obvious is that some bureaus may have considerable support in Congress and override the department in that way. Still, the Secretary and his staff might well decide to just push their preferences if that were all that had to be considered. One difficulty is that a record of recommending far less than Congress appropriates may lead to a general disregard of what the Secretary proposes. Why pay attention if he is obviously a loser? Another difficulty is that the department officials may be in need of bureau support in other matters and may find that hostility over deep cuts interferes with the necessary good relations. After all, the bureaus are administering the programs and have the day-to-day experience and information the Secretary needs. The need for cooperation also appears in balancing requests among the bureaus. For the feeling that one or another bureau has been unfairly treated may lead to serious internal dissension, foot-dragging, and other evils. So the department often finds it wise to temper its preferences with a strong dose of calculations as to what would be acceptable to the other participants.

Just allowing each bureau to ask the Budget Bureau for what it wants has obvious disadvantages. The Secretary may lose a position of leadership and the request may be turned down severely by the Budget Bureau and Congress. There are times, however, when this approach may appear to be necessary. One Secretary of Health, Education and Welfare (HEW) found that Congress was vastly increasing departmental, not to say Budget Bureau, requests for the National Institutes of Health (NIH). Submitting low estimates had obviously failed.

[18] See Simon, et al., "The Struggle for Existence," in *Public Administration* (New York, 1950) pp. 381-422.

So the Secretary decided that it might be better to come in much higher in the hopes of assuming at least part of the leadership for health research and thus having some say in determining the program. Adopting the notion of joining them if you cannot beat them may have been the lesser evil.

Considerations such as these involve the various departments (whether they know it or not) in resolving a basic question of political theory. Shall each bureau ask for what it wants or shall it give priority to the total departmental situation in making requests? (Put in a different way the question might be phrased: Is it best for each interest to pursue its own advantage or shall each seek a solution it believes is in the interest of all?) "One of my most difficult tasks," a budget official asserted, "is finding out what these bureau people really want so I will know how to deal and bargain and oppose them if I have to. Many [bureaus] won't speak up. I don't want them to tell me what's good for the department. That's the Secretary's job and my job and his staff's too. But it is difficult to divide the pie if you don't know for sure how much of a piece each one really wants." Of course, if every bureau just shoots for the moon, the total reaches astronomical figures and that is not much help. Except in years when there are exceedingly powerful reasons for keeping budget totals down, the approach preferred by most department officials is a modified version of "tell us what you really want." Fortunately, we have an acute statement by William Jump expressing this view:

> . . . By and large in normal times we start out on the theory that while every bureau and program head . . . is expected . . . to have fully in mind probable over-all budgetary limitations . . . nevertheless the Department ought to give each bureau a chance to express its ideas of what is necessary or desirable. . . . That is one way you can be sure . . . of determining the extent to which the various bureaus have a constructive approach . . . and a carefully planned program. . . . If . . . you get the original estimates . . . too

strictly inhibited to start with . . . you will never see . . .
the plans which the head of program may have in mind.
. . . [T]hen the Department . . . [may] make such revisions as may be necessary, in the light of many over-all considerations. . . .[19]

The usual practice is for a high department official to lay the whole budget down in front of the bureau heads in an effort to explain why they cannot get any more than their share despite the fact that their programs are eminently deserving. Some budget officials are extremely talented at cutting without getting the blame.

THE BUREAU OF THE BUDGET: ROLES AND PERSPECTIVES

The dominant role of the Bureau of the Budget, in form and in fact, is to help the President carry out his purposes.[20] The orientation of the Bureau depends, therefore, on that of the President. His concerns about the relative priorities of domestic and foreign policy programs, his beliefs about the desirability of a balanced budget, his preferences, in the areas where he has them, determine a good deal of what the Bureau tries to do. Thus the Bureau finds itself trying to get appropriations from Congress for Presidential programs and, at times, prodding agencies to come in with new or enlarged programs to meet the President's desires. Yet the Budget Bureau ordinarily does not give as much weight to advocating Presiden-

[19] Jump, House Agriculture Appropriations Committee, *op. cit.*
[20] See Fritz Morstein Marx, "The Bureau of the Budget: Its Evolution and Present Role, II," XXXIX *American Political Science Review* (October 1945) pp. 869-898; Richard Neustadt, "Presidency and Legislation: The Growth of Central Clearance," XLVIII *American Political Science Review* (September 1954) pp. 641-671; Arthur Maas, "In Accord with the Program of the President?" in Carl Friedrich and Kenneth Galbraith, editors, IV *Public Policy* (Cambridge, Mass., 1954) pp. 77-93; Frederick J. Lawton, "Legislative-Executive Relationships in Budgeting as Viewed by the Executive," XIII *Public Administration Review* (Summer 1953) pp. 169-176; Aaron Wildavsky, *Dixon-Yates: A Study in Power Politics* (New Haven, 1962) p. 64.

tial programs as to seeing that they do not go beyond bounds, because everyone expects the agencies to perform the functions of advocacy. That can be seen in the responses of Budget Director Maurice Stans to a question on the role of the Bureau:

> Mr. Tufts: Did you conceive it as part of your job as Director to advise the President, then, whether departmental programs were adequate for what you call great purposes?
>
> Mr. Stans: I considered it our responsibility to do that just as much as to indicate that programs were excessive or unnecessary.
>
> I might say that the occasions for us to make recommendations along that line were very much less frequent because the agencies themselves did a pretty good job in asking for all the things that they thought they could effectively carry out.[21]

After all, if the President could count on the agencies to express his preferences, he would have less need for the Budget Bureau.

There are, of course, always some people in the Budget Bureau who identify more closely with an agency or program than do others, or who develop policy preferences independent of the President. They have a creative urge. "I don't like to think of myself as a red-pencil man." They see themselves as doing the right thing by pursuing policies in the public interest and they may convince themselves that the President would support them if only he had the time and inclination to go into the matter as deeply as they had. They would rarely resist a direct Presidential command, but these are few at any one time and ordinarily leave much room for interpretation. The role adopted by its budget examiners is important to an agency even if the general orientation of the Budget Bureau is different.

Even within the same Administration, different budget di-

[21] *Jackson Committee Hearings*, pp. 1104-1111.

rectors can have an impact of their own on the Budget Bureau's decisions. Some Directors have much better relationships with the President than others; they get in to see him more often and without going through subordinates; he backs them up more frequently on appeals from the agencies. This kind of information is eagerly sought and circulates rapidly. Not only did the four Directors under President Eisenhower differ in these respects, but their policy preferences also varied within the wide meaning of conservatism, and they exhibited rather striking differences in qualities like judgment, tenacity, and initiative.

Should the President turn down an appeal, the agency and its supporting interests may seek to discover how much of an increase they can get from Congress without risking a Presidential veto or strong opposition from him. The President really cannot insist on precise and strict limitation of funds. If he says $500 million, he can hardly object to $503 or probably $510 million and the agency may seek the highest point in this game. This tactic may encourage setting a lower figure to compensate for the expected small increase.

In bargaining on recommendations a Budget Director who is close to the President has an important advantage since he knows how much leeway he has within the Chief Executive's desires. In the final instance the President, though he lacks an item veto, may halt the spending of appropriations by impounding the funds. He cannot go too far lest he raise a great outcry in Congress; he can only choose a few items.[22] But there is today far more acceptance of impounding than in previous years. Congressmen sometimes object to impounding because it diminishes their power over appropriations. Upon hearing that the Department of Agriculture had secured a Presidential directive freezing funds for the Soil Conservation Service that had been appropriated only three weeks before,

[22] See Inter-University Case Program, "The Impounding of Funds by the Bureau of the Budget," ICP Case Series No. 28, November 1955.

Representative Whitten remarked angrily that, "To freeze these funds means that the policy expressed by Congress was not controlling." Yet Congressmen are ready enough to use it, as Representative Thomas did when he said, "I do not think the money [expanding the Air Force] should be used. I think it should be impounded, and I have the impression that if the money is appropriated it may not be used."

Congressmen manifest ambivalent feelings about the Bureau of the Budget; they regard it essentially as a necessary evil. The ambivalence comes through when a member of the House Appropriations Committee speaks at one time with a trace of contempt of Bureau officials as a bunch of bureaucrats who think they are making the budget, and at another occasion reviles them for not having done enough. The Bureau may be regarded as a rival for control of appropriations. Representative Flood dramatized this feeling when he said, "Mr. Secretary [of Defense] . . . you are a very important man in the Government . . . but you are a minor deity, believe me, compared to the Director of the Budget. He is the Poo-Bah of this town. . . . I feel so strongly about it and many members of the committee and Congress, that we think the Bureau of the Budget as it is now set up should be ripped out altogether. . . ." But it does help set the agenda of the appropriations committees by establishing a starting point, and it does serve to reduce the crushing amount of work for even the most conscientious member.

Attitudes toward the Bureau shift according to the degree to which its actions are believed to promote or hinder the particular program in which a Congressman or agency official is interested. Congressmen sometimes find the Bureau insensitive to considerations of practical politics both in relation to their constituency demands and to their requirements as members of a legislative social system who have to get along with their colleagues. "Don't they know we have to live, too?" says a Congressman. People in the Budget Bureau return the favor by viewing many Congressmen as people overly concerned with local advantage to the detriment of national interest. "All they care about is taking care of their parochial little corner," says a Bureau man.

Every agency and its officials have to decide what kind of relationship to maintain with the Budget Bureau and particularly with the examiners it assigns. Since no examiner can know everything unless the information is volunteered, the agency may decide to provide only that information which is specifically requested. More and more, however, there is a tendency to actually push information at the examiners all the time and not merely when they ask. Why? First, abundant information helps the examiners to be competent defenders of the agency's viewpoint at Budget Bureau meetings when agency personnel is not represented. Second, the examiners may become converted into advocates of particular programs. Third, the examiners' knowledge can be turned to advantage by getting them to secure Administration assistance in clearing up some difficulty. The major disadvantage, of course, is that the examiners "get to know where the bodies are buried this way," as one budget officer put it. But, he continued in words echoed by many others, "you can't hide serious weaknesses for very long anyway, and so the advantages far outweigh the disadvantages."

Budget Bureau and agency personnel have certain beliefs about one another which both vehemently deny but which are widespread. One belief is that Budget Bureau people get promotions on the basis of how successful they are in coming up with a figure that is not changed much by Congress. "You won't believe it, and they will deny it, and I can't prove it, but I am not alone in my belief that Budget people get ahead by how close Congress comes to what they recommend." A corresponding belief is that budget officers get promoted by the degree of success they have in getting the Bureau and Congress to raise appropriations.[23] Whether these beliefs are correct or not, the fact that they are so readily accepted suggests much about the images they have of one another. Where agency personnel have formerly worked for the Bureau, or where the Bureau has managed to help secure difficult appropriations, its image is much more positive. In general, however, the Bureau is regarded as an essentially negative institution. "It can hurt you," a typical response goes, "but it can't and won't help you very much."

Agency people agree that Budget Bureau support is worth having if you can get it without sacrificing too much in Congress. Given Congressional propensity to cut, what the Budget Bureau proposes for an agency is likely to be the upper limit (see Table 2-2). In addition, there are multitudes of small items which Congress would not ordinarily investigate but which might get into trouble if the Bureau's approval were lacking. On occasion, Bureau backing may be helpful in gaining support, particularly if the President is known to approve. Yet agency men recognize two basic limitations on Budget Bureau influence.

A most serious handicap under which the Budget Bureau labors is not so much that Congress may raise its estimates (though this is obviously important) but that it cannot guarantee that a cooperating agency will receive the amount it has recommended. (See Table 2-2, number 3, which shows that Bureau estimates are reduced about three-fourths of the time.) If agencies could depend on receiving the Budget Bureau's figures, they would have much greater incentive to cooperate. The Bureau thus becomes another important road-

---

[23] On the basis of interviews, David S. Brown reports that ". . . Budget officers know the success of their programs. One reported '1,000 batting average,' based on the fact Congress had not cut a penny from his agency estimates in six years. . . ." "The Staff Man Looks in the Mirror," XXIII *Public Administration Review* (June 1963) p. 63.

block in the governmental process; after agencies surmount this hurdle they still have to get money from Congress.

TABLE 2-2*

Congress frequently cuts Budget Bureau estimates.**

	No difference	Estimates greater than recommended	Estimates less than recommended	Other
(1) Budget estimate as compared to House Committee recommendation	74 cases	342 cases	27 cases	1 case
(2) Budget estimate compared to House Bill	70	344	29	1
(3) Budget estimate compared to final appropriation	62	316	66	

* Figures supplied by Richard Fenno.
** Table shows summary of appropriations histories of 37 bureaus dealing with domestic policies for 12 years (1947-59) (444 cases in all).

The most serious obstacle to acceptance of Budget Bureau leadership is that Congress determines appropriations. Everyone knows that agencies make end-runs around the Bureau to gain support from Congress. If they do so too often, the Budget Bureau finds that its currency has depreciated. Hence the Bureau frequently accepts consistent Congressional action as a guide. A close eye is kept on Congressional action for the preceding year before an agency's total is set for the next one. Failure to do so might leave the Bureau with a record of defeat that jeopardizes its effectiveness in other areas.

The basic situation is immediately apparent to other participants in budgeting. The man whose requests are continually turned down in Congress finds that he tends to be rejected in the Budget Bureau and in his own department as well. Again, the Budget Bureau follows Congressional action.

This fact is of enormous significance because it leads to pivotal strategic moves. Suppose an agency must choose between alternatives, one favored by Congressmen, another by the Budget Bureau. The strategy indicated would be to side with Congress because one's record with Congress determines how one is viewed and treated by the Budget Bureau and the Department. These considerations weaken the Bureau of the Budget in the eyes of the agency.

A popularity poll would no doubt reveal a strong tendency for agencies that get much more than the Budget Bureau recommends to be unpopular in that institution. This attitude is understandable. No one likes to be overruled. The Budget Bureau may go so far as to scrutinize the requests of such agencies with special care. But the political realities take most of the pleasure out of this practice. What is the point of more careful scrutiny if you cannot implement your findings and, in any event, do not want your recommendation to be consistently too far off? The Bureau finds itself treating agencies it dislikes much better than those it may like better but who cannot help themselves nearly as much in Congress. The "popularity" of those who cannot help themselves is bound to wane in the Budget Bureau as annoyance at having to take over the job of pushing the agency's programs if they are to be pushed at all (when the President would rather use his resources elsewhere) triumphs over the agency's willingness to accord deference.

DECIDING HOW MUCH TO RECOMMEND

The Bureau of the Budget (BOB) faces in an extreme form the perplexing problem of deciding how much it believes should be spent on particular programs. An agency may solve the problem by getting as much as it can. But in the absence of specific Presidential guidance, the BOB is put in the position of trying to decide how desirable a program might be on its intrinsic merits.

Let us take an extreme case. How much should be devoted to medical research sponsored by the Federal Government? Most of us would say, "quite a lot." But how much is that? A million, a hundred million, a billion? BOB personnel do not have the technical competence in medical research to evaluate specific proposals and they are not certain they should spend their limited time in this way; they would rather set priorities. Technical criteria like cost-benefit ratios would be helpful if they existed, but even so the determination of what may qualify as a benefit would be crucial. (Having decided how much one wants to spend, standards may be devised that permit that much to be justified.) No one really knows how much medical research might be carried on profitably in some sense,[24] and the BOB people have discovered that there seems to be no end to the work qualified people believe it desirable to attempt. With painful awareness that they are violating deeply held notions of rationality, the responsible officials leave the area of intrinsic merits because it does not help them make decisions and turn instead to other criteria which may not be "rational" but which do help them.

They may try to give the question a political cast—how much is our society willing to spend?—and come up with what we have described as an expected level of appropriations, which narrows their burden of calculation considerably by giving them directions.[25] But in the case of the NIH

[24] A beginning in discussing some economic guide lines has been made by Burton A. Weisbrod in *The Economics of Public Health; Measuring the Economic Impact of Diseases* (Philadelphia, 1961), but the implications of using pure economic criteria are startling, if not inhuman.

[25] In addressing himself to the question of evaluating program effectiveness, Elmer B. Staats, an experienced, high-level official in the Bureau of the Budget, declared: "I think basically and foremost there is the political test—'Political' in the broad policy and program sense, but also in the more traditional sense of party labels and political campaigns.

(which I have chosen for this very reason) there is not yet (though the time may be approaching) agreement on a fair share. Nor is there another formula, however arbitrary—such as devoting 1 per cent of the Gross National Product or allowing a rise of 10 per cent a year—which justifies a course of action. So the BOB has the choice of cutting NIH arbitrarily and being drastically overridden by Congress, or of raising it arbitrarily and feeling that the situation has gotten out of hand.

Here is a story of one actual attempt to wrestle with this problem.

Respondent: My day to day work was not very effective. It was a desperate attempt at wondering how to grasp ahold of this whole business. . . . We couldn't get a meaningful standard to judge as to how much medical research the Government should support.

Interviewer: How did the BOB decide where and how much to cut the NIH request?

Respondent: This is a very good question. I wonder how we did decide. I would say as a generalization that it was some kind of a mechanical factor like "let's hold it to last year's budget" or "last year's budget plus 10% of new grants" . . . or just "10% increase over last year."

Interviewer: How did you arrive at this figure?

Respondent: We do it on an ad hoc basis. 10% sounds right. . . . They [the NIH] may point out that it doesn't demonstrate a 10% growth due to certain factors, so we will give them say 12.5%. . . . We were playing around with graphs and figures. Curves . . . projecting growth to 1965

This is the real test of program effectiveness. Society is constantly applying this test to the party organizations, to the Congress, to the President who is the only person elected by all of us, to the pressure group that is concerned with a particular program—and the test is the measure of whatever it is that causes people to identify themselves with one party or candidate rather than another." From "Evaluating Program Effectiveness," in D. L. Bowen and L. K. Caldwell, editors, *Selected Papers on Public Administration*, Institute of Training for Public Service, Department of Government, Indiana University (Bloomington, Ind., 1960) p. 62.

and say the figure was 1.3 billion. The people in the BOB will say, let's reach 1.3 billion not by 1965 but by 1975. So we cut the figure by the percent to reach it [by 1975]. . . . There was an argument on what to start with as the base, the unobligated balance to be included or not. If we take the lower figure we could give them the same rate of growth but it would be say $60 million less than they asked. . . . I would get the [NIH] estimate and come up with my recommendation. This would have to be a little lower than the department request.

Interviewer: Why?

Respondent: Because I didn't think it was appropriate to give the same amount the department asked, so I cut a little. From here my recommendation went to the division review meeting. . . . I would say they [the NIH] asked for say a 32% increase and I allowed 23%. Comments might go like this. "We have to put a stop to this NIH." "Congress will up it anyway no matter what we do. . . ." Then somebody will say, "Let's hold it to last year's level." But somebody else would reply, "No, that is no good. That isn't realistic at all. There has to be some increase." Then another would say, "Can we raise them 10% and get a rationalization for this?" and we will try to figure one out." . . .

Interviewer: How about apportionment of appropriations?

Respondent: Usually what happened was the President's budget got shot to hell with major increases. The staff [of the BOB] would consider the possibility of a veto. But you can't veto a health bill politically. It makes the President in favor of cancer. But you can't just crawl under a rock. What can you do?

There are several alternatives and we can at least set down the type of calculations that go into each one. The most obvious is for the BOB to shoot from the hip and let the bodies fall where they may. The feeling here may be that if the BOB does what it believes is right and protests long enough something will be done. The opposite rationale holds that it is foolish to continually estimate under or over what Congress will probably give. (Similar cries like "they'll roll us on the floor," or "the Senate will put the item in and get the credit," are also heard on the House Appropriations Committee.) Note the dialogue in which a Census Bureau official explained why the BOB turned down a request. "Representative Stefan: Apparently they [the BOB] anticipated what this committee might do. Mr. Hauser: That was exactly the language they used." Another possibility is for the BOB to come in just a little low in the hopes that it can slowly apply a brake to a program it believes is expanding too fast. Or the BOB may on rare occasion seek to take leadership by proposing greatly increased expenditures itself and in this way hope to exercise a larger voice in determining the content of the program. Now the Bureau appears to have adopted an incremental approach whereby it uses various rules of thumb to estimate the relative importance of the last proposed increases, and it is apparently making progress.

The case of the NIH is an unusual one but like a medical case history it does serve to highlight factors operating to a lesser degree in more normal organisms. The extreme case is especially valuable for our purposes because of the understandable reluctance of people to admit that their decisions are sometimes based on something less than the epitome of reasoned judgment. In many areas of budgeting, of course, there are more explicit criteria of judgment. Experience has been accumulated and it is possible to speak more securely of consequences of doing this or that. A level of funds has been reached through the political process. Work-load data or cost-benefit analysis has been developed to some degree. A close look at this kind of criterion, however, shows that most of the standards are not directly based on intrinsic merit—as an ideal cost-benefit analysis might be—but on "extrinsic" criteria such as limits beyond which Congress will not go. Yet the problems of calculation would be so vast without the extrinsic standards—where would one begin?—that it is difficult to see how decisions could be made unless some person or group dictated them. Hence the paradox that the extrinsic factors most often criticized—historical development, self-evident meeting points, stress on agreement—provide essential means for limiting the range of calculation so that factors intrinsic to the worth of the program have an opportunity to be given some weight.

THE APPROPRIATIONS COMMITTEES:
ROLES AND PERSPECTIVES

When Representative Preston asked, "Is there anything fantastic about this 18th Decennial Census that . . . we should know about as guardians of the taxpayer's money?" he was describing the prevailing role played by members of the House Appropriations Committee. As guardians of the public purse, committee members are expected to cast a skeptical eye on the blandishments of a bureaucracy ever anxious to increase its dominion by raising its appropriations. After an administrator spoke of the wonderful things accomplished by research in forestry, Representative Clarence Cannon struck the proper note by replying, "All these Government researchers every year come in here and outline . . . great progress that has been made in the various industries and claim credit for them where it would have gone ahead if they had not been in existence, and you are no exception to that rule."

There is perhaps something here of the romantic conception of the sheriff warding off the mob, Horatio at the bridge, or of the unknown and unappreciated but faithful servant who guards his master's fortune against the pernicious schemes of wasteful relatives. Fenno quotes a veteran committee member to the effect that "No subcommittee of which I have been a member has ever reported out a bill without a cut in the budget. I'm proud of that record."[26] In typical comments John Rooney, who guards the State Department budget, says, "I am questioning you for the taxpayer. I ap-

---

[26] Fenno, *op. cit.*, pp. 311-312.

proach [the budget] with the idea that it can be cut. It's an asking price." Another committee member says, "Here we look at the bright side. We see a reduction." In order to provide an objective check on the effectiveness of this orientation, Fenno examined the appropriations histories of 37 bureaus concerned with domestic policies from 1947-1959 and discovered that the committee reduced the estimates it received 77.2 per cent of the time.[27]

It cannot be emphasized too often, however, that we are describing the most generally accepted role, and not the only one, which guides all committee members in all cases. There are members who identify completely with an agency or its programs. "To me forestry has become a religion . . ." said Representative Walter Horan. In a profound violation of House Committee norms, he took his protest against his own appropriations subcommittee to the Senate hearings, declaring that "The items are totally inadequate and I do not care particularly which way *we* get them, but *we* do need funds. . . ." (Emphasis supplied.) There are also subcommittees such as the one headed by Representative Fogarty on the National Institutes of Health, which obviously see their role as proponents of greater spending. And there are also Congressmen like Daniel Flood who switch roles from one subcommittee to the next, acting like the protector of national defense in one place and an economy advocate in another.

At times, then, the sense of having served a great cause expressed in terms of public interest may create a sense of identification with an agency or program that overwhelms other considerations. This feeling comes through in the poignant remarks Representative Anderson addressed to the Administrator of the Soil Conservation Service.

> You know every man serving in Congress hopes to leave his imprint in some small way upon work in which he is interested.

[27] *Ibid.*, p. 312.

The activities of our Government and the responsibilities are so vast that we are fortunate if we leave Congress even after twenty or thirty years and have our name attached even in a slight degree to something really worthwhile, and I am proud of the fact that sixteen years ago, gentlemen, I was fighting to increase in this very room the money set aside for soil conservation operations.

The desire to cut the budget may conflict with the desire not to damage programs vital to the nation. At such a time a Congressman may try to get the best of both worlds by asking the agency to assume the responsibility of reconciling the divergent roles. As Representative Jensen once put it to the Atomic Energy Commission:

> The members of this committee certainly would not take it upon themselves to blindly make a cut in your appropriation because of the fact that it is such an important function. However, it may be that after this so-called post mortem of your budget request for this committee you might be able to find an item or two that you could reduce to a degree. . . . I would not like to have it on my conscience.

In the case of local constituency interests, the deviation from guardianship of the budget is exceedingly powerful because it touches on the most basic relationship a Congressman may have—that with the people who elect him and might conceivably defeat him—and because Congressmen are prone to take as an article of faith another of their roles as defender of constituency interests. Where their constituencies are affected, appropriations committee members use all the vast leverage over men and money which their positions give them to secure favorable outcomes. The battle-royal that Representative John Rooney engaged in to keep a Department of Commerce office in New York City so that his constituents would not lose their jobs would make a fascinating story in itself. An Assistant Secretary of Commerce had the temerity to suggest that this was not exactly an example of ideal administration, and Rooney lit into him. "Do you mean that employees of long standing, who, for instance, live right in my Congressional district . . . have no right to . . . raise their voices to prevent the loss of jobs . . . ? Were any of the employees who came to this committee from that New York office penalized . . . ?" "I can assure you that was not done, Mr. Congressman," said the Assistant Secretary. Then there was Representative Ivor Fenton's tenacious campaign to have an anthracite laboratory located in Schuylkill Haven instead of Hazleton, Pennsylvania. Fenton said that he got no action until he got on the Appropriations Committee. At that time he accused the Secretary of the Interior of "the cheapest kind of politics" and decided "that no funds now available for the laboratory be obligated until this matter is clarified to the satisfaction of the Appropriations Committee." The funds were denied. In the other chamber, Senator Meyers spoke of "exceptional energy on the part of one of the subcommittee members in seeking to establish some sort of political plot to locate the laboratory in a district other than his." The law that was passed specified that the laboratory had to be built in Schuylkill Haven. A little arm-twisting was applied by Senator Lyndon Johnson in order to make certain that a prison was built in the right place. "I sure would hate to put in this money to build a prison in Congressman Grey's district and Senator Dirksen's state in Illinois and find out that they got it in X, Y, Z, somewhere." It is not surprising to discover that the new space center is being constructed in the home city of Representative Thomas, the subcommittee chairman dealing with the space agency.

Tough as they may be in cutting the budgets of their agencies, appropriations committee members, once having made their decision, generally defend the agencies against further cuts on the floor.[28] This kind of action is in part self-

[28] In an exchange with a member of the Appropriations Committee, Representative Clarence Brown complained that when an amendment is

interest. The power of the appropriations subcommittees would be diminished if their recommendations were successfully challenged very often. Members believe that the House would "run wild" if "orderly procedure"—that is, acceptance of committee recommendations—were not followed. But the role of defender also has its roots in the respect for expertise and specialization in Congress, and the ensuing belief that members who have not studied the subject should not exercise a deciding voice without the presence of overriding considerations. An appeal to this norm is usually sufficient to block an attempt to reduce appropriations, as Senator Douglas has discovered many times. Appropriations Committee members, McKellar cried on one occasion, had "worked almost like slaves on the bill. . . . Here at the last moment comes an amendment offered by a Senator who has not taken part in any hearings." Douglas was squashed then as he has been ever since on the same grounds.

A member of the Senate Appropriations Committee is likely to conceive of his proper role as the responsible legislator who sees to it that the irrepressible lower House does not do too much damage either to constituency or to national interests. Though members of the House Appropriations Committee tend to view their opposite members in the Senate as frivolous dilettantes who swap favors and do not care what happens to the public purse, Senators tend to reverse the compliment by regarding their brethren in the other chamber as jealous and power-hungry types who do not care what happens to "essential" programs so long as they can show that they have made cuts. Senator Mundt expressed this feeling in 1957 when he said, in regard to a Bureau of Indian Affairs ap-

---

offered "to reduce an appropriations item, the Appropriations Committee stands like a stone wall most of the time, saying 'No, you mustn't touch this.' That is one of the things that has brought complaint against your committee, sir, and you know it. . . ." House Government Operations Subcommittee, *Improving Federal Budgeting and Appropriations*, 85th Congress, 1st Session, 1957, p. 139.

propriation, "I think it is important to have in the record . . . that the House finds no fault with the program of construction. They just failed to provide the money. The need is there and it is our responsibility to meet that need. . . ." House members would say that there is also a need for restraint. The difference in perspective between the two committees was illustrated by Senator Dirksen, who used to glory in his role as tough guardian of the purse. Referring to a House action to reduce from ten to six the number of employees, Dirksen said, "It was great, good fun when I was on the House Appropriations Committee to cut four [positions]. Too often you discover that the six positions depend in large measure on the four. You just wasted the money for the six. I would rather give you nothing or whatever it takes to do a good job."

The Senators are rather painfully aware of the House Committee's pre-eminence in the field of appropriations and they know that they cannot hope to match the time and thoroughness that the House body devotes to screening requests. For this reason, the Senate Committee puts a high value on having agencies carry appeals to it. "We all know," said Senator Richard Russell, "that almost since the inception of the Government, the Senate Appropriations Committee has served as an appeal body and has heard requests . . . that deal principally with items that have been changed or reduced or eliminated by the House of Representatives." The Senators value their ability to disagree on items in dispute as a means of maintaining their influence in crucial areas while putting the least possible strain on their time and energy. The dominant Senate role of responsible appeals court is dependent upon agency advocacy and House committee guardianship.

Although it is true the Senate frequently increases the amount of appropriations voted by the House, this relationship varies with the agency, the issue area, and the particular item. Given significant differences in the degree of success with which various agencies secure their appropriation goals, it is not overly helpful to say that the Senate generally grants more than the House. For we must account for the differences between agencies and programs, occasions when this relationship does not hold at all, and the broad differences in the percentages of increase offered by the Senate.

In policy areas such as natural resources, in which the Senate increases the amount passed by the House, the result may be a product of two factors. First, the interests desiring the increased appropriation are better represented in the Senate. The fact, for example, that the Reclamation Bureau works in seventeen western states gives it a much greater influence in the Senate than in the House, where a much smaller percentage of representatives are directly concerned. Second, the House, knowing that the Senate will increase funds, lowers its amount for bargaining purposes and the Senate correspondingly increases its amount in a pattern of reciprocal expectations. House and Senate members claim that the others do more of this than they do.

The impact of gerrymandering and failure to reapportion on representation in the House may be a third factor affecting its desire to spend. State legislatures are commonly strongholds of conservatism that resist giving more equality of representation to voters from urban areas who would elect men with a more favorable view on certain kinds of spending. Senators give more representation to constituencies that wish to spend. The result is that the Senate today is more liberal than the House in several senses of that word.[29]

Keenly aware of the particular roles adopted by the members of the appropriations subcommittees who deal with their programs, the predominant view that agency officials have of these legislators is that they are very powerful people. "They

[29] See Lewis A. Froman, Jr., "Why the Senate Is More Liberal than the House" in *Congressmen and Their Constituencies* (Chicago, 1963), pp. 69-97.

can do you a world of good and they can cut your throat."
"These men, notably the Chairman, can murder you and also
make things easy." The figures in Table 2-3, which show that
Appropriations Committee recommendations in both houses
are accepted almost nine out of every ten times, bear elo-
quent testimony to the accuracy of these perceptions. Experienced, tough, coming from safe districts, recognized as
pre-eminent in their specialized domains by other legislators,
these men are in a position to control the financial life of the
agencies within fairly wide zones of tolerance. So long as they
do not violate widespread and intense preferences among fellow legislators, they can do much to reward or punish agencies
and their personnel without much fear of being contradicted.
Newsweek (April 7, 1958) quotes a State Department official
as saying, "Let's face it. When Rooney whistles, we've just
got to dance." Another investigator reports that "one otherwise articulate official was so unstrung after testifying that he
offered his resignation as soon as he returned to his office. Another was caught by his wife arguing with an imaginary
Rooney."[30] There is no getting away from it: a single individual in these key committee positions can wield great
power, as the careers of Representatives John Rooney and
John Fogarty and Senators Carl Hayden and Lister Hill,
among many others, demonstrate.

Staff members of the Appropriations Committees view
themselves as neutral servants of Congressmen. Of course,
they know that they have opinions and that personal preferences may influence their opinions. But they try to serve
members of their committee well regardless of whether or not
they agree with them. Unless their relationship is close, the
staff rarely proffers advice to a Congressman on their own;
they wait to be asked. Then the staff will answer in terms of
the question and say that if the Congressman wants X, then

[30] Peter Wyden, "The Man Who Frightens Bureaucrats," *Saturday
Evening Post* (January 31, 1959) p. 87.

he should do Y. Or a staff man may confine himself to specifying the likely consequences of policy moves proposed by Congressmen. At all times the staff shuns publicity as an invasion of the prerogative of Congressmen.

TABLE 2-3*

Recommendations of the appropriations committees are usually adopted.**

	No difference	Committee recommendation greater than bill	Committee recommmendation less than bill	Other
House Committee recommendations compared with final House bill	387 (87.4%)	30	26	1
Senate Committee recommendations compared with Senate bill	390 (88.0%)	14	40	
Summary of floor action on committee recommendations in both houses	777 (87.6%)	44	66	

* Figures supplied by Richard Fenno.
** Table is based on histories of 37 bureaus dealing with domestic policies for 12 years (1947-59) (888 cases in all).

When the subcommittee chairman is less competent than usual and not very industrious, committee staff may find themselves shaping more policy. They may mold the line of inquiry, order the consideration of alternatives, and take a larger part in writing recommendations about appropriations. Even under different circumstances, however, the staff has extensive influence over the disposition of small items which may have escaped the attention of Congressmen or which may or may not be lost in the shuffle at the end of a session, depending on how the staff acts.

Many agencies choose to keep subcommittee staff informed

months and sometimes years ahead on new developments. This expedient enables the staff to have ready explanations if and when Congressmen make inquiries. At times, the agency is placed in a position in which it would not like to reveal certain information to the staff but fears that failure to do so will be considered a breach of confidence. Career officials and political appointees who look forward to years of service are often willing to make some sacrifices by providing information in the hope that they will gain by the increase in confidence that may result. They also tend to believe that it is better to provide the information themselves than to have it turn up without their cooperation and without their being able to put the best possible interpretation on it.

Although it appears that agency personnel are more dependent on committee staff than vice versa, the relationship is by no means a one-way proposition. The staff man knows that he can do a more effective job if he has the cooperation of the budget officer. For much of the staff's work is dependent on securing information from the agency about current programs and the possible effects of various changes. The staff may be blamed for not informing Congressmen of changes in agency plans and expenditures. And when complex problems arise, the agency may actually do the work for the staff. Mutual dependence is the order of the day and both sides generally regard their contacts as prerequisites to doing their best work. Yet mutual dependence is, of necessity, tinged with the realization that committee staff and budget officers represent different organizations, whose roles are not completely compatible.

DECIDING HOW MUCH TO GIVE:
THE APPROPRIATIONS COMMITTEES

The ways in which the appropriations committees go about making budgetary calculations are profoundly affected by their central position in the Congressional system. Their power to make budgetary decisions is in a sense dependent upon their ability to help keep the system going by meeting the needs of other Congressmen. Appropriations must be voted each year if the government is to continue to function. (The experience of the Fourth French Republic, in which the practice of voting "twelfths" [one month's appropriations] because of inability to agree sapped the stability of the regime, is instructive on this point.) To put together budgets running into the billions of dollars and involving innumerable different activities is a huge task. In order to make the necessary decisions the committees must reduce the enormous burden of calculation involved in budgeting. Otherwise, the necessity for decision might propel them into making random or wholly capricious choices that would throw governmental operations out of kilter by sudden stops and headlong starts. Nor could Congress as a whole take on the burden. The bulk of Congressmen are busy with other things. They can hardly hope to become knowledgeable in more than a few areas of budgeting, if that. Some way of reducing their information costs must be found unless they are to abdicate their powers. And the way they have adopted of doing so is to accept the verdict of the appropriations committees most of the time, intervening just often enough to keep the committees roughly in line.

Budgeting is specialized. There are multiple levels of specialization within Congress—the House and Senate Appropriations Committees, their subcommittees, the subject areas within these subcommittees, the Senate Appropriations Committee appeals procedure, the Conference Committee, and the authorizations functions of the substantive committees and their specialized subcommittees. Most of the decisions in the House Appropriations Committee are taken in its specialized subcommittees. "Why, you'd be branded an impostor," a House subcommittee chairman said, "if you went into one of those other subcommittee meetings. The only time I go is by appointment, by arrangement with the chairman at a special time. I'm as much a stranger in another subcommittee as I would be in [a substantive committee]. Each one [subcommittee] does its work apart from all others."[31] The full committee rarely acts and even then only in regard to a few items. Members ordinarily take the position that each subcommittee accepts the results of the others in their respective jurisdictions and that the House and Senate follow the recommendations of the committees. "Had I been sitting on this [sub]committee," a House member said, "I undoubtedly would not have agreed with all the items. I am not on that [sub]committee. It is not my responsibility." And within their subcommittees members ordinarily concentrate on a particular area such as mental health or small watersheds. Statements such as, "I will leave the questioning to our great expert on . . ." abound in appropriations hearings. The situation in the Senate differs somewhat in that there is considerable overlap of membership between substantive and appropriations subcommittees and outsiders from the substantive subcommittees are welcome at hearings. The Senate does, however, add another level of specialization through its appeals procedure. Each level of specialization, then, is wrapped within the other with the applicable decision-rule in most cases being that the most specialized member or members carry the day. Coupled with the preferred political style of long hours and hard work, especially in the House, specialization confers considerable influence upon those who practice it.

Budgeting is historical. Since members usually serve in Congress for several years before getting on the appropriations committees, and they are expected to serve an apprenticeship before making themselves heard, the more influential among

[31] Fenno, *op. cit.*, p. 316.

them typically have years of experience in dealing with their specialties. They have absorbed a series of past moves and are prepared to apply the results of their previous calculations to present circumstances. In this way the magnitude of any one decision at any one time is reduced and with it the burden of calculation. An historical approach is facilitated by a line-item budgetary form. Instead of necessarily focusing attention on various programs as a whole, the committees usually concentrate on changes in the various items—personnel, equipment, maintenance, specific activities—which make up the program. ". . . we will take an awfully long look when we come to the part of your budget that adds 5 additional people to the agency," Representative Jensen assured the Fish and Wildlife Service in 1960. By keeping the categories constant over a number of years, and by requiring that the previous and present year's figures be placed in adjacent columns, the calculations made in the past need not be gone over again completely. And though the members know that the agency is involved in various programs, the line-item form enables them to concentrate on the less divisive issue of how much for each item.

Budgeting is fragmented.   Budgets are made in fragments. Each subcommittee, and sometimes specialists within these bodies, operates as a largely autonomous unit concerned only with a limited area of the budget. Even the subcommittees do not attend to all the items in the budget but pay special attention to instances of increases or decreases over the previous year. In this way, it might be said, the subcommittees deal with a fragment of a fragment of the whole. Fragmentation is further increased by the Senate Appropriations Committee, which focuses its attention on items that are appealed from House decisions. The Senators, therefore, often deal with a fragment of what is already (through House action) a fragment of a fragment.

Budgeting is treated as if it were non-programmatic. This statement does not mean that appropriations committee people do not care about programs; they do. Nor does it mean that they do not fight for or against some programs; they do. What it does mean is that they view most of their work as marginal, monetary adjustments to existing programs so that the question of the ultimate desirability of most programs arises only once in a while. "A disagreement on money isn't like a legislative program . . ." one member said in a typical statement, "it's a matter of money rather than a difference in philosophy." An appropriations committee member explains how disagreements are handled in the mark-up session when members retire behind closed doors to work out their recommendations. "If there's agreement, we go right along. If there's a lot of controversy we put the item aside and go on. Then, after a day or two, we may have a list of ten controversial items. We give and take and pound them down till we get agreement."[32]

Budgeting is repetitive. Decision making in budgeting is carried on with the knowledge that few problems have to be "solved" once and for all. Everyone knows that a problem may be dealt with over and over again. Hence considerations that a Congressman neglects one year may be taken up by himself another year or in a supplementary action during the same year. Problems are not so much solved as they are worn down by repeated attacks until they are no longer pressing or have been superseded by other problems.

Budgeting is sequential. The appropriations committees do not try to solve every problem at once. On the contrary, they do not deal with many problems in a particular year, and those they do encounter are dealt with mostly in different places and at different times. They allow many decisions made in previous years to stand or to vary slightly without

[32] *Ibid.*

question. Then they divide up subjects for more intensive inquiry among subcommittees and their specialists. Over the years the subcommittees center now on one and then on another problem. When the budgetary decisions made by one subcommittee adversely affect those of another the difficulty is handled by "fire-truck tactics"; that is, by dealing with each problem in turn in whatever jurisdiction it appears. Difficulties are overcome not so much by central coordination or planning as by attacking each manifestation in the different centers of decision in sequence.[33]

The Conference Committee carries on the process of sequential calculation by concentrating on the items of difference between the Senate and House. The bargaining is carried on in great secrecy to facilitate give and take. For the Conference Committee to fail to reach agreement on many items would disrupt the entire legislative process, especially since their deliberations frequently take place at the tail end of the session. One way to secure agreement is to swap items in dispute. Referring to a Conference Committee session on the United States Information Agency, Representative Coudert reported that the House agreed to raise its figure and "in return the Senate yielded on these little things. . . . When you have different things in dispute the two [subcommittee] chairmen [Representative Rooney and Senator Kilgore] just trade them off, back and forth." Another way of reaching agreement has been described by T. C. Schelling[34] as the presence of a unique solution that is evident to everyone. Given the necessity for arriving at agreement, and inability to decide what it should be, the conferees may settle on a formula that appears to be intuitively satisfying. They may split

---

[33] The method of calculation described here independently bears a striking similarity to those attributed to social scientists by David Braybrooke and Charles E. Lindblom in their *A Strategy of Decision* (New York, 1963), and to private firms by Richard Cyert and James March in their *A Behavioral Theory of the Firm* (Englewood Cliffs, N. J., 1963).

[34] See his *The Strategy of Conflict* (Cambridge, 1962).

the difference, choose the highest amount for each item, or the lowest amount for each item. Inevitably, there is a premium on raising or lowering amounts voted in the House or Senate so as to leave room for "concessions" to the other side.

SUMMARY

Although much more remains to be discovered about budgetary calculations, we have now completed a broad survey of the subject. Aids to calculations commonly used in dealing with the problem of complexity have been described. Budgeting turns out to be an incremental process, proceeding from a historical base, guided by accepted notions of fair shares, in which decisions are fragmented, made in sequence by specialized bodies, and coordinated through repeated attacks on problems and through multiple feedback mechanisms. The role of the participants, and their perceptions of each other's powers and desires, fit together to provide a reasonably stable set of criteria on which to base calculations. A variety of rules for decision, depending on a reading of "the signs of the times," and on differing attitudes toward time, innovation, and other goals, have at least been sketched out. We have been made aware of the kind of calculations that go into such basic choices as deciding how much to ask for and how much to appropriate. Now I would like to extend the range of budgetary behavior under consideration by turning to a separate (though related) set of questions: how do the agencies—the advocates in the process of budgeting—go about trying to get what they want? Which strategies are used under which circumstances? What are some of the counter-strategies employed by the other participants? What are some of the primary conditions associated with the achievement of budgetary goals?

STRATEGIES

3

BUDGETARY STRATEGIES are actions by governmental agencies intended to maintain or increase the amount of money available to them. Not every move in the budgetary arena is necessarily aimed at getting funds in a conscious way. Yet administrators can hardly help being aware that nothing can be done without funds, and that they must normally do things to retain or increase rather than decrease their income.

Our major purpose in this chapter is to describe in an orderly manner the major budgetary strategies currently being employed and to relate them to the environment from which they spring. In this way we can, for the first time, describe the behavior of officials engaged in budgeting as they seek to relate their requirements and powers to the needs and powers of others. Strategies are the links between the intentions and perceptions of budget officials and the political system that imposes restraints and creates opportunities for them. When we know about strategies we are not only made aware of important kinds of behavior, we also learn about the political world in which they take place.

Strategic moves take place in a rapidly changing environment in which no one is quite certain how things will turn out and new goals constantly emerge in response to experience. In this context of uncertainty, choice among existing strategies must be based on intuition and hunch, on an "educated guess," as well as on firm knowledge. Assuming a normal capacity to learn, however, experience should eventually provide a more reliable guide than sheer guesswork. When we discover strategies that are practiced throughout the entire administrative apparatus, we suspect that officials have discovered paths to success which may not be wholly reliable but which have proved to be more advantageous than the available alternatives.

UBIQUITOUS AND CONTINGENT STRATEGIES

What really counts in helping an agency get the appropriations it desires? Long service in Washington has convinced high agency officials that some things count a great deal and others only a little. Although they are well aware of the desirability of having technical data to support their requests, budget officials commonly derogate the importance of the formal aspects of their work as a means of securing appropriations. Budget estimates that are well prepared may be useful for internal purposes—deciding among competing programs, maintaining control of the agency's operations, giving the participants the feeling they know what they are doing, finding the cost of complex items. The estimates also provide a respectable backstop for the agency's demands. But, as several informants put it in almost identical words, "It's not what's in your estimates but how good a politician you are that matters."

Being a good politician, these officials say, requires essentially three things: cultivation of an active clientele, the development of confidence among other governmental officials, and skill in following strategies that exploit one's opportunities to the maximum. Doing good work is viewed as part of being a good politician.

Strategies designed to gain confidence and clientele are ubiquitous; they are found everywhere and at all times in the budgetary system. The need for obtaining support is so firmly fixed a star in the budgetary firmament that it is perceived by everyone and uniformly taken into account in making the calculations upon which strategies depend.

"Contingent" strategies are particular; they depend upon conditions of time and place and circumstance; they are especially dependent upon an agency's attitude toward the opportunities the budgetary system provides for. Arising out of these attitudes, we may distinguish three basic orientations toward budgeting in increasing order of ambition. First, defending the agency's base by guarding against cuts in old programs. Second, increasing the size of the base by moving ahead with old programs. Third, expanding the base by adding new programs. These types of strategies differ considerably from one another. An agency might cut popular programs to promote a restoration of funds; it would be unlikely to follow this strategy in adding new programs. We shall take up ubiquitous and contingent strategies in turn.

CLIENTELE

Find a clientele. For most agencies locating a clientele is no problem at all; the groups interested in their activities are all too present. But for some agencies the problem is a difficult one and they have to take extraordinary measures to solve it. Men and women incarcerated in federal prisons, for instance, are hardly an ideal clientele. And the rest of society cares only to the extent of keeping these people locked up. So the Bureau of Prisons tries to create special interest in its activities on the part of Congressmen who are invited to see what is going on. "I wish, Mr. Bow, you would come and

visit us at one of these prison places when you have the time.
. . . I am sure you would enjoy it." The United States Information Agency faces a similar problem—partly explaining its mendicant status—because it serves people abroad rather than directly benefiting them at home. Things got so bad that the USIA sought to organize the country's ambassadors to foreign nations to vouch for the good job it said it was doing.

Serve your clientele. For an agency that has a large and strategically placed clientele, the most effective strategy is service to those who are in a position to help them. "If we deliver this kind of service," an administrator declared, "other things are secondary and automatic." His agency made a point of organizing clientele groups in various localities, priming them to engage in approved projects, serving them well, and encouraging them to inform their Congressmen of their reaction. Informing one's clientele of the full extent of the benefits they receive may increase the intensity with which they support the agency's request.

Expand your clientele. In order to secure substantial funds from Congress for domestic purposes, it is ordinarily necessary to develop fairly wide interest in the program. This is what Representative Whitten did when he became a member of the Appropriations Committee and discovered that soil conservation in various watersheds had been authorized but little money had been forthcoming: "Living in the watersheds . . . I began to check . . . and I found that all these watersheds were in a particular region, which meant there was no general interest in the Congress in this type of program . . . . It led me to go before the Democratic platform committee in 1952 and urge them to write into the platform a plank on watershed protection. And they did." As a result, Whitten was able to call on more general support from Democrats and increase appropriations for the Soil Conservation Service watersheds.

Concentrate on individual constituencies. After the Census Bureau had made an unsuccessful bid to establish a national housing survey, Representative Yates gave it a useful hint. The proposed survey "is so general," Yates said, "as to be almost useless to the people of a particular community. . . . This would help someone like Armstrong Cork, who can sell its product anywhere in the country . . . but will it help the construction industry in a particular area to know whether or not it faces a shortage of customers?" Later, the Bureau submitted a new program that called for a detailed enumeration of metropolitan districts with a sample survey of other areas to get a national total. Endorsed by mortgage holding associations, the construction material industry, and Federal and state housing agencies, the new National Housing Inventory received enthusiastic support in Congress where Representative Preston exclaimed, "This certainly represents a lot of imaginative thinking on your part . . . ." In another case the National Science Foundation made headway with a program of summer mathematics institutes not only because the idea was excellent but also because the institutes were spread around the country, where they became part of a constituency interest Congressmen are supposed to protect.

Secure feedback. Almost everyone claims that his projects are immensely popular and benefit lots of people. But how do elected officials know? They can only be made aware by hearing from constituents. The agency can do a lot to ensure that its clientele responds by informing them that contacting Congressmen is necessary and by telling them how to go about it if they do not already know. In fact, the agency may organize the clientele in the first place. The agency may then offer to fulfill the demand it has helped to create. Indeed, Congressmen often urge administrators to make a show of their clientele.

> Senator Wherry: Do you have letters or evidence from small operators . . . that need your service that you can introduce into the record . . . . Is that not the test on how much demand there is for your services?
>
> Ralston [Bureau of Mines]: Yes. . . . If it is important, as a rule they come to talk.

When feedback is absent or limited, Congressmen tend to assume no one cares and they need not bother with the appropriation. ". . . A dozen or more complaints do not impress me very much. . . . We cut this out last spring and we did not hear any wild howls of distress . . . ." When feedback is present it can work wonders, as happened with the Soil Conservation Service's Small Watershed program. Representative Andersen waxed enthusiastic:

> . . . Will you point again to Chippewa-Shakopee? I know that project well because it is in my district. I wish the members of this subcommittee could see that Shakopee Creek watershed as it is today. The farmers in that neighborhood were very doubtful when we started that project. Now many of them tell us, Mr. Williams, that the additional crops they have obtained . . . have more than repaid their entire assessment . . . .

Guarding the treasury may be all right but it becomes uncomfortable when cuts return to haunt a Congressman. This is made clear in Representative Clevenger's tale of woe.

> Clevenger: I do not want to economize on the Weather Bureau. I never did. I do want an economical administration . . . . I have been blamed for hurricane Hazel. My neighbor, who lived across the road from me for 30 years, printed in his paper that I was to blame for $500 millions in damage and 200 lives . . . . His kids grew up on my porch and yet he prints that on the first page and it is not "maybe." I just "am." He goes back to stories that related to cuts that I made when I was chairman of the Committee.

Most agencies maintain publicity offices (under a variety of titles) whose job is to inform interested parties and the general public of the good things the agency is doing, creating a favorable climate of opinion. There may be objections to this practice on the part of Congressmen who do not like an agency and/or its programs, but those who favor the agency consider it desirable. House subcommittee Chairman Kirwan urged this course on the Bureau of Indian Affairs in connection with its Alaskan Native Service, a worthy but not overly popular program. "Why don't you make some arrangement to tell the Americans every year," Kirwan suggested, "instead of telling this committee what is going on? If you write a letter when you go back to Alaska . . . I will guarantee you the press will get it." The Weather Bureau was urged to put out some publicity of its own by Representative Flood, who observed that

> . . . forecasts . . . were obviously, literally and figuratively all wet. Somebody pointed out in this [New York Times] editorial where this . . . forecast has been "a little cold, a little wet, a little snow, but not bad." . . . But something took place which . . . dumped the whole wagonload of snow on Broadway and made them very unhappy. This happened repeatedly over a period of 30 days, which did not make you look very good, if I can understate it . . . . All right. Why do you not prepare a statement for the many newspaper readers in the area and point out to them that you know the problem is there, and that this is what you want to do about it. . . .

A final example comes from a student who wrote away for a summer job and received in reply a letter from an administrator refusing him on account of budgetary limitations. "Because of our inadequate funds at this critical time," the official wrote, "many students, like yourself, who would otherwise receive the professional training that this work provides, will be deprived of that opportunity . . . . Only prompt action by Congress in increasing these funds can make the success of our mission possible."

Divided we stand. The structure of administrative units may be so arranged as to obtain greater support from clientele. It may be advantageous for a department to create more bureaus or subunits so that there are more claimants for funds who can attract support. "We have had the rather disillusioning experience that too often when we create a new agency of Government or divide up an existing agency," a Representative concluded, "that we wind up with more people on the payroll than we ever had before . . . ." There can be little doubt the division of the NIH into separate institutes for heart research, cancer research, and so on has helped mobilize more support than lumping them together under a general title with which it would be more difficult for individuals to identify.

United we fall. The Weather Bureau is an example of an agency that did rather poorly until it took the many suggestions offered by its supporters in Congress and established a separate appropriation for research and development. The new category was the glamorous one and it was easier to attract support alone; being lumped in with the others hurt its appeal. Indeed, putting projects under the same category may be a way of holding down the expenditures for some so that others will not suffer. One of the imposing difficulties faced in building up the Polaris missile program was the fear that it would deprive traditional Navy activities of resources.

Advisory committees always ask for more. Get a group of people together who are professionally interested in a subject, no matter how conservative or frugal they might otherwise be, and they are certain to find additional ways in which money could be spent. This apparently invariable law was stated by Representative Thomas when he observed that "All architects [doctors, lawyers, scientists, Indian chiefs] are for more and bigger projects, regardless of type. I have not seen one yet that did not come into that classification."

Advisors may be used to gather support for a program or agency in various ways. They may directly lobby with Congress or the President. "I happened to have lunch with Dr. Farber [a member of the quasi-governmental advisory committee of the NIH] the other day," Congressman Fogarty reveals, "and I learned there is considerable sentiment for these [clinical research] centers." Congressman Cederberg did not know of "anyone who would in any way want to hamper these programs, because I had lunch with Dr. Farber . . . ." Advisors may provide a focus of respectability and apparent disinterest to take the onus of self-seeking from the proponents of greater spending. They may work with interest groups and, indeed, may actually represent them. They may direct their attempts to the public media of information as anyone can see by reading the many columns written by Howard Rusk, M.D., a writer on medical subjects for the *New York Times*, requesting greater funds for the NIH.

Do not admit giving in to "pressure."

Civil Aeronautics Board official: . . . One of the reasons there has been such substantial expansion in local airline service, believe it or not, is largely due to the members of Congress.

Representative Flood: I hope you are talking about Hazleton, Pa.

CAB official: I am talking about Pennsylvania as well as every other state. I do not want to leave the impression here that there has been undue pressure or that we have been unduly influenced by members of Congress, but we have tried to cooperate with them.

Representative Flood: I do not care what the distinction is.

But if they press make them pay.

CAB official: . . . Senator . . . if there are any members of Congress apprehensive about the increasing level of

> subsidy, this has not been evident to the Board . . . . I cannot think of any local service case in which we have not had at least 15, 20, or 25 members of Congress each one urging an extension of the local service to the communities in his constituency as being needed in the public interest . . . . We felt that they, if anyone, knew what the public interest required . . . as to local service . . . with full knowledge that this would require additional subsidy.

Avoid being captured. The danger always exists that the tail will wag the dog and the agency must exercise care to avoid being captured. Rival interests and Congressmen may be played against each other. New clientele may be recruited to replace the old. The President and influential Congressmen may be persuaded to help out. Or the agency may just decide to say "no" and take the consequences. Dependence upon the support of clientele, however, implies some degree of obligation and the agency may have to make some compromises. The interests involved may also have to compromise because they are dependent upon the administrators for access to decisions, and they may have many irons in the fire with the agency so that it is not worth jeopardizing all of them by an uncompromising stand on one.

Spending and cutting moods. Unfortunately, no studies have been made about how cutting and spending moods are generated. Yet changes in the climate of opinion do have an impact on appropriations. Possibly a great many groups and individuals, working without much direct coordination but with common purpose, seize upon events like reaction to World War II controls and spending to create a climate adverse to additional appropriations, or upon a recession to create an environment favorable for greater expenditures.

Budget balancing and end-runs. It is clear that the slogan of the balanced budget has become a weapon in the political wars as well as an article of belief. This is not the place to inquire whether the idea has merit; this is the place to observe that as a belief or slogan budget balancing is one determinant of strategies.

When the idea of a balanced budget becomes imbued with political significance, the Administration may seek appropriations policies that minimize the short-run impact on the budget although total expense may be greater over a period of years. In the Dixon-Yates case a proposed TVA power plant was rejected partly because it involved large immediate capital outlays. The private power plant that was accepted involved much larger expenditures over a 25 year period, but they would have had comparatively little impact during the Eisenhower Administration's term of office.[1]

When clientele are absent or weak there are some techniques for making expenditures that either do not appear in the budget or appear much later on. The International Monetary Fund may be given a Treasury note that it can use at some future date when it needs money. Public buildings may be constructed by private organizations so that the rent paid is much lower in the short run than an initial capital expenditure. The Federal Government may guarantee local bond flotations. An agency and its supporters who fear hostile committee action may also seek out ways to avoid direct encounter with the normal budgetary process. This action is bitterly opposed, especially in the House Appropriations Committee, as back-door spending.

I do not mean to suggest that getting constituency support is all that counts. On the contrary, many agencies lay down tough criteria that projects must meet before they are accepted. The point is that there are ordinarily so many programs that can be truly judged worthwhile by the agency's standards that its major task appears to be that of gaining political support. Priorities may then be assigned on the basis

[1] See the author's *Dixon-Yates: A Study in Power Politics* (New Haven, 1962).

of the ability of the program and its sponsors to garner the necessary support.

The sheer complexity of budgetary matters means that some people need to trust others because they can check up on them only a fraction of the time. "It is impossible for any person to understand in detail the purposes for which $70 billion are requested," Senator Thomas declared in regard to the defense budget. "The committee must take some things on faith." If we add to this the idea of budgeting by increments, where large areas of the budget are not subject to serious questions each year, committee members will treat an agency much better if they feel that its officials will not deceive them. Thus the ways in which the participants in budgeting try to solve their staggering burden of calculation constrains and guides them in their choice of means to secure budgetary ends.

Administrative officials are unanimously agreed that they must, as a bare minimum, enjoy the confidence of the appropriations committee members and their staff. "If you have the confidence of your subcommittee your life is much easier and you can do your department good; if you don't have confidence you can't accomplish much and you are always in trouble over this or that." How do agency personnel seek to establish this confidence?

Be what they think they are. Confidence is achieved by gearing one's behavior to fit in with the expectations of committee people. Essentially, the desired qualities appear to be projections of the committee members' images of themselves. Bureaucrats are expected to be masters of detail, hard-working, concise, frank, self-effacing fellows who are devoted to their work, tight with the taxpayer's money, recognize a political necessity when they see one, and keep the Congressmen informed. Where Representative Clevenger speaks dourly of how "fewer trips to the coffee shop . . . help make money in most of the departments . . . ," Rooney demonstrates the other side of the coin by speaking favorably of calling the Census Bureau late at night and finding its employees "on the job far later than usual closing hours." An administrator is highly praised because "he always knows his detail and his work. He is short, concise, and to the point. He does not waste any words. I hope when it comes to the economy in your laundry soap it is as great as his economy in words."

To be considered aboveboard, a fair and square shooter, a frank man is highly desirable. After an official admitted that an item had been so far down on the priority list that it had not been discussed with him, Senator Cordon remarked, "All right, I can understand that. Your frankness is refreshing." An administrator like Val Peterson, head of the Federal Civil Defense Agency, will take pains to stress that "There is nothing introduced here that is in the field of legerdemain at all . . . I want . . . to throw the cards on the table. . . ."

The budget official needs to show that he is also a guardian of the treasury: sound, responsible, not a wastrel; he needs to be able to defend his presentations with convincing evidence and to at least appear to be concerned with protecting the taxpayer. Like the lady who gets a "bargain" and tells her husband how much she has saved, so the administrator is expected to speak of economies. Not only is there no fat in his budget, there is almost no lean. Witness Dewey Short, a former Congressman, speaking on behalf of the Army: "We think we are almost down to the bone. It is a modest request . . . a meager request. . . ." Agency people soon catch on to the economy motif: "I have already been under attack . . . for being too tight with this money . . ." Petersen said. "I went through it [a field hospital] very carefully myself to be sure there were no plush items in it, nothing goldplated or fancy."

If and when a subcommittee drops the most prevalent role and becomes converted into an outright advocate of a program, as with the Polaris missile system, the budget official is expected to shoot for the moon and he will be criticised if he emphasizes petty economies instead of pushing his projects. Democratic Subcommittee Chairman Kirwan and ranking Republican Jensen complained that the Bureau of Land Management did not ask for enough money for soil conservation. "It is only a drop in the bucket," Kirwan said, "they are afraid to come in." "This committee has pounded for the seven years I know of," Jensen responded, "trying to get them to come in with greater amounts for soil conservation and they pay no attention to it." The norm against waste may even be invoked for spending, as when Kirwan proclaimed that "It is a big waste and loss of money for the U.S. Government when only 6 million is requested for the management of fish and wildlife." In 1948 the head of the Cancer Institute was told in no uncertain terms, "The sky is the limit . . . and you come in with a little amount of $5,500,000. . . ." It is not so much what administrators do but how they meet the particular subcommittee's or chairman's expectations that counts.

Play it straight! Everyone agrees that the most important requirement of confidence, at least in a negative sense, is to be aboveboard. As Rooney once said, "There's only two things that get me mad. One is hare-brained schemes; the other is when they don't play it straight." A lie, an attempt to blatantly cover up some misdeed, a tricky move of any kind, can lead to an irreparable loss of confidence. A typical comment by an administrator states, "It doesn't pay to try to put something over on them [committee members] because if you get caught, you might as well pack your bags and leave Washington." And the chances of getting caught (as the examples that follow illustrate) are considerable because interested committeemen and their staffs have much experience and many sources of information.

Administrators invariably mention first things that should not be done. They believe that there are more people who can harm them than can help and that punishments for failure to establish confidence are greater than the rewards for achieving it. But at times they slip up and then the roof falls in. When Congress limited the amount of funds that could be spent on personnel, a bureau apparently evaded this limitation in 1952 by subcontracting out a plan to private investors. The House Subcommittee was furious:

> Representative Jensen: It certainly is going to take a house-cleaning . . . of . . . all people who are responsible for this kind of business.
> Official: We are going to do it, Mr. Chairman.
> Representative Jensen: I do not mean "maybe." That is the most disgraceful showing that I have seen of any department.
> Official: I am awfully sorry.

If a committee feels that it has been misled, there is no end to the punitory actions it can take. Senator Hayden spoke of the time when a bureau was given a lump-sum appropriation as an experiment. "Next year . . . the committee felt outraged that certain actions had been taken, not indicated in the hearings before them. Then we proceeded to earmark the bill from one end to the other. We just tied it up in knots to show that it was the Congress, after all, that dictated policy."

Four months after a House subcommittee had recommended funds for a new prison, a supplemental appropriation request appeared for the purchase of an institution on the west coast that the Army was willing to sell. Rooney went up in smoke. "Never mentioned it at all, did you?" "Well," the Director replied, "negotiations were very nebulous at that time, Mr. Rooney." "Was that," Rooney asked, "because of the fact that this is a first-rate penal institution . . . and would accommodate almost 1,500 prisoners?" It developed that Rooney, catching sight of the proposed supplemental, had sent a man out to investigate the institution. The supplemental did not go through.

Integrity. The positive side of the confidence relationship is to develop the opinion that the agency official is a man of high integrity who can be trusted. He must not only give but must also appear to give reliable information. He must keep confidences and not get a Congressman into trouble by what he says or does. He must be willing to take blame but never credit. Like a brand name, a budget official's reputation comes to be worth a good deal in negotiation. (This is called "ivory soap value," that is, 99 and 44/100% pure.) The crucial test may come when an official chooses to act contrary to his presumed immediate interests by accepting a cutback or taking the blame in order to maintain his integrity with his appropriations subcommittee. It must not be forgotten that the budget official often has a long-term perspective and may be correct in trying to maximize his appropriations over the years rather than on every single item.

If you are believed to have integrity, then you can get by more easily.

> Rooney: Mr. Andretta [Justice Department], this is strictly a crystal ball operation; is it?
> Andretta: That is right.
> Rooney: Matter of an expert guess?
> Andretta: An expert guess. . . .
> Rooney: We have come to depend upon your guesswork and it is better than some other guesswork I have seen.

A good index of confidence is ability to secure emergency funds on short notice with skimpy hearings. No doubt Andretta's achievement was related to his frequent informal contact with Rooney.

Rooney: I am one who believes we should keep in close contact with one another so we understand one another's problems.

Andretta: I agree.

Rooney: You very often get in touch with us during the course of the year when you do not have a budget pending, to keep us acquainted with what is going on.

Andretta: Exactly. . . .

Make friends: The visit. Parallel in importance to the need for maintaining integrity is developing close personal relationships with members of the agency's appropriations subcommittee, particularly the Chairman. The most obvious way is to seek them out and get to know them. One official reports that he visited every member of his subcommittee asking merely that they call on him if they wanted assistance. Later, as relationships developed, he was able to bring up budgetary matters. Appropriations hearings reveal numerous instances of personal visitation. A few examples should suggest how these matters work: Representative Jensen: "Mr. Clawson [head of the Bureau of Land Management] came in my office the other day to visit with me. I don't know whether he came in purposely or whether he was just going by and dropped in, and he told me that he was asking for considerably more money for . . . administrative expenses and we had quite a visit. . . ." A subordinate employee of that bureau showed that he had caught the proper spirit when he told Representative Stockman, "If you would like some up-to-date information from the firing line, I shall be glad to call at your office and discuss the matter; will you like for me to do that?"

When columnist Peter Edson editorially asked why the Peace Corps did so well in appropriations compared to the difficult times had by the State Department and the Agency for International Development, he concluded that Sargeant Shriver, head of the Corps, "has tried to establish congres-

sional confidence in him and his agency. Of the 537 members
of Congress, he has called on at least 450 in their offices."

The pay-off. Wherever possible, the administrators seek
to accommodate the Congressman and impress him with their
interest and friendliness. This attitude comes through in an
exchange between a man in the Fish and Wildlife Service and
Senator Mundt.

> Official: Last year at the hearings . . . you were quite in-
> terested in the aquarium there [the Senator's state], particu-
> larly in view of the centennial coming up in 1961.
> Mundt: That is right.
> Official: Rest assured we will try our best to have every-
> thing in order for the opening of that centennial.

The administrator recognizes and tries to avoid certain disagreeable consequences of establishing relationships with Congressmen. The Congressman who talks too much and quotes
you is to be avoided. The administrator who receives a favor
may get caught unable to return one the following year and
may find that he is dealing with an enemy, not just a neutral.

I'd love to help you but . . . . Where the administrator's
notion of what is proper conflicts with that of a Congressman
with whom it is desirable to maintain friendly relations, there
is no perfect way out of the difficulty. Most officials try to turn
the Congressman down by suggesting that their hands are
tied, that something may be done in the future, or by stressing
some other project on which they are agreed. After Representative Natcher spoke for the second time of his desire for
a project in his district, Don Williams of the Soil Conservation Service complimented him for his interest in watershed
activity in Kentucky but was "sorry that some of the projects
that were proposed would not qualify under the . . . law
. . . but . . . they are highly desirable."

The "it can't be done" line was also taken by the Weather
Bureau in an altercation with Representative Yates.

> Weather Bureau official: We cannot serve the public by telephone . . . because we cannot put enough telephone lines or the operators to do the job. . . . We expect them [the public] to get it through the medium of newspapers, radio, television. If you have six telephones you have to have six people to deal with them. You have no idea. . . .
>
> Yates: Yes; I do have an idea, because I have been getting calls from them. What I want to do is have such calls transferred to you. . . . But as long as you have only one phone, I shall get the calls and you will not. . . .
>
> Weather Bureau official: We find we must do it on the basis of mass distribution.

Sometimes, action may be delayed to see if the committee member will protest. The Weather Bureau tried for a while to cut off weather reports from Savannah to the northern communities that constitute its major source of tourists despite the fact that the Bureau's House subcommittee chairman represented that city.

> Representative Preston: I wrote you gentlemen . . . a polite letter about it thinking that maybe you would [restore it] . . . and no action was taken on it. Now, Savannah may be unimportant to the Weather Bureau but it is important to me. . . .
>
> Weather Bureau official: I can almost commit ourselves to seeing to it that the Savannah weather report gets distribution in the northeastern United States.

Give and take. At other times some compromise may be sought. Secretary of Commerce Averell Harriman was faced with the unpalatable task of deciding which field offices to eliminate. He first used internal Department criteria to find the lower one-third of offices in point of usefulness. Then he decided which to drop or curtail by checking with the affected Congressmen, trying to determine the intensity of their reactions, making his own estimate of whom he could and could not afford to hurt. Harriman's solution was a nice mixture of internal and political criteria designed to meet as many goals as possible or at least to hold the Department's losses down.[2]

Truth and consequences. In the end, the administrator may just have to face the consequences of opposing Congressmen whose support he needs. Even if he were disposed to accommodate himself to their desires at times, he may find that other influential members are in disagreement. He may play them off against one another or he may find that nothing he can do will help. The best he may be able to do is to ride out the storm without compounding his difficulties by adding suspicions of his integrity to disagreements over his policies. He hopes, particularly if he is a career man, that the Congressmen will rest content to damn the deed without damning the man.

Emphasis. The administrator's perception of Congressional knowledge and motivation helps determine the kind of relationships he seeks to establish. The administrator who feels that the members of his appropriations subcommittees are not too well informed on specifics and that they evaluate the agency's program on the basis of feedback from constituents, stresses the role of supporting interests in maintaining good relations with Congressmen. He may not feel the need to be too careful with his estimates. The administrator who believes that the Congressmen are well informed and fairly autonomous is likely to stress personal relationships and demonstrations of good work as well as clientele support. Certain objective conditions may be important here. Some subcommittees deal with much smaller areas than others and their members are likely to be better informed than they otherwise would be. Practices of appointment to subcommittees differ between House and Senate and with passing time. Where

[2] Kathryn Smul Arnow, *The Department of Commerce Field Offices*, The Inter-University Case Program, ICP Case Series, No. 21, February 1954.

Congressmen are appointed who have direct and important constituency interests at stake, the information they get from back home becomes more important. If the composition of the committee changes and there are many members without substantial background in the agency's work, and if the staff does not take up the slack, the agency need not be so meticulous about the information it presents. This situation is reflected in the hearings in which much time is spent on presenting general background information and relatively little on specifics.

Subcommittee and other staff. Relationships of confidence between agency personnel and subcommittee staff are also vital and are eagerly sought after. Contacts between subcommittee staff and budget officers are often frequent, intensive, and close. Frequency of contacts runs to several times a day when hearings are in progress, once a day when the bill is before the committee, and several times a month during other seasons. This is the principal contact the committee staff has with the Executive Branch. Even when the staff seeks information directly from another official in the agency, the budget officer is generally apprised of the contact and it is channeled through him. Relationships between ordinary committee staff members and Budget Bureau personnel are infrequent, although the people involved know one another. The top-ranking staff members and the Budget Bureau liaison man, however, do get together frequently to discuss problems of coordination (such as scheduling of deficiency appropriations) and format of budget presentation. At times, the BOB uses this opportunity to sound out the senior staff on how the committee might react to changes in presentation and policy. The staff members respond without speaking for the committee in any way. There also may be extensive contact between committee staff and the staff attached to individual Congressmen, but there is not a stable pattern of consultations. House and Senate Appropriations Committee staff may check with one another; also, the staff attached to the substantive committees sometimes may go into the financial implications of new bills with appropriations staff.

When an agency has good relations with subcommittee staff it has an easier time in Congress than it might otherwise. The agency finds that more reliance is placed on its figures, more credence is given to its claims, and more opportunities are provided to secure its demands. Thus one budget officer received information that a million-dollar item had been casually dropped from a bill and was able to arrange with his source of information on the staff to have the item put back for reconsideration. On the other hand, a staff man can do great harm to an agency by expressing distrust of its competence or integrity. Asked if they would consider refusing to talk to committee staff, agency officials uniformly declared that this refusal would be tantamount to cutting their own throats.

CONGRESSIONAL COMMITTEE HEARINGS

The observer who knows that Congressmen and bureaucrats frequently engage in mutually profitable transactions during the year may make the mistake of discounting the hearings as mere ritual. In some cases it is true that the conclusions have been arrived at in advance and that the hearings serve only to create a record to convince others to support the committee's action.[3] But most of the time hearings do have an importance of their own so that what happens may have an effect on the committee's decision. Some agencies are rather wary of too close a relationship with Congressmen; their top officials may lack a gift for the personal touch; they prefer to make their

[3] It is worth noting that one of the functions that hearings may serve consists of getting administrators to make public commitments of private agreements. Once the administrator has committed himself in public, it is difficult for him to alter his position.

case in the open at the hearings. Even when personal relationships are close and continuous the pressure of time on the parties concerned may mean that prior consultation has been kept to a minimum. Not all items have previously been discussed and it may be necessary to muster support for them at the hearings. Not every Congressman on an appropriations subcommittee may have been included in personal visits and these votes may be needed when the subcommittees go into the mark-up session. Confidence may rapidly be dissipated by a poor performance. No one wants to trust incompetents.

The rehearsal. For all these reasons, administrators are aware that an effective presentation at hearings can help an agency whereas a poor one can nullify its efforts. It has become standard practice to hold mock hearings in which administrators can take turns in playing the roles of leading Congressmen. Based on past experience, tough questions are asked and answers prepared. "You'd be surprised," a budget officer commented, "how often we discover that something we thought was perfectly defensible turns out to lack a convincing rationale."

Avoid surprise. One of the basic rules of thumb arising out of hard experience is to avoid being surprised. A diligent search of hearings, a review of the agency's programs, are all useful. But there is nothing like some inside information on what is likely to come up.

The office of a budget official turns into a complex communication center in which the phone is always ringing and a constant flow of information is coming in and being sent out. Calls are received from the Executive Office, other agencies, Congressmen, interest groups, appropriations committee staff, the agency head, and many others. The budget official particularly conceives it to be his task to be a trouble shooter and head off difficult situations. This function requires him to keep informed and to inform others of what is going on, so he is continually engaged in coordination.

The plant.   What are the sources of the questions asked at committee appropriations hearings? The truly expert and hard-working subcommittee chairman who knows his subject may frame all his own questions without assistance from anyone. Men who know less or who find they cannot be fully informed may receive aid from committee staff, agency personnel, interest groups, experts, or other Congressmen. At one extreme there is the agency official who has strong personal connections with the committee member and may submit an entire list of questions and have all of them used. The men with seniority who do most of the questioning like to look alert and supplying them with perceptive but not dangerous questions is one way of satisfying this need. One official reported some embarrassment when he not only answered the first question he had planted but, inadvertently, the next one as well. On other occasions the agency may suggest just a few key questions or at least be informed by a friendly Congressman that it had better be prepared to answer some difficult ones.

The interchange between agency personnel and committee staff is often subtle. During the year, the staff and some Congressmen may ask questions about agency operations. If the question has an answer that will put the agency in a favorable light, the official may suggest that the hearings would be a good time to deal with it. If the answer might be difficult or damaging, the agency official may try to head it off by delay or partial answer or diversion of attention. Moreover, there are countless conversations during the year in which the budget officer may drop a hint as to a question, or the staff member may act so as to suggest that a certain question is likely to be asked. The staff member knows about planted questions, though he may not care much if they are useful. He is likely to take hints much more readily from officials in whom he has confidence.

The portrait. Hearings present an excellent opportunity for an agency to paint a self-portrait that not only reflects credit upon it but also helps create a favorable mood. The Bureau of Prisons, for example, portrays itself as a guardian of the country, protecting the populace against vicious criminals, doing a splendid job in spite of financial difficulties. Increases in the budget are always due to forces the Bureau cannot control, such as increasing prison population, and these increases are always necessary. Its personnel are dedicated career administrators who are selflessly serving the public without being overly concerned for material rewards and without ever receiving due recognition. The NIH and various science agencies, to choose another instance, play on the "dedicated-man-of-science" theme. Sincere, warm, devoted to suffering humanity, professional from head to toe, they work their wonders in ways mysterious to behold. Who would expect men who devote their careers to saving lives to know about material things like budgets? This portrait may be used to ward off deep probing as when a top official referred to "budget and fiscal considerations about which I am certainly not qualified to comment."

Know your budget. There is no substitute for knowing what you are talking about. The administrator who can answer questions, who can explain his agency's operations, is likely to have a much easier time. Department heads vary enormously in their interest in and knowledge of their budgets and this shows up at hearings if nowhere else.

Though they provide plenty of detail to back up their presentations, most budget officials find it advisable to make their presentations brief and to the point. Otherwise, busy Congressmen may lose patience and all the detailed work that goes into justifications may be wasted. At the same time, it is inadvisable to give the Congressmen the impression that important items are being slighted. When in doubt, top officials may ask Congressmen and staff for advice about which witnesses are likely to prove effective, how long the statements should be, whether or not charts would be helpful, points of special salience to individual members, and so on. When the presentation has been done well, an administrator like Chairman Herzog of the National Labor Relations Board may receive a compliment. ". . . You rank very high . . . in . . . being able to inform the committee of the operations of your agency. . . . Unfortunately, all agency heads are not in that position."

The kind of repartee that delights an administrator occurs when his preparation pays off. When Representative Rooney comments, "You always tell such a convincing story when you come up here on the Hill that you always have enough fat to absorb pretty nearly everything," Chief Administrator James Bennett parries with a modest rejoinder: "You do me too much credit." Rooney feels good when he can show that some of his lower estimates of costs were more accurate than Bennett's. But there are times when Bennett puts up such an airtight case that Rooney can only say, "We are stymied. What can we do with this to prevent giving you any of the taxpayer's money?" "You cannot do very much, Congressman," Bennett replies with evident satisfaction.

Play the game.   The Bureau of the Budget, under Presidential direction, lays down the rule that members of the Executive Branch are not to challenge the Executive Budget. But everyone knows that the administrative officials want more for their agencies and are sometimes in a position to get it in league with supporting Congressmen. The result on these occasions is a formalized game, which any reader of appropriations hearings will recognize. The agency official is asked whether or not he supports the amounts in the President's Budget and he says "yes" in such a way that it sounds like yes but that everyone present knows that it means "no." His manner may communicate a marked lack of enthusiasm or he may be just too enthusiastic to be true. A committee member will then inquire as to how much the agency originally requested from the Budget Bureau. There follows an apparent refusal to answer in the form of a protestation of loyalty to the Chief Executive. Under duress, however, and amidst reminders of Congressional prerogatives, the agency man cites the figures. Could he usefully spend the money, he is asked. Of course, he could. The presumption that the agency would not have asked for more money if it did not need it is made explicit. Then comes another defense of the Administration's position by the agency, which, however, puts up feeble opposition to Congressional demands for increases.

When the game is played according to the rules, the administrator has a proper rejoinder available. Senator Ellender asked Admiral Burke how the House committee ever got the idea that the Navy wanted nine Polaris submarines when the Budget Bureau allowed only two. "Did you ever give [that number] to them?" The Admiral replied, "No, sir; however, let me amplify that. This number was brought out under specific questioning by the Defense Subcommittee of the House. We had recommended to the Secretary of Defense that there be nine."

The psychology of hearings is important. Some departmental budget officers believe that they can tell when a bureau man has "sold his goods" to a Congressman before the hearings and is merely responding to questions that have been set up before. If a man is too spontaneous, answers too readily, this reaction may give him away. When there is reason to believe that this is going on, the Department head may threaten and (more rarely) take disciplinary action. Word will go out warning others not to sell their goods on the Hill. At other times this technique works in reverse and word goes out that a bureau need not fight increases too hard.

It is often difficult to tell whether the game is played by pre-arrangement or not. Congressmen know all about it and often do not have to be prompted to ask the questions that the game calls for if they favor a particular program. Interest groups may spur a Congressman on to this kind of behavior. Demonstrating a violation of the Presidential directive may not be easy and it is difficult to decide when an offense gets so bad as to fire someone. The game is sufficiently widespread that if all suspected violators over a period of years were punished, there would be few top agency officials left.

RESULTS

Confidence rests to some extent on showing the Budget Bureau and Congress that the programs are worthwhile because they lead to useful results. The word "results" in this context has at least two meanings, which must be disentangled. In one sense it means that some people feel they are being served. In a second sense it means that the activity accomplishes its intended purposes. This sense of "result" itself involves a basic distinction. There are programs that involve a product or a service that is concrete, such as an airplane, and others that involve activities that resist measurement, such as propaganda abroad. The demonstration of results differs in both cases, as do the strategies employed.

Serve an appreciative clientele. The best kind of result is one that provides services to a large and strategically placed clientele, which brings its satisfaction to the attention of decision makers. (The clientele may be producers of services, as in the case of defense contractors.) The kinds of strategies involved have been discussed under "clientele," and we shall go on to others in which the second sense of "result" is implicated.

It works: the problem of criteria. Outside of overwhelming public support, there is nothing that demonstrates results better than tangible accomplishment. The Polaris does fire and hit a target with reasonable accuracy; a nuclear submarine actually operates; a range-reseeding project makes the grass grow again. Interpretation of accomplishments as being worthwhile depends on finding criteria and on how tough these criteria are permitted to be. The Nike-Zeus missile may be fine if it is only supposed to knock down a few missiles or half of an enemy's missiles; it may be utterly inadequate if the criterion is raised to all missiles or most missiles or is changed to include avoidance of decoys. There is great temptation to devise a criterion that will enable a project's supporters to say that it works. At the same time, opponents of a project may unfairly propose criteria that cannot be met. And there are times when men reasonably disagree over criteria because no one knows what will happen. We hope and pray to avoid nuclear war. But if it comes, what criteria should a civil defense program have to meet? If one argues that it must save everyone, then no program can show results. Suppose, however, that one is willing to accept much less—say half or a third or a fifth of the population. Then everything depends on estimates which can surely be improved upon but which nobody can really claim to be reliable as to likely levels of attack, patterns of wind and radiation, and a multitude of other factors.

The invitation. Most governmental activity is conducted outside Washington and may seem somewhat remote to the Congressman or Budget Bureau official in the nation's capital. An impression of need, activity, heroic efforts by an overworked staff, may be much easier to substantiate on the spot than it would be through words on paper. A basic strategy, therefore, is to invite officials who pass on the budget to visit the agency and observe its work at first hand. The common belief is that the more these officials know, the more friendly they tend to be. True, it may work the other way and enable them to see some "soft spots" they might otherwise have missed, but the risk is usually thought to be worth taking.

When the "come up and see my installation" approach works well it can bring splendid results, as we can see from these comments:

> Representative Jensen: I can see the need up in Alaska for more help in the General Land Office. That is one place where I am going to be very liberal. . . . I was up there and saw with my own eyes what a big job it was.

> Senator Thye: I was out at the University of Minnesota last year during the time we were considering the appropriations, and they showed me a terrifically crowded laboratory. . . . That is one reason why I felt that we had to increase some of this research money, because I saw it with my own eyes.

But visits must be handled carefully lest they have unanticipated consequences.

Sometimes Congressmen must be "educated" so that they see things in the right way from the agency viewpoint. A Congressman may sweep through an office and draw negative conclusions because it is mostly empty, not realizing that the employees are legitimately out in the field. Despite all precautions, a favorable observation may have unfortunate implications for the agency concerned, as when Representative Laird was so impressed with the spirit shown by scientists at the University of Wisconsin that he inquired and was told that working together in a small group helped promote this wonderful spirit. "It seemed to me," Laird reported to his colleagues on the NIH subcommittee, "that maybe some of this spirit is destroyed if you put too much emphasis on large research installations . . ." like those sponsored by NIH. Sudden visits may show the agency at a disadvantage. Representative Engle said that his trip to the Air Transport Command had not been impressive. "You saw it, I am afraid, at a bad time," a General volunteered. Only ". . . in the sense that they did not know we were coming," Engle replied. There is also such a thing as overdoing it so that legislators, particularly on defense committees where junketing has reached epidemic proportions, complain that "there were so many public relations men running around to see what they could do for me that I was embarrassed."

Simplify or make complex. The difficulties in understanding budgetary subject matter, a major problem of calculation, creates strategic problems for budget officials. Items on which Budget Bureau people and especially Congressmen feel expert are much more difficult to justify than those which are technical and complex. One can see this problem in military construction, where Congressmen feel knowledgeable, as compared to complicated missile and observation systems. From the strategic point of view, the agency can adopt one of two general lines. If it feels that the Congressmen are likely to be sympathetic it may make special efforts to simplify presentations in order to enlist their informed support. If it feels that interested Congressmen would not appreciate the program, the agency may present the matter in its full complexity. The risk here is that Congressmen may be disposed to slash what they do not understand.

Avoid too good results. The danger of claiming superb accomplishments is that Congress and the Budget Bureau may reward the agency by ending the program. "Why would you need five more people in the supervisory unit?" John Rooney inquired of the Justice Department. "Since you are doing so well, as we have heard for fifteen minutes, you surely do not need any more supervision." However good it may be said that results are, it is advisable to put equal stress on what remains to be done. "Progress has been realized in the past," the Civil Defense agency asserted, "but we cannot permit these past accomplishments to lull us into a false sense of security."

Now we turn to strategies pursued by agencies that do not produce tangible items that are easy to measure.

Our program is priceless. If it is true that "In the final analysis the only thing in the world that can save the American people . . . is civil defense," then the conclusions drawn by Civil Defense Administrator Petersen—"Congress . . . should not exercise undue frugality"—would appear to be a huge understatement even if the agency could show little in the way of results. To agree with Dr. Sidney Farber—"one cannot put a dollar value on medical research if it pertains directly to the saving of human lives . . ."—is to say that there should be no monetary limits on medical research whatsoever regardless of the "state of the art" or other claims on the treasury.

It can't be measured. The USIA lacks confidence partly because it is particularly vulnerable to a line of attack based on the lack of results. "I have been on this committee now for twenty years," Senator Ellender told the agency, "and I have not seen any results from the money we have expended." A USIA official could only say that ". . . It would be very good to have a fine and exact measure of total results. We just don't have it. We will never get it. . . ." When an affluent agency that has confidence runs into this kind of difficulty the approach is quite different. "I wish," Representative Fogarty said, "that you would supply the committee with a list of things that the National Institutes of Health have accomplished . . . because we are being continually reminded that we are appropriating a lot of money for research and nothing ever comes of it." The best response is a scientific breakthrough, when a disease is brought under control.

Tomorrow and tomorrow. If there are no results today, they can always be promised for some remote future.

Representative Kirwan: Can you give us a few recent results of your research?

Bureau of Mines: [Reads a prepared statement.]

Representative Kirwan: . . . that is something that you are going to undertake, is it not?

Bureau of Mines: It is something that is under way.

Representative Kirwan: But there are no results. . . .

Bureau of Mines: That is correct. There have been no immediate results by industry at the present time but as the program proceeds, new findings are made continually which will lead to further research on the subject.

Representative Kirwan: . . . Were there any results. . . ?

This program's estimate was cut by $150,000 by the committee.

Statistics. Research of all kinds is a complicated subject because the results are difficult to measure and there is always hope that something good will turn up. Since significant results are not easily demonstrable, the advocates of a research program may resort to presenting a procession of figures that may or may not have any relevance. Take a look at a doctor's testimony:

To mention just a few of the research contributions . . . merely as being indicative of progress. There have been . . . 2,800 compounds tested which have some tumor-damaging properties. Four hundred of these have proved to be very interesting and, narrowing these down, twelve of them have been found to have very, very interesting possibilities in the future treatment of cancer.

Is this research valuable? No one can tell from this presentation.

Stretching things. Should results directly germane to the agency's program not be forthcoming, it is always possible to stretch things a little. A claim like the one by the Weather Bureau that follows is not only difficult to prove; it is virtually impossible to disprove.

Representative Rooney: [Do you take] editorial credit for the sentence near the top of page two: "Guidance to motorists regarding the use of antifreeze is estimated to be worth $50 million per year"? . . . How do you arrive at that figure?

Weather Bureau Official: Total value of motor vehicles is of the order of billions. . . . Some $3 billion is the estimated value of all automotive equipment in the United States. . . . It does not take a very high percentage of motor blocks in terms of the millions of motor vehicles that are to be protected, to roll up a total of $50 million a year preventable loss. That figure has been very carefully arrived at.

Avoid extreme claims that can be tested. There are times when a desire to show direct results boomerangs because of the very absurdity of the claim. Such is the unhappy tale of the State Department official who refused to admit that a Chinese language program would necessarily have a deferred pay off in view of the fact that we had no formal diplomatic relations with Communist China and the number of men we could send to Formosa was limited.

Representative Rooney: I find a gentleman here, an FSO-6. He got an A in Chinese and you assigned him to London.

Mr. X: Yes, sir. That officer will have opportunities in London—not as many as he would have in Hong Kong, for example—

Representative Rooney: What will he do? Spend his time in Chinatown?

Mr. X: No, sir. There will be opportunities in dealing with officers in the British Foreign Office who are concerned with Far Eastern affairs. . . .

Representative Rooney: So instead of speaking English to one another, they will sit in the London office and talk Chinese?

Mr. X: Yes, sir.

Representative Rooney: Is that not fantastic?

Mr. X: No, sir. They are anxious to keep up their practice. . . .

> Representative Rooney: They go out to Chinese restaurants and have chop suey together?
>
> Mr. X: Yes, sir.
>
> Representative Rooney: And that is all at the expense of the American taxpayer?

Procedures, not predictions. As a result of the daily requirement that the Weather Bureau "stick its neck out" in its forecasts, and the frequent public humiliation of wrong predictions and consequent ridicule, the Bureau is reluctant to engage in any activity for which it can be called to strict account by an input-output formula. The best kind of activity from the Bureau's point of view is one that involves the passive, repetitive measurement or collection of some sort of meteorological data, which is then filed, analyzed, and tested —but from which no prediction need be issued. Funds are sought on the basis of the procedures involving the analysis of weather.

> Weather Bureau official: This observer is extremely busy . . . He has certain scheduled observational functions he must perform. . . . Those have to go on the teletype circuit on the hour every hour. Then he has another scheduled report that has to go in between 15 and 20 minutes after the hour, and another between 35 and 40 minutes after the hour. During the rest of the hour he is busy posting the weather charts for pilots to look at and he is busy taking teletype reports that come in from roughly 250 stations in the area and posting those on clipboards. Some stations have 10 or 12 clipboards. Every 20 minutes or so he has . . ."
>
> Representative Flood: He had better not have any trouble with his personal plumbing. What does this fellow do?
>
> Weather Bureau official: He has to wait.

Faith. The foreign aid operation has a hard time showing results. Part of the difficulty lies in the presence of so many other variables—the strength of local subversive movements, the resources of the recipient nation, the cultural habits of a people—that it is difficult to single out any one factor as making a special contribution. But this difficulty is minor compared to that of measuring results when you are not clear about your goals. Is the program supposed to keep nations free, make them beholden to us, keep communists out, raise living standards even if it increases communist strength? If we adopt the goal of keeping a country out of communist hands, we have no theory to guide us in accomplishing this purpose. The basic idea behind foreign aid is that economic development will do the trick. Conceivably, an investment of $200 million would keep a nation outside this bloc, $400 million would bring it closer, $600 million even closer, $800 million would bring it back, and so on. And if any of these eventualities occur we cannot now be certain of the part played by foreign aid.

STRATEGIES DESIGNED TO CAPITALIZE
ON THE FRAGMENTATION OF POWER IN NATIONAL POLITICS

The separation of powers and the internal divisions of labor within Congress and the Executive Branch present numerous opportunities to play one center of power off against another.

Compensation. Supporters of a program who have superior access to one house of Congress may seek to raise the program's grant to allow for bargaining with the other branch. If they can get their way or arrange to split the difference in the Conference Committee, they are that much ahead. A Congressman may ask the agency for the lowest addition that would make a project possible so he will know how far he can go in Conference. Thus Senator McCarran told the Census Bureau that he "just wanted to see . . . how much we could lose in the conference, and still give you some assistance to be of value." Frequently, appeals are taken to the Senate in the hope of securing an increase. This procedure works both ways, however, and an agency that expects hostility in the

Senate may get its friends to prepare questions and answers in the House hearings and floor debates in anticipation of trouble with the other chamber.

Cross fire. Although the presence of differing interests and degrees of confidence in the House and Senate may provide the agency with room to maneuver, it may also subject it to a withering cross fire from which there is no immediate escape. In the controversy over grazing fees on public lands the House was for increases and the Senate was opposed. Representative Tarver asked the Forest Service whether anything could be done to expedite a study of the fee situation and the following exchange ensued:

> Forest Service official: I guess you really ought to try to get the Senate to go along with you. The Senate told us not to and you told us to do it; so that we are between two fires.
>
> Representative Tarver: I was wondering whether there was some place in this appropriation where we would make a substantial cut for the purpose of impressing upon you the desirability of making this study.

Both ends against the middle. The separation between appropriations and substantive committees creates another opportunity to exploit differences between dual authorities. Appropriations committees often refuse funds for projects authorized by substantive committees. And substantive committees, with or without agency backing, sometimes seek to exert influence over appropriations committees. A familiar tactic is the calling of hearings by substantive committees to dramatize the contention that an authorized program is being underfinanced or not financed at all. Knowing that the appropriations committees have the final say, the substantive committees can afford to authorize any project they deem good without too much concern for its financial implications. Appropriations committees sometimes seek to write legislation into appropriations bills; this effort may lead to a conflict with the substantive committee that spills over onto the floor of the houses of Congress. Participants believe that there is now greater awareness, particularly on the part of staff members, of the need to maintain contact between the two kinds of committees in regard to the financial implications of legislation and the legislative implications of appropriations.

Agencies stand to gain by exploiting these conflicts to their own advantage. They try to use an authorization as a club over the head of the appropriations committees by pointing to a substantive committee as a source of commitment to ask for funds. In seeking an increase for fishery research, the Fish and Wildlife Service declared that it "came about through direction of a Congressional Committee. . . . The [substantive] committee directed that hereafter the department should include this item for their appropriations." This strategy does not create much difficulty in the Senate, where some members of the substantive committees are likely to sit on the Appropriations Committee. But the House members do not like it at all—though a member may from time to time brag about how he got through a pet appropriation without a real authorization—and they are quick to remind administrators of their prerogatives.

> State Department official: I believe the legislation includes a specific amount of $8,000.
> Representative Rooney: We would not be discussing this at all if the legislation did not permit such a thing as entertainment, but never lose sight of the fact that the Appropriations Committees are the saucers that cool the legislative tea. Just because you have an authorization does not mean a thing to us. . . .
> State Department official: I understand, sir.

The conference committee adds another level of decision to an already fragmented power structure in Congress. Perhaps the most common device is to aim at resolution in Conference Committee by pushing an appropriations measure up in one of the houses of Congress. An item may be put in an appropriations measure for the sole purpose of providing the conferees with something to give in the bargaining sessions. A project may deliberately be given a low appropriation in one chamber so that its supporters on the Conference Committee will have to give something else.

The commitment. The Conference Committee is an ideal place in which to use the commitment strategy, whereby one side paradoxically increases its bargaining power by depriving itself of the ability to act.[4] A chamber may take an adamant position, thus giving notice that it will not back down so that the conferees from the other chamber will have to give in if Government activity is to continue. House conferees, for example, have been known to seek votes from their chamber in support of a motion insisting that they not give in. To get around this obstacle, no attempt may be made to secure an appropriation in the House where, once voted down, it could not be offered in conference. Instead, the appropriation is brought up in the Senate, where its chance of passage and inclusion in the Conference Committe bill are much better. It is difficult to overturn a Conference Committee decision.

CONTINGENCY AND CALCULATION

Because budgets are calculated incrementally from a base representing a widespread notion of fair shares, attention is focused on significant departures from what has gone before. "Naturally," says a Representative, "we are concerned about a project which shows an increase of 200 percent in cost to the Government and it is going to be very important that we have a full and detailed statement of the program." In the absence of attention-directing signals—a substantial increase or decrease in a going program or a new venture—the expecta-

[4] See T. C. Schelling, *The Strategy of Conflict* (Cambridge, Mass., 1960).

tion is that the base will remain undisturbed. Congressmen who specialize in appropriations lose no status if they continue the program base of an agency; they can serve as guardians of the public purse by resisting new programs or they can appear to play this role by admitting new ones in the guise of the old. In budgeting, as in other aspects of social life, appearances are tremendously important.

Under the historical frame of reference created by the incremental, base, fair-share types of calculation, agency officials are faced with a series of related problems. How can they keep their base intact so as to have an advantageous starting point next time around? How can they increase their appropriations income without giving the appearance of increasing them drastically? How can they make new programs look like old ones? How can they secure funds for new programs that are presented as just what they are? Another way of putting it is to ask how they can do what they believe is required in the public interest as they define it within the context of the budgetary system?

The answer to all these questions appears to be: by following strategies that take into account fundamental facts about human perception. It is not an event but its interpretation in comparison to other events that counts. Strategies involving calculations, therefore, revolve around the crucial question of what kind of frame of reference, inviting what kind of comparisons, will be used.

DEFENDING THE BASE:
GUARDING AGAINST CUTS IN THE OLD PROGRAMS

Cut the popular program. No one should assume that most agencies engage in perpetual feasting. There is always the specter of cuts. A major strategy in resisting cuts is to make them in such a way that they have to be put back.

Rather than cut the national office's administrative expenses, for instance, an agency might cut down on the handling of applications from citizens with full realization that the ensuing discontent would be bound to get back to Congressmen, who would have to restore the funds. When the National Institutes of Health wanted to get funds for a new, struggling institute such as one devoted to dental research, it would cut one or all of the popular institutes. The committee would be upset that heart, cancer, or mental health had been cut and would replace the funds. The same strategy was used in transferring funds from the popular research to the unpopular operating expenses category.

Cut the less-visible items. Counter-strategies are available to legislators. Many Congressmen feel a need to cut an agency's requests somewhere. Yet the same Congressman may be sympathetic to the agency's program or feel obliged to support it because people in his constituency are thought to want it. Where, then, can the cuts be made? In those places which do not appear to directly involve program activities. The department office or general administrative expenses, for example, may be cut without appearing to affect any specific desirable program. And this fits in well with a general suspicion current in society that the bureaucrats are wasteful. Housekeeping activities may also suffer since it often appears that they can be put off for another year and they do not seem directly connected with programs. The result may be that deferred maintenance may turn out to be much more expensive in the end. But cutting here enables the Congressman to meet conflicting pressures for the time being.

Promotional activities, non-tangible items, are also difficult to support. Unless the appropriations committee members trust the agency officials more than it ordinarily happens, they will inevitably be suspicious of items that resist measurement and concrete demonstration of accomplishment. Here, again, is a place to cut where the bureaucracy can be chastised and where powerful interest group support is likely to be lacking.

All or nothing.   The tactic is to assert that if a cut is made the entire program will have to be scrapped. "Reducing the fund to $50,000 would reduce it too much for us to carry forward the work. We have to request the restoration . . ." said the Bureau of Mines. The danger is that Congress may take the hint and cut out the whole program. So this strategy must be employed with care in connection with a program that is most unlikely to be abolished.

Squeezed to the wall.   "It so happens," the Fish and Wildlife Service told the Senate Committee, that our budget is so tight that we have no provision at all for any leeway in this amount. This will simply result in a lower level of production at our fish hatcheries."

Alter the form.   We have seen that appearance counts for a great deal and that a program viewed and calculated in one light may be more attractive than when viewed in another. The form of the budget, therefore, may become crucial in determining the budgetary outcomes. Suppose that an agency has strong clientele backing for individual projects. It is likely to gain by presenting them separately so that any cut may be readily identified and support may be easily mobilized. Lumping a large number of items together may facilitate cuts on an across-the-board basis. Items lacking support, on the other hand, may do better by being placed in large categories. A program budget may help raise appropriations by focusing attention on favored aspects of an agency's activities while burying others. The opposite result is also possible and an agency may object to presenting its budget in categories that do not show it off to best advantage.

Shift the blame. A widespread strategy is to get the other party to make the difficult decisions of cutting down on requests, thus shifting the onus for the cuts. If he has to take the blame he may not be willing to make the cut. In many bureaus it is the practice to submit initial requests to the agency head or budget officer that are considerably above expectations for support either in the Executive Branch or Congress. By including many good projects the bureau hopes to compel the department head to make the difficult choice of which ones are to be excluded. As a counter-strategy, the agency head may set down a ceiling and insist that the subdivision decide which of its desired projects are to be included. Both the agency head and the subdivision may be restrained, however, by their desire not to come in so high or so low that they risk loss of confidence by others.

Everyone knows that many agencies raise their budgetary requests (among other reasons) in order to show their supporting interests that they are working hard but are being thwarted by the Administration. So the Budget Bureau is disposed to cut. The most frustrating aspect of this activity is that when an agency's budget is squeezed it is often not the "wasteful" things that come out; priorities within the agency and Congress vary greatly and the legendary obsolete munitions factory may survive long after more essential activities have disappeared. Thus the Budget Bureau may be caught between its desire to make the agency responsible for cuts and the need to insist that they be made in certain places rather than others.

After reviewing their program, agency officials often find that they have many programs in which they believe and which cost more than they think the Budget Bureau will allow. Rather than choose the priorities themselves, the officials may try to get the Bureau to do the paring on the very best items. In this way they maintain their reputation for submitting only first-class programs and let the Budget Bureau take the blame for denying some of them. When clientele groups complain, the agency can always say that it tried but the Budget Bureau turned it down.

The ceiling.   This is the context in which setting a ceiling becomes highly attractive for the Budget Bureau. The agency is thereby compelled to establish priorities at the top and when complaints are made the Director can say that the agency chose certain projects in preference to others. In order to prevent an agency from excluding vital items that every-one knows Congress will support, instructions may be given to specifically include key items in the agency's budget.

We love them all.   One device that Congressmen use is to get the agencies to set priorities among programs. Should any-one protest a cut later on, the legislator would be able to say that he was not to blame; the agency had a choice and made it. Agencies are reluctant to set priorities and counter with a strategy of their own. Representative Stefan wondered what Director Capt of the Census Bureau would do if he were a Congressman and had to consider the poor taxpayer. "What is your opinion of the most vital item among these ten items?" The administrator gallantly replied that "It is something like asking a parent which one of his five children he would hate most to give up."

It may not be so much a question of preference as of the relationships among things; such is another standard reply to a call for priorities. "In view of the inter-relationships of the three activities—mail-rate cases, route cases, and field audits —it would be extremely difficult to determine which one . . . should be accorded the highest priority . . ." a Civil Aeronautics Board witness said.

You choose.   An agency may try to turn the tables by en-ticing a Congressman into choosing priorities so that he becomes committed to what has become his own choice. James Bennett of the Bureau of Prisons put the choice squarely up to his committee: "A question arises—which I think you are as well able to answer as I—as to whether it would be wise to put the $3.5 million . . . into reconstruction of Alcatraz, or whether to take the money and add a little more to it and locate the institution a little more centrally." Another time, when Bennett talked about a project in a what-do-you-think manner, Representative Rooney called him up on it: "Mr. Bennett, you have now repeated a couple of times certain language, from which I deduce you are trying to pass the ball to us."

They made me. Congressmen have developed strategies of their own for making cuts without taking full responsibility. Just as budget officials say that circumstances have compelled them to ask for increases, so do Congressmen assert that outside forces—a climate of opinion against spending, the strong views of influential colleagues, attempts by the other party to make spending an issue, the overriding need to balance the budget—leave them with little choice. Representative Mahon spoke in this vein about the Army's construction activities: "Day before yesterday one of the most influential members of the House of Representatives stopped me in the corridor and asked me how the hearings were progressing. He is a great friend of the military forces and the cause of national defense. He said to me, George, heretofore I have stayed with you on military appropriations, but this year I am going to vote to cut, and to cut deep, because the military people are wasting so much money." Senator Johnson told the Bureau of Prisons, "We are going to be accused of being spenders here if we are not careful. . . . Now, Mr. Bennett, I wonder if you would not give consideration to our postponing the new power-plant." The plant was postponed. The USIA was told that "The general feeling among the Senators that I have talked to is that they want to keep the budget not in excess of what you had last year . . . and they want to cut it if they can." A favorite tactic is hiding behind the Budget Bureau, as when Representative Sikes told the Bureau of Prisons, "Historically, the administration has generally refused to allow money to be spent that the Bureau of the Budget did not request. We are in a box, too, when it comes to meeting these problems."

When cuts mean increases. There are times when an agency wishes to cut its own budget because it has lost faith in a program, for internal disciplinary reasons, or because it would like to use the money elsewhere. If the agency is particularly well endowed with effective clientele groups, however, it may not only fail in this purpose but may actually see the appropriation increased as this threat mobilizes the affected interests. One budget officer tried to convince the Budget Bureau to continue two projects which the agency did not want but which several influential Congressmen felt strongly about. Otherwise, the official argued, the Congressmen would secure their desires by offering additional projects to their colleagues. The Budget Bureau turned him down and the result was nine projects instead of two.

As a result of unhappy experiences in attempting to cut their own budgets, agencies may mobilize for this purpose in the same way that they do to get substantial increases. They may assemble a task force of program administrators, Congressional liaison men, executive office personnel, sympathetic interests, and others to explain the logic of their position and head off stiff resistance.

INCREASING THE BASE:
INCHING AHEAD WITH EXISTING PROGRAMS

Old stuff. Since appropriations for new programs are particularly difficult to obtain, agencies are motivated to claim that what they want to do is just what they have been doing. The funds requested are said to be part of the agency's base, its continuing program, rather than some new way to spend money. "Our programs have grown a lot," an official confided, "but we have never begun anything we described as fundamentally new in the twenty years I have been here."[5]

Don't stand pat. Although agencies may at times find it advantageous to follow a strategy of asking or appearing to ask for what they received the previous year, they may run into difficulty if they forget to vary it a little so as to show that they are thinking. "You are not asking any change," a Congressman comments in defense hearings, "that always makes me suspicious." In a revealing statement, Representative Michael Kirwan, a power in the resource field, gave some homely advice to the Bureau of Mines when it came up with identical requests two years in a row. "It would look better," the experienced Congressman said, "if you just juggled around the numbers, for example, from 7 to 3 . . . so it will not look stereotyped."

The advantages of rounding. The rules for rounding off figures are not universally agreed upon, presenting opportunities for gaining a little. A neat case was found by John Rooney:

> Representative Rooney: . . . You suggest an increase in limitation to $1.8 million for administrative expenses. You actually need, you say, but $1,782,900. You have delightfully rounded this out so as to increase the amount of the limitation by $17,100. Did you know that this was done?

[5] In his book, *On Thermonuclear War* (Princeton, 1960) p. 339, Hermann Kahn describes the strategic situation: ". . . It is always easier to 'sell' something that can be presented as carrying out an existing program, or (a last resort) as a necessary modification of such a program. Barring a crisis or an exceptionally 'glamorous' idea, it is usually risky to phrase the recommendation as an expansion of an existing program and disastrous to let it look like the initiation of a new program."

State Department official: That it was rounded out?
. . . No, sir; I did not notice that figure.

Like most others, this game can be played in two ways and we find a house subcommittee proposing to round off a large sum for the military to $68 million, a reduction of some $155,000.

The transfer.   One way of moving ahead while appearing to stand still is to keep appropriations for particular categories constant so that no change seems to be made although various expenditures of the past are no longer being made and have been replaced with others. Items may be transferred from one category to another so that no particular one stands out as being too far out of line. Transfer may be made between agencies to effect the same purpose. Representative Rooney saw this tactic when he said, "The taxpayer cannot win with this kind of business. You are going to have the $50,000 covered in the Department of Commerce budget and now use the $50,000 that was in this budget for other purposes." If a committee or the Budget Bureau is concerned over increases in administrative expenses, ways may be found of transferring these expenditures to other items by including them as part of less suspect costs. Some agencies include administrative expenses under each program instead of under the administrative category.

Congressmen realize how dependent they are on a historical and comparative approach to budgeting and try to keep the categories constant from one year to the next so they will know what they are doing. Their dependence on consistency helps account for the insistence of appropriations committee members that budgetary forms not be changed too often.

The numbers game.   There are other ways of increasing income without making it obvious. Rather than pay attention to total appropriations, an agency may try to establish a right to a specific number of categories of appropriations and then increase the content while keeping the number constant. The NIH has done so by increasing the size of research grants and complaining that the total number—its preferred comparison —has gone down.

Herman Kahn has noted that for many years it was widely believed that the Air Force was entitled to a set number of wings. Costs soared as the planes had to meet higher standards of performance and as the Air Force used many more planes per wing. Given a choice between renovating 100 units of old equipment or keeping the old and buying 50 new ones, the former might be more expensive but it would be much preferred because the latter would look like an increase in the size of the force.[6] In the American belief system a high value is put on repair and making do; it seems so much more thrifty than buying something new. In response to this type of situation an agency may deliberately engage in irrational behavior, like spending more for maintenance than it would cost to buy a new item, in order to secure at least some of its budgetary requests. Kahn reports that:

> One of the most amusing and brazen examples of disguised procurement occurred in the early days of the Republic. It seemed that Congress was unwilling to retire old naval ships and replace them with new ones, so the Navy disguised its replacement program as a repair and maintenance program. They took old ships, tied them up at the docks and let them deteriorate. The money was saved, and as soon as it amounted to enough a new ship was bought and given the same name as the old ship.[7]

EXPANDING THE BASE: ADDING NEW PROGRAMS

The wedge or the camel's nose. A large program may be begun by an apparently insignificant sum. The agency then claims that (1) this has become part of its base and that (2)

---

[6] *Ibid.*, pp. 339-340.
[7] *Ibid.*

it would be terrible to lose the money already spent by not going ahead and finishing the job. As Representative Rooney observed, "This may be only $250 but this is the camel's nose. These things never get out of a budget. They manage to stay and grow." It was for a long time common practice for agencies to submit a request for a relatively small sum to begin a project without showing its full cost over a period of years. Congress has sought to counter this strategy by passing legislation requiring a total estimate for a project before any part can be authorized. But estimates are subject to change and a small sum one year rarely seems imposing even if a larger amount is postulated for the future.[8]

An agency may engage in wedging by requesting a small sum for research and using it to justify the feasibility of a big new project. The agency may borrow some personnel and equipment, use a few people part time in order to develop a program, and then tease Congress and the Budget Bureau with an established operation that has generated support for its continuance. A change in the wording of authorization legislation may then be sought so that the agency does not appear to be building empires.

The desire of budget officials to keep items in the budget,

---

[8] In arguing against a change in accounting procedures, Representative Mahon sketched the strategic implications:

"Now let me say that the accrued expenditure procedure is used now, as everyone knows, to some extent. I believe it was last year that we appropriated $1 million, just a little $1 million to start a public works project of the Army Engineers which is to cost $1 billion. Why, if I go to Congressmen Kilgore and say, 'Listen, Joe, we have been colleagues a long time, can't you vote for just this little $1 million for my area to help me and my people?

"Well, Joe, I am sure he would do whatever was right and proper, but it might be something tempting, particularly if I had voted for a million-dollar project for Joe on a former occasion to vote for my proposal. But if I go up to Joe and I say, 'Listen, Joe, I want you to vote for this project, it costs a billion dollars over a period of years, and if you start it, it is going to be completed." (*Improving Federal Budgeting and Appropriations*, House Subcommittee on Government Operations, 85th Congress, 1st Session, pp. 132-133.)

even if they are small and underfinanced, is readily explained once it is understood that they may one day serve to launch full-blown programs when conditions are more favorable. Research projects are often not terminated when they have proven successful or have failed; a small item concerning applicability of the research is kept in the budget so that if the agency wishes to resume it has a foot in the door, and if it wishes to begin a new project that may be connected with the old one.

Just for now. "Is there anything more permanent than a temporary agency of the Government?" Representative Phillips wanted to know. His colleague, Mr. Thomas, spoke with some asperity of a temporary activity that had begun four years ago. "Of course, [the agency] said it would take them about two years to clear it up and then they would be off the payroll. Since then I think you have added 30 to this group." A temporary adjustment to a passing situation results in an emergency appropriation for a fixed period, which turns out to be a permanent expenditure.

So small. When an increase is presented as one, a first line of defense is to say that it is so small as to be eminently justifiable or, if not, then certainly not worth bothering about. Here, as elsewhere, much depends on the basis of comparison. Administrator Petersen was fond of comparing the "negligible" costs of Civil Defense with the "outrageous" advertising costs of a certain beer. "The costs of the investigations that we make," the Fish and Wildlife Service asserted, "are tiny in relation to the total project costs of the engineering agencies. Normally they can be accomplished for a few thousand dollars on a project that cost millions. . . ." A more extreme example was furnished by Representative Siemanski who defended the Narcotics Bureau by asserting that it would cost $279 million to run for one hundred years. "Stack that against the two billion cargo that vanished in 1950 and the issue is clear. In 100 years, at 500 tons a year, opium runners at present prices would net 200 billion."

This strategy is also meant to suggest that a particular item or class of items is too insignificant to warrant study. A Justice Department Official spoke of "a net increase of $162,000 made up of a number of small items. I question seriously whether the committee wants to spend time on them, they are so small." He was wrong. But it is impossible to go into everything and the way in which the agency presents its budget, the kinds of emphasis it gives, the comparisons it suggests, may serve to direct attention to and from various objects. A miscellaneous category is unlikely to excite anyone's imagination. Every once in a while a Congressman will say, "Give us a breakdown here of 'other objects,' $2,264,000," as happened to the Weather Bureau in 1961.

Absorb it if it is so small. The tables may be turned in Congress or the Budget Bureau when agencies are told that if the increase they want is so terribly small they must surely be able to find some other money in their accounts. Representative Flood wanted to know why a mere $130,000 could not be absorbed by the Defense Department with their billions. "Why," he said, "it is hard to get a general you can discuss such a small sum with." Senator Hayden asks, "Can't you pinch out the $2,000?" An official of the Bureau of Mines knows defeat when he sees it—"Certainly it would be foolish for me to say we could not . . ."—but he takes a stab at suggesting some awful consequences. As Dr. Reichelderfer of the Weather Bureau so aptly expressed it, "Well, whenever there is a cut of a relatively small amount of that kind one is between the devil and the sea. . . . We felt that it could be taken as quibbling if we appealed for its restoration because, in an appropriation of $38 million, the point can always be made that certainly the Bureau can absorb a cut of $100,000."

The commitment or no choice. Although expenditures may rise and requests for money may increase, an agency can hardly be blamed if it had no choice. As one official put it, "The increases are in every case presented as either related to commitments . . . or other uncontrollable factors. . . ."

A favorite strategy is to lay down long-range goals for an existing program, which the agency can use to say that its requirements are not being met. The very statement that there are so many acres not yet under soil conservation practices or so many Indian children who need schooling may serve to create an implied commitment to meet the demand. The NIH and its Congressional allies go one step further by speaking of "moral obligations" for continuing projects mounting up to tens of millions of dollars.

If this, then that. If it can be shown that new projects are an integral part of old ones included in the agency's base, then the implied obligation to go on with the old passes on to the new. "This whole series of items . . . tie together very closely," a spokesman for the Bureau of Indian Affairs stated. "The question of supervision of forest and range land . . . tie in with the soil conservation practices in those areas . . . including some of the irrigation work that have to do with development . . . go together more or less in one bundle." One thing leads to another. The Congress was interested in bettering the education of American Indians. So the Bureau made a tie-in: ". . . As they become better educated, they are more apt to come and ask assistance to move to another area." If you appropriate more for education as you intend, then you must also do more for relocation.

The backlog. Nobody loves a backlog. The very use of the term suggests that there is an obligation to do something about it. Thomas tells the Federal Communications Commission that "It is well known that we do not like backlogs and we always try to get rid of them and cut them down."

The agency has to be careful, however, lest Congress or the Budget Bureau suggest that other employees be devoted to the task of catching up with the work. "There are 90 employees in the Office of Management," Thomas said. "Could you take 15 or 20 . . . and . . . cut down this backlog?"

Look, no hands. Strategies involving the use of work-load data fit nicely into those using the idea of an accepted base with a commitment to continue the program. Once acceptance of a particular kind of project has been gained, increases may be presented as an inevitable outgrowth of increases in the tasks to be performed. It is often easier to secure appropriations when the work can be broken down into easily quantifiable units and work-load data can be supplied to give an estimate of costs. There is something about categories like the number of applications processed, or number of operations performed, which appears to be reasonable. The Budget Bureau and Congress may be impressed with a computer program arranged so that the ultimate figure appears to pop out untouched by human hands.

In mandatory programs such as veterans' benefits or farm price supports, appropriations are largely dependent upon securing an agreement on workload data. Where the work is routine and history provides a fund of experience, the area of dispute may be reduced to small dimensions. The agency does well to establish a record of correct estimation or to choose those units for quantification which will permit it to do well. Chairman Herzog hoped that his statement did not sound boastful but he assumed "this [House] committee will want to take into consideration the fact that the [National Labor Relations Board] has not been inflating its estimates in order to look as though we are going to get a lot of work which we do not really expect to get."

Work loads and work loads. Yet there are many ways to skin a cat: a work load based on number of inquiries may disregard the differences in time and skill that inquiries take; there is room for disagreement on the appropriate unit of measurement. Observe the following colloquy:

> Representative Thomas: I note you have 60 people handling 268 loans; that represents about 4½ loans per person. Are they not a little overworked . . . ?
> Housing and Home Finance official: . . . This . . . is . . . the most difficult program . . . with which I ever had any experience. . . .

Yet it is not obvious that this work load is any less appropriate than the fourteen convictions per agent in the field used by the Narcotics Bureau. If quantification does not seem advantageous an agency may resist the implementation of a work-load plan as a scheme to derogate the character of its operations by breaking them up into oversimplified units. Or it may devise a measure that results in a more favorable appearance. Agencies may use the concept of "man-years," which assumes that an employee will work 365 days a year, instead of "jobs," a practice that enables them to present a figure lower than the number of positions to be filled because it takes more than one person to work a man-year. This practice may create difficulties for the Congressmen who must interpret the concept. "For 1957, you want 34.5 man-years at a cost of $233,000 which is about 38 or 39 or 40 jobs against 28 man-years in 1956, or about 31 or 32 jobs." Finally, Congressman Thomas flared up saying, "We'd like to have it [the table] in jobs rather than man-years as we can understand what jobs mean."

It pays for itself; it makes a profit. An increase may not seem like an increase if it can be shown that it brings in revenue equal to or greater than the cost. Although government is presumably not conducted for profit, the delight Congressmen take in finding an activity that returns money to the Treasury is indicated by the frequency with which they use this fact to praise administrators and to support programs they prefer. Senator Dworshak told the Fish and Wildlife Service that "when you return money like that [$1 million from seal furs] back in, you should be proud of it and have the record show it." Not to be outdone, J. Edgar Hoover pointed out that the FBI had recovered $73 million more through its investigation activities over a ten-year period than it had received in appropriations.

Spend to save. Of certain activities it may be claimed that the more you spend the more the government earns. Properly conceived, this may seem more like a decrease than an increase in spending. The Soil Conservation Service, for example, declared that any money spent on soil erosion studies would soon be repaid by reduced costs in dredging channels and reservoirs. It made a study that demonstrated that "the extra income taxes paid by farmers as a result of their soil conservation work and by retailers, processors and distributors who profit by the extra business would total $69,-192,185. Thus it appears that in 1948 the Federal Government recovered, in increased income tax, the entire amount spent by the SCS (a total of $39,189,654) and made 76% profit on its investment." The slogan, "we are going to save billions," used in this case by Senator Thye to support cancer research, is also used as an inducement to loosen the public purse by advocates of slum clearance, accounting reforms, education, and other advocates of spending.

The crisis. There comes a time, however, when it is necessary to admit that a new program is in the offing or that substantial increases in existing ones are desired. This situation calls for a special campaign in which three techniques—the crisis, salesmanship, and advertising—are often called into play. Their purpose is to generate extraordinary support so that the agency or program does not merely inch ahead but secures sizable new appropriations.

Events do not have meaning in themselves; they are given meaning by observers. From time to time situations arise— war, drought, depression, plant disease, atomic energy—which virtually everyone recognizes as crises. The agency in a position to meet a crisis, as TVA was by supplying huge amounts of power to atomic-energy installations, can greatly increase its appropriations. Soon after a jet plane had crashed because of contact with a flock of starlings, the Fish and Wildlife Service was able to obtain funds for research into the habits of these birds. There is also a borderline area of discretion in which crises may be made to appear more real. A number of agency officials are famous in budgetary circles for their ability to embellish or make use of crises. By publicizing a situation, dramatizing it effectively, and perhaps asking for emergency appropriations, an agency may maneuver itself into a position of responsibility for large new programs.

Good examples of crises are the Bureau of Land Management's emergency program for controlling the noxious weed, halogeton, the Polaris system, and the reaction in many areas to the Soviet sputnik. But not every such appeal succeeds. The unpopular USIA was slapped down while others were successfully crying crisis: "What have you to say about this statement that you used the Suez crisis as an excuse for increasing the information efforts?" Arthur Larson, its hapless Director, was asked.

Salesmanship runs the gamut from a cops-and-robbers appeal—"agents of our [Narcotics Bureau] . . . engaged in a 45-minute gun battle with Mexican smugglers"—to the "agony sessions" at the NIH hearings. Who could resist Senator Hill's plea:

> As we begin today's hearings on appropriations . . . we take notice of the passing of . . . John Foster Dulles [who] fell victim to the most dread killer of our time, cancer.
>
> Cancer, that most ancient and accursed scourge of mankind, has . . . robbed the U.S. Senate of some of its greatest

leaders: Robert A. Taft, Arthur Vandenberg, Kenneth Wherry, Brian McMahon, and Matthew Neely. What more fitting . . . memorial . . . could there be than a high re-solve . . . to re-double our research efforts against the mon-strous killer which . . . will claim the lives of 250,000 more Americans before this year has ended? . . . We are very happy to have with us our colleague, Senator Neuber-ger. . . .

The impact on a Congressman of many vivid descriptions of disease is described by Representative Scrivner:

A week ago, Mr. Chairman, after this hearing about cancer, I went home and checked all the little skin flecks and felt for bumps and bruises. I lay awake that night and could have convinced myself I had cancer. And then more re-cently I lay awake listening to my heart after hearing the heart-trouble talk. I listened to see if it went too fast or if it was too weak or if it was irregular or whether it was pump-ing too hard. . . . And here I am listening to all this mental health talk . . . and I wonder what I am going to dream about tonight.

Who would vote against appropriations for medical research after being subjected to this treatment?

The crisis strategy is well known to appropriations com-mittee members. Rooney begins exclaiming, "That is the magic word this year, Africa. That is the gimmick that is really giving the taxpayer the business. . . ." His colleague obligingly responds with, "It is taking the place of sputnik." And Rooney comes back with, "Every year it is something different." But this does not mean that Congressmen are im-mune. They recognize the signs of the times as a fact of life.

Advertising and salesmanship. Proponents of new pro-grams or of greatly increased old ones, be they agency per-sonnel, interest group leaders, or Congressmen, stress the need for advertising and salesmanship to garner the necessary sup-port. A program may be dressed up by giving it a dramatic name such as Mission 66 (a ten-year program designed to improve facilities in national parks by 1966) or by giving it a glamorous label like Polaris or Titan. These designations are supposed to make the programs easier to remember and to refer to in publicity releases. Much thought is given to the name. The B-70 bomber became the RS-70 (reconnaissance strike) overnight as soon as the Air Force discovered that it could not get funds by attempting to justify the plane as useful for its original mission and had to find a new one with more appeal. What some call "Peter Rabbit" presentations—fancy brochures, stirring pictures, simple graphs—are used to advertise the program in Congress and the public media of information. Congressmen are taken on grand guided tours and constituency response is encouraged. An astronaut is paraded before a committee to make a pitch. Releases are distributed to the press. Attempts are made to tie the program to heartfelt needs—a cure for cancer, protection against old age, the joys of outdoor living.

Let us look at "Operation Outdoors," the Forest Service's answer to Mission 66. For some time the Forest Service had a rather ordinary $3 million program with the uninspiring name of "Recreation-public use" in budgetary documents. In 1957, however, the Service made a special field survey, occasioned, it said, by increased public use of its facilities. It was determined that additional funds were urgently needed and a revitalized program, Operation Outdoors, carried a proposed $85 million price tag to be raised over the next five years. By 1960 the Forest Service had succeeded in more than tripling the usual appropriation for this activity. Thanks to hurricanes Carol, Edna, Hazel and others, for example, the Weather Bureau appropriations rose from $28 million to $42 million in 1956.

The defense motif.   From the beginning of World War II national defense retained an aura of necessity and importance shared by few other activities. It is ideal for crisis strategies.

The temptation to say that almost anything one can think of has implications for national defense is overwhelming and few agencies have been able to resist it. The National Labor Relations Board in 1952 was no exception: "I recognize that every agency of the government will come before you and say, 'Well, we may not nominally be a defense agency, but what we do is essential to the . . . war effort.' In spite of that, I am going to make that statement." A list of all the projects said to be connected with national defense would fill up a good many pages. "I notice," Chairman Thomas wryly remarked to the House and Home Finance Agency, "in the summary statement . . . everything pointed at the national defense. . . . The author of the language is putting on a good act of walking the tight wire with two buckets of water on each shoulder . . . —national defense, national defense." Mental health is related to national defense by statements like "During World War II . . . more people were kept out of the service for mental illnesses than there were men and women under arms in the Pacific Theater of Operations." We also learn that "during the last war 32,000 were rejected for cancer and other neoplasms. This would have been sufficient to man at least two Army infantry divisions. . . ." Everyone knows, to be sure, that our national defense depends upon such things as a prosperous farm and urban population (that is, everybody), conservation of resources, utilization of resources, etc. A twist is performed by the military and civil defense agencies, which are prone to argue that their programs will have valuable secondary results for peacetime purposes. The Space Agency will not only get us to the moon but will also improve our existence on the way up through many new discoveries.

Overselling.   Occasionally, a program may be oversold in the sense that it becomes so popular that the large sums appropriated to it threaten to deprive others of support. This has happened to Polaris. The result was that the Navy, knowing that Polaris would do well, concentrated on building up less popular projects such as new aircraft carriers. The possibility of creating a sort of budgetary Frankenstein exists but it does not seem to deter advertising and salesmanship.

OUTCOMES

Having described the major kinds of calculations and strategies used in federal budgeting, we are now in a position to develop (in Chapter 4) a critique of the usual proposals for budgetary reform and to appraise (in Chapter 5) the main features of the existing process. But at this early stage in the study of budgeting, descriptions of calculations and strategies, however helpful in improving our understanding, are not sufficient for the purpose of accounting precisely for the outcomes of the budgetary process. Although we have been able to elucidate basic strategic requirements such as confidence, clientele, and response to crises, we cannot now (in the absence of intensive studies of a wide range of strategies employed under specific historical circumstances)[9] explain precisely which strategies are most efficacious under which conditions. Nor is this difficulty surprising, since particular historical conditions were taken as given, and we dealt only with those parts of the budget within the control of the participants. It is possible, however, to suggest how the propositions in this volume might be connected with a general theory accounting for the pattern and level of public expenditures over an extended period of time. Fortunately, a recent attempt in this direction has been made.

In a pioneering work, Peacock and Wiseman propose an explanation accounting for the long-term trend—stability, sharp rise, plateau, stability at new level, and continuation of the cycle—in governmental expenditures.

[9] The author is in the midst of preparing such a study for Resources for the Future, Inc.

. . . In settled times [they write] notions about taxation are likely to be more influential than ideas about desirable increases in expenditure in deciding the size and rate of growth of the public sector. There may thus be a persistent divergence between ideas about desirable public spending and ideas about the limits of taxation.[10] This divergence may be narrowed by large-scale social disturbances, such as major wars. Such disturbances may create a displacement effect, shifting public revenues and expenditures to new levels. After the disturbance is over new ideas of tolerable tax levels emerge, and a new plateau of expenditure may be reached, with public expenditures again taking a broadly constant share of gross national product, though a different share from the former one.

This displacement effect has two aspects. People will accept, in times of crisis, methods of raising revenue formerly thought intolerable, and the acceptance of new tax levels remains when the disturbance has disappeared. It is harder to get the saddle on the horse than to keep it there. Expenditures which the government may have thought desirable before the disturbance, but which it did not then dare to implement, consequently become possible. At the same time, social upheavals impose new and continuing obligations on governments both as the aftermath of functions assumed in wartime (*e.g.*, payments of war pensions, debt interest, reparation payments) and as the result of changes in social ideas.[11]

---

[10] For validation of this proposition in the American context, see Eva Mueller, "Public Attitudes Toward Fiscal Programs," LXXVII *The Quarterly Journal of Economics* (May 1963), pp. 210-235. The article is based on a national survey conducted by the Survey Research Center of the University of Michigan.

[11] Alan T. Peacock and Jack Wiseman, *The Growth of Public Expenditures in the United Kingdom* (Princeton, 1961) p. xxiv. We assume here that the theory is also useful for the United States. See the following sources cited by the above authors: R. A. Musgrave and J. M. Culbertson, "The Growth of Public Expenditures in the United States, 1890-1948," VI *National Tax Journal* (June 1953) pp. 97-115; G. Colm and M. Helzner, "The Structure of Governmental Revenue and Expenditure in the United States," in *L'Importance et la Structure des Recettes et des Dépenses Publiques,* International Institute of Public Finance (Brussels, 1960).

A similar trend for the United States is described by Mosher and Poland:

> The upward trend in [governmental] expenditures . . . has conformed rather consistently to the following patterns:
>
> *Defense-related spending* rises sharply during war, then declines after hostilities but steadies at a plateau considerably higher than before the war. . . . *General domestic spending* moves in nearly opposite directions. During wars, it stays about the same or declines. . . . At the onset of major depressions . . . it increases greatly. During other peacetime periods, it tends to rise gradually.[12]

Peacock and Wiseman provide one kind of explanation for the periodic rise in expenditures and for the plateau and stability that follows until the next social disruption. We can add to their theory by answering questions appropriate to our level of exposition: why do expenditures (except those mandated by the disturbance) not sharply decrease to their former level? Why, in more ordinary times, do we observe steady (though comparatively) gentle increases in expenditures? Explanations based on the calculations and strategies used in budgeting are available to us.

Budgetary calculations are incremental, using a historical base as the point of departure. The existing level of expenditures is largely taken for granted and, for the most part, only small changes are seriously considered. The distribution of roles among the participants operates in such a way that most transactions involve reductions in the increased amounts proposed by agency advocates, thus helping account for the slightly rising trend of expenditures. The use of strategies by the affected administrative units and their supporters also helps account for the difficulty of sharp reductions as well as the likelihood that the new conditions created by a depression or war or other social disturbance will be seized upon

[12] Frederick C. Mosher and Orville F. Poland, *The Cost of Governments in the United States: Facts, Trends, Myths,* (Mimeo., August, 1963) p. II-9.

through crisis stategies. Disturbances are evidently more likely to affect some areas of expenditure more severely than others. The analysis in this volume makes a beginning in accounting for the distribution of funds by explaining why some agencies are in a better position to exploit their environment than others.

In devising models of budgeting it may be possible to build in "shocks" (that is, social disturbances) to the system and simulate the reaction of a budgetary process that operates much like the one described in these pages.[13] By creating an artificial but realistic approximation of the budgetary process, and subjecting it to shocks of various kinds, we may be able to emancipate ourselves from complete dependence on knowledge of individual cases and still be able to explain the general shape and trend of budgetary outcomes.

Perhaps the "study of budgeting" is just another expression for the "study of politics"; yet one cannot study everything at once, and the vantage point offered by concentration on budgetary decisions offers a useful and much-neglected perspective from which to analyze the making of public policy. The opportunities for comparison are ample, the outcomes are specific and quantifiable,[14] and a dynamic quality is assured by virtue of the comparative ease with which one can study the development of budgetary items and programs over a period of years.

[13] The close connection between the types of calculations described in Richard Cyert and James March, *A Behavioral Theory of the Firm* (Englewood Cliffs, N. J., 1963), and those found in the budgetary process suggests that elements of organization theory may be applicable to studies of budgeting. The participants who normally deal with budgets and programs of particular agencies might be considered as members of an organizational coalition whose goals, roles, aspiration levels, decision rules, search behavior, and feedback mechanisms might be studied to provide predictions of likely kinds of budgetary behavior under various conditions.

[14] The author and Otto Davis, an economist at the Carnegie Institute of Technology, are now engaged in a statistical analysis of federal appropriations since the end of World War II. They hope to test various propositions concerning relationships among participants in budgeting and to discover new relationships that demand explanation.

REFORMS

4

A LARGE PART OF THE LITERATURE on budgeting in the United States is concerned with reform. The goals of the proposed reforms are couched in similar language—economy, efficiency, improvement, or just better budgeting. The President, the Congress and its committees, administrative agencies, even the interested citizenry are all to gain by some change in the way the budget is formulated, presented, or evaluated. There is little or no realization among the reformers, however, that any effective change in budgetary relationships must necessarily alter the outcomes of the budgetary process. Otherwise, why bother? Far from being a neutral matter of "better budgeting," proposed reforms inevitably contain important implications for the political system; that is, for the "who gets what" of governmental decisions. What are some of the major political implications of budgetary reform? We begin with the noblest vision of reform: the development of a normative theory of budgeting (stating what ought to be) that would provide the basis for allocating funds among competing activities.

A NORMATIVE THEORY OF BUDGETING?

In 1940, in what is still the best discussion of the subject, V. O. Key lamented "The Lack of a Budgetary Theory." He called for a theory that would help answer the basic question of budgeting on the expenditure side: "On what basis shall it be decided to allocate X dollars to Activity A instead of Activity B?"[1] Although several attempts have been made to meet this challenge,[2] not one has come close to succeeding. No progress has been made for the excellent reason that the task, as posed, is impossible to fulfill.[3] The search for an unrealizable goal indicates serious weaknesses in prevailing conceptions of the budget.

If a normative theory of budgeting is to be more than an academic exercise, it must actually guide the making of governmental decisions. The items of expenditures that are passed by Congress, enacted into law, and spent must in large measure conform to the theory if it is to have any practical effect. This is tantamount to prescribing that virtually all the activities of government be carried on according to the theory. For whatever the government does must be paid for from public funds; it is difficult to think of any policy that can be carried out without money.

The budget is the lifeblood of the government, the financial reflection of what the government does or intends to do. A theory that contains criteria for determining what ought to be in the budget is nothing less than a theory stating what the

[1] V. O. Key, Jr., "The Lack of a Budgetary Theory," XXXIV *The American Political Science Review* (December 1940) pp. 1137-1144.

[2] Verne B. Lewis, "Toward a Theory of Budgeting," XII *Public Administration Review* (Winter 1952) pp. 42-54; "Symposium on Budget Theory," X *Public Administration Review* (Winter 1950) pp. 20-31; Arthur Smithies, *The Budgetary Process in the United States* (New York, 1955).

[3] Key, in fact, shies away from the implications of his question and indicates keen awareness of the political problems involved. But the question has been posed by subsequent authors largely as he framed it.

government ought to do. If we substitute the words "what the government ought to do" for the words "ought to be in the budget," it becomes clear that a normative theory of budgeting would be a comprehensive and specific political theory detailing what the government's activities ought to be at a particular time. A normative theory of budgeting, therefore, is utopian in the fullest sense of that word: its accomplishment and acceptance would mean the end of conflict over the government's role in society.

By suppressing dissent, totalitarian regimes enforce their normative theories of budgeting on others. Presumably, we reject this solution to the problem of conflict in society and insist on democratic procedures. How then arrive at a theory of budgeting that is something more than one man's preferences?

The crucial aspect of budgeting is whose preferences are to prevail in disputes about which activities are to be carried on and to what degree, in the light of limited resources. The problem is not only "how shall budgetary benefits be maximized?" as if it made no difference who received them, but also "who shall receive budgetary benefits and how much?" One may purport to solve the problem of budgeting by proposing a normative theory (or a welfare function or a hierarchy of values) which specifies a method for maximizing returns for budgetary expenditures. In the absence of ability to impose a set of preferred policies on others, however, this solution breaks down. It amounts to no more than saying that if you can persuade others to agree with you, then you will have achieved agreement. Or it begs the question of what kind of policies will be fed into the scheme by assuming that these are agreed upon. Yet we hardly need argue that a state of universal agreement has not yet arisen.

Another way of avoiding the problem of budgeting is to treat society as a single organism with a consistent set of desires and a life of its own, much as a single consumer might be assumed to have a stable demand and indifference schedule. Instead of revenue being raised and the budget being spent by and for many individuals who may have their own preferences and feelings, as is surely the case, these processes are treated, in effect, as if a single individual were the only one concerned. This approach avoids the central problems of social conflict, of somehow aggregating different preferences so that a decision may emerge. How can we compare the worth of expenditures for irrigation to certain farmers with the worth of widening a highway to motorists and the desirability of aiding old people to pay medical bills as against the degree of safety provided by an expanded defense program?

The process we have developed for dealing with interpersonal comparisons in government is not economic but political. Conflicts are resolved (under agreed-upon rules) by translating different preferences through the political system into units called votes or into types of authority like a veto power. There need not be (and there is not) full agreement on goals or the preferential weights to be accorded to different goals. Congressmen directly threaten, compromise, and trade favors in regard to policies in which values are implicitly weighted, and then agree to register the results according to the rules for tallying votes.

The burden of calculation is enormously reduced for three primary reasons: first, only the small number of alternatives politically feasible at any one time are considered; second, these policies in a democracy typically differ only in small increments from previous policies on which there is a store of relevant information; and, third, each participant may ordinarily assume that he need consider only his preferences and those of his powerful opponents since the American political system works to assure that every significant interest has representation at some key point. Since only a relatively few interest groups contend on any given issue and no single item is considered in conjunction with all others (because budgets are made in bits and pieces), a huge and confusing array of interests is not activated all at once.

In the American context, a typical result is that bargaining takes place among many dispersed centers of influence and that favors are swapped as in the case of log-rolling public-works appropriations. Since there is no one group of men who can necessarily impose their preferences upon others within the American political system, special coalitions are formed to support or oppose specific policies. Support is sought in this system of fragmented power at numerous centers of influence —Congressional committees, the Congressional leadership, the President, the Budget Bureau, interdepartmental committees, departments, bureaus, private groups, and so on. Nowhere does a single authority have power to determine what is going to be in the budget.

THE POLITICS IN BUDGET REFORM

The seeming irrationalities of a political system that does not provide for even formal consideration of the budget as a whole[4] (except by the President, who cannot control the final result) has led to many attacks and proposals for reform. The tradition of reform in America is a noble one, not easily to be denied. But in this case it is doomed to failure because it is aimed at the wrong target. If the present budgetary process is rightly or wrongly deemed unsatisfactory, then one must alter in some respect the political system of which the budget is but an expression. It makes no sense to speak as if one could

[4] See Charles E. Lindblom, "The Science of 'Muddling Through,'" XIX *Public Administration Review* (Spring 1959) pp. 79-88, for a description and criticism of the comprehensive method. See also his "Decision-Making in Taxation and Expenditure," in National Bureau of Economic Research, *Public Finances: Needs, Sources, and Utilization* (Princeton, 1961) pp. 295-336, and his "Policy Analysis," XLVIII *American Economic Review* (June 1958) pp. 298-312. His recent book (with David Braybrooke), *A Strategy of Decision* (New York, 1963) contains the most extensive statement of his position.

make drastic changes in budgeting without also altering the distribution of influence. But this task is inevitably so formidable (though the reformers are not directly conscious of it) that most adversaries prefer to speak of changing the budgetary process, as if by some subtle alchemy the intractable political element could be transformed into a more malleable substance.

The reader who objects to being taken thus far only to be told that the budget is inextricably linked to the political system would have a just complaint if the implications of this remark were recognized in the literature on budgeting. Since these implications have not been spelled out, it seems worthwhile to do so now. One implication is that by far the most significant way of influencing the budget is to introduce basic political changes (or to wait for secular changes like the growing industrialization of the South). Provide the President with more powers enabling him to control the votes of his party in Congress; enable a small group of Congressmen to command a majority of votes on all occasions so that they can push their program through. Then you will have exerted a profound influence on the content of the budget.

A second implication is that no significant change can be made in the budgetary process without affecting the political process. There would be no point in tinkering with the budgetary machinery if, at the end, the pattern of budgetary decisions was precisely the same as before. On the contrary, reform has little justification unless it results in different kinds of decisions and, when and if this has been accomplished, the play of political forces has necessarily been altered. Enabling some political forces to gain at the expense of others requires the explicit introduction and defense of value premises that are ordinarily missing from proposals for budgetary reform.

Since the budget represents conflicts over whose preferences shall prevail, the third implication is that one cannot speak of "better budgeting" without considering who benefits and who loses or demonstrating that no one loses. Just as the supposedly objective criterion of "efficiency" has been shown to have normative implications,[5] so a "better budget" may well be a cloak for hidden policy preferences. To propose that the President be given an item veto, for example, is to attempt to increase the influence of the particular interests that gain superior access to the Chief Executive rather than, say, to the Congress. Only if one eliminates the element of conflict over expenditures, can it be assumed that a reform that enables an official to do a better job from his point of view is simply "good" without considering the policy implications for others.

A TYPICAL REFORM

Arthur Smithies may stand as a typical proponent of a typical reform. Identifying rationality with a comprehensive overview of the budget by a single person or group, Smithies despairs of the fragmented approach taken by Congress and proposes a remedy. He suggests that a Joint (Congressional) Budget Policy committee be formed and empowered to consider all proposals for revenue and expenditure in a single package and that their decisions be made binding by a concurrent resolution. And he presents his reform as a moderate proposal to improve the rationality of the budget process.[6] If the proposed Joint Committee were unable to secure the passage of its recommendations, as it would surely be, it would have gone to enormous trouble without accomplishing anything but a public revelation of futility. The impotence of the Joint Commit-

[5] Dwight Waldo, *The Administrative State* (New York, 1948); Herbert A. Simon, "The Criterion of Efficiency," in *Administrative Behavior*, 2nd edition (New York, 1957) pp. 172-197.

[6] Smithies, *op. cit.*, pp. 192-193 ff. See also Jesse Burkhead, *Government Budgeting* (New York, 1956), for a useful historical account of proposals for reform.

tee on the Legislative Budget,[7] the breakdown of the single
Congressional attempt to develop a comprehensive legislative
budget,[8] and the failure of Congressional attempts to control
the Council of Economic Advisers[9] and the Budget Bureau,[10]
all stem from the same cause. There is no cohesive group in
Congress capable of using these devices to affect decision
making by imposing its preferences on a majority of Congressmen. Smithies' budgetary reform presupposes a completely
different political system from the one that exists in the
United States. To be sure, there is a name for a committee
that imposes its will on the legislature and tolerates no rival
committees—it is called a Cabinet on the British model. In
the guise of a procedural change in the preparation of the
budget by Congress, Smithies is actually proposing a revolutionary move that would mean the virtual introduction of the
British parliamentary system if it were successful.

Smithies (pp. 188-225) suggests that his proposals would
be helpful to the President. But the membership of the Joint

[7] Avery Leiserson, "Coordination of Federal Budgetary and Appropriations Procedures Under the Legislative Reorganization Act of 1946,"
I *National Tax Journal* (June 1948) pp. 118-126.

[8] Robert Ash Wallace, "Congressional Control of the Budget," III
Midwest Journal of Political Science (May 1959) pp. 151-167; Dalmas
H. Nelson, "The Omnibus Appropriations Act of 1950," XV *Journal of
Politics* (May 1953) pp. 274-288; Representative John Phillips, "The
Hadacol of the Budget Makers," IV *National Tax Journal* (September
1951) pp. 255-268.

[9] Roy Blough, "The Role of the Economist in Federal Policy-Making,"
LI *University of Illinois Bulletin* (November 1953); Lester Seligman,
"Presidential Leadership: The Inner Circle and Institutionalization,"
XVIII *Journal of Politics* (August 1956) pp. 410-426; Edwin G. Nourse,
*Economics in the Public Service; Administrative Aspects of the Employ-
ment Act* (New York, 1953); Ronald C. Hood, "Reorganizing the
Council of Economic Advisors," LXIX *Political Science Quarterly*
(September 1954) pp. 413-437.

[10] Fritz Morstein Marx, "The Bureau of the Budget: Its Evolution and
Present Role, II," XXXIX *The American Political Science Review* (October 1945) pp. 869-898; Richard Neustadt, "Presidency and Legislation: The Growth of Central Clearance," XLVIII *ibid.* (September
1954) pp. 641-671; Seligman, *op. cit.*

Committee would be made up largely of conservatives from safe districts, who are not dependent on the President, who come from a different constituency than he does, but with whom he must deal in order to get any money for his programs. Should the members of the Joint Committee ever be able to command a two-thirds vote of the Congress, they could virtually ignore the President in matters of domestic policy and run the executive branch so that it would be accountable only to them.

PROGRAM BUDGETING VERSUS TRADITIONAL BUDGETING

The basic idea behind program budgeting is that instead of presenting budgetary requests in the usual line-item form, which focuses on categories like supplies, maintenance, and personnel, the presentation is made in terms of the end-products, of program packages like public health or limited war or strategic retaliatory forces. The virtues of the program budget are said to be its usefulness in relating ends to means in a comprehensive fashion, the emphasis it puts upon the policy implications of budgeting, and the ease with which it permits consideration of the budget as a whole as each program competes with every other for funds.[11] Interestingly enough, the distinguishing characteristics of the program procedure are precisely the reverse of those of the traditional practice. Federal budgeting today is incremental rather than

[11] On program budgeting see A. E. Buck, *Municipal Finance* (New York, 1926) and *Public Budgeting* (New York, 1929); The (Hoover) Commission on the Organization of the Executive Branch of the Government, *Budgeting and Accounting* (Washington, D.C., 1949); Arthur Smithies, *op. cit.*; Jesse Burkhead, *op. cit.*; Gladys Kammerer, *Program Budgeting: An Aid to Understanding* (Gainesville, Fla., 1959); Symposium, "Performance Budgeting: Has the Theory Worked?" XX *Public Administration Review* (Spring 1960) pp. 63-85; Stanley T. Gabis, *Mental Health and Financial Management: Some Dilemmas of Program Budgeting*, Public Administration Program, Department of Political Science Research Report, No. 3 (East Lansing, Mich., 1960).

comprehensive, calculated in bits and pieces rather than as a whole, and veils policy implications rather than emphasizing them.

This brief account will focus on three major consequences resulting from the differences in budgetary procedure. First, the traditional procedure increases agreement among the participants whereas the program device decreases it. Second, the program budgeting procedure increases the burden of calculation on the participants; the traditional method decreases it. And, third, the specific outcomes in the form of decisions are likely to be different.

The incremental, fragmented, non-programmatic, and sequential procedures of the present budgetary process aid in securing agreement and reducing the burden of calculation. It is much easier to agree on an addition or reduction of a few thousand or a million than to agree on whether a program is good in the abstract. It is much easier to agree on a small addition or decrease than to compare the worth of one program to that of all others. Conflict is reduced by an incremental approach because the area open to dispute is reduced. In much the same way the burden of calculation is eased because no one has to make all the calculations that would be involved in a comprehensive evaluation of all expenditures. Calculations are made sequentially, in small segments, by subcommittees, and are accepted by the Congress as a whole. Were each subcommittee to challenge the results of the others, conflict would be greatly exacerbated. Were each Congressman to fail to accept the decisions of the subcommittees most of the time there would be (assuming that time was available to make the necessary calculations) continual disagreement over most items instead of only a few as at present. Finally, agreement comes much more readily when the items in dispute can be treated as differences in dollars instead of basic differences in policy. Calculating budgets in monetary increments facilitates bargaining and logrolling. It becomes possible to swap an increase here for a decrease there or for an increase elsewhere without always having to consider the ultimate desirability of programs blatantly in competition.

Procedures that de-emphasize overt conflicts among competing programs also encourage secret deliberations, non-partisanship, and the recruitment of personnel who feel comfortable in sidestepping policy decisions most of the time. The prospects for agreement within the House Appropriations Committee are enhanced by closed hearings and mark-up sessions, and by a tradition against publicity. Were deliberations to take place in public—"open covenants openly arrived at"—committee members might find themselves accused of "selling out" as they made concessions. Willingness to compromise, to be flexible, is a quality sought in choosing members to serve on the appropriations committees.

Party ties might be disruptive of agreement if they focused attention on the policy differences between the two political persuasions. Instead, party differences are submerged during committee deliberations. Thus the usual process of taking something from a program here, adding to a program there, swapping this for that, can go on at the committee stage without having to take the kind of "yes" or "no" party positions that may be required at the voting stage on the floor.

Consider by contrast some likely consequences of program budgeting. The practice of focusing attention on programs means that policy implications can hardly be avoided. The gains and the losses for the interests involved become far more evident to all concerned.[12] Conflict is heightened by the stress on policy differences and increased still further by an in-built tendency to an all-or-nothing, "yes" or "no" response to the policy in dispute. The very concept of program packages sug-

---

[12] Gabis, *op. cit.*, p. 46, writes that "under program budgeting the increase or decrease in the power and influence of each program would be spelled out in detail. It would be surprising if each addition or subtraction were not accompanied by a complicated process of maneuver and counter-maneuver among the affected program heads."

gests that the policy in dispute is indivisible, that the appropriate response is to be for or against rather than bargaining for a little more or a little less. Logrolling and bargaining are hindered because it is much easier to trade increments conceived in monetary terms than it is to give in on basic policy differences. Problems of calculation are vastly increased by the necessity, if program budgeting is to have meaning, of evaluating the desirability of every program as compared to all others, instead of the traditional practice of considering budgets in relatively independent segments. Conflict would become much more prevalent as the specialist whose verdict was usually accepted in his limited sphere gave way to the generalist whose decisions were fought over by all his fellow legislators who could claim as much or (considering the staggering burden of calculation) as little competence as he. The Hobbesian war of all against all, though no doubt an exaggeration, is suggestive on this score.

I wish to make it clear that I am not saying that the traditional method of budgeting is good because it tends to reduce the amount of conflict. Many of us may well want more conflict in specific areas rather than less. What I am saying is that mitigation of conflict is a widely shared value in our society, and that we ought to realize that program budgeting is likely to affect that value.

THE PROGRAM BUDGET IN THE DEPARTMENT OF DEFENSE

By 1960 it had become clear that the major decisions of the Department of Defense revolved around the choice of hugely expensive weapons systems designed to accomplish the military missions of the nuclear era. In order to produce the data most relevant to the choice of alternative weapons systems, including the full cost of development, procurement, and maintenance, the Defense Department, under the aegis of Comptroller Charles J. Hitch, undertook the installation of a program budget. The nation's defense effort was categorized into seven basic programs—strategic retaliatory forces, continental air and missile defense forces, general purpose forces, airlift and sealift forces, special research and development, reserve and national guard forces, and general support—each composed of a number of program elements, such as Polaris submarines and Minuteman missiles, which were devoted to the accomplishment of a common military mission.[13] As it happened, the new program budget was used mainly for internal purposes; it was deemed desirable to present the defense budget to Congress by converting the program categories into the more traditional rubrics such as procurement, construction, and personnel. Although it might be good practice to use different kinds of budgets for internal and external purposes—or even to devise several different budget formulations for use by department officials—the installation of the program budget under these circumstances does raise interesting political problems that have largely been ignored in the debate over the superior efficiency of the old or new budget formulations.

Hearings before Senator Henry Jackson's Subcommittee on National Policy machinery in 1961,[14] in which program budgeting was discussed by knowledgeable participants, gives us an opportunity to suggest some of its likely policy implications. The hearings were held to help determine whether the newly installed program budget in the Defense Department was likely to have desirable consequences for defense policy.

Committee consultant Robert Tufts kept hammering away at the question of why the new program budget in defense would lead to different results than prior practice if the participants remained the same as they had in the past. Ulti-

[13] See Charles J. Hitch and Roland N. McKean, *The Economics of Defense in the Nuclear Age* (Cambridge, 1960), and Hitch's "Management of the Defense Dollar," XI *The Federal Accountant* (June 1962) pp. 33-44.

[14] *Jackson Subcommittee Hearings.*

mately, Defense Department Comptroller Charles Hitch admitted that one difference would be that "Program decisions . . . are decisions of the sort which can only be made by the Secretary and, therefore, the role of the Secretary *and of the Secretary's advisers* will be greater" (italics supplied) (pp. 1031-32). The most significant result of the program budget may turn out to be the increased power it gives to the Secretary of Defense.

Former Comptroller Wilfred McNeil asserted that program packages

> would not be conducive to economy of force. . . . I would assume the number of destroyers in active service is probably around 225. I can assure you that if you broke that package up . . . budgetwise, and allocated and assigned . . . separate groups of destroyers to the carrier force, to a possible convoy force, to an antisubmarine force, and to the various odd jobs they do, that you will find requirements above 225. . . . By budgeting for the maintenance of 225 destroyers and then thinking flexibly about their use, . . . you will find you don't need quite as many as you would if you divided them up in neat packages (p. 1066).

The point is that the way a budget is arranged suggests ways of thinking and comparison and that if you change the form you change the kinds of calculations and the probable outcomes.[15]

---

[15] In *Governing New York City*, Wallace Sayre and Herbert Kaufman show that "an almost incredibly detailed 'line item' budget, which the Budget Director has in fact prepared and of which only he and his staff are masters" is a potent factor in increasing that official's influence over budgetary decisions. They also observe that "Some of the city's most articulate interest groups have within the last decade found a weapon . . . by seizing upon a demand (widely supported by new budget doctrine in national, state, and local governments elsewhere) for a change . . . to a 'program' or 'performance' budget. This change would open up the budget process to more critical public scrutiny, increase the discretion of the Mayor and agency heads to make budget decisions, and restrict the opportunities of the Board of Estimate and the Budget Director to make their traditional detailed expenditure decisions." (New York, 1960) pp. 368-369.

Senator Jackson chimed in with the observation that "What troubles me is that if . . . under the program package approach, the service finds that with the big increase occurring [say] . . . in the strategic striking force—other items are cut back, maybe they would be reluctant to push the newer and more costly programs that would tend to offset the so-called balance of forces within their own department." "All I can say," Hitch replied, "is that . . . under the program package procedures there is less chance of those cutbacks affecting the same service so that the tendency to hold back for this reason should be considerably less" (p. 1019). Perhaps. But if Hitch were correct, then inter-service rivalry would be increased and these severe conflicts might lead to similar difficulties. And if we take McNeil's hint and note that "almost the entire Army, with the exception of Air Defense, is in one grouping [program package]" (p. 1063), the Army would have to defend the strategic concept behind that program to the bitter end or else see the service disappear with a change in program.

Another kind of jurisdictional problem was brought up by Senator Jacob Javits. "If you [the Defense Department] are going to bring programs to the Appropriations Committee rather than the Armed Service Committees of the House and Senate," Javits asked, "do you think that we are going to have to do something about our congressional review of your programs . . . ? You are coming now with the basic program concept. When Congress approves your budget it approves the concept" (p. 1027). Speaking of program packages seems mild enough. But who is brave enough to tell the Armed Services Committees to abdicate their present responsibilities and powers?

The late Senator Mundt had his own worries. Although he was perfectly willing to accept the idea of program packages, he was disturbed by Budget Director David Bell's talk about country program packages in foreign aid budgeting.

To me [Mundt declared] that opens up a Pandora's box of undesirable possibilities. I think if the word gets out that the U.S. Government, in its annual budgeting, is providing a country program . . . in Africa, Asia, and Latin America . . . that we are not too far away from the day when, in addition to the Appropriations Committees . . . listening to delegations from every one of our 50 States who come in for public works projects, we can anticipate we will have delegations from every one of 100 different countries (pp. 1150-51).

Whether or not program budgeting will lead to "better budgeting" in some sense is a moot point. (McNeil felt that those in authority might want to consider all sorts of packages at different times rather than being stuck with one in the budget. They might want to consider the portion of the effort allocated to offense as compared to defense of the United States, to look at the effort allocated to the defense of the fighting forces themselves in forward areas, and to group expenditures by geographic area to be defended and by proportion of defense effort going into research and testing versus actual procurement of military hardware [p. 1062]). What is clear is that the kind of categories used and the procedures of program budgeting are likely to have important consequences for our defense policies.

EFFICIENCY

I do not mean to disparage in any way the important problem of efficiency, of finding ways to maximize budgetary benefits given a specified distribution of shares. In principle, there seems to be no reason why policy machinery could not be so arranged as to alter the ratio of inputs to outputs without changing the distribution of shares. One can imagine situations in which everyone benefits or where the losses suffered in one respect are made up by greater gains elsewhere. It may happen that such losses as do exist are not felt by the participants and they may be happy to make changes that increase their benefits. The inevitable lack of full information and the disinclination of participants to utilize their political resources to the fullest extent undoubtedly leave broad areas of inertia and inattention open for change. Thus, the "slack" in the system may leave considerable room for ingenuity and innovation in such areas as benefit cost analysis and the comparability and interrelatedness of public works without running into outstanding political difficulties or involving large changes in the system. Most practical budgeting may take place in a twilight zone between politics and efficiency. Without presenting a final opinion on this matter, it does seem to me that the problem of distributing shares has either been neglected entirely or has been confused with the problem of efficiency to the detriment of both concerns. The statements in this chapter should be understood to refer only to the question of determining shares in the budget.

KNOWLEDGE AND REFORM

The overriding concern of the literature on budgeting with normative theory and reform has tended to obscure the fact that we know very little about the budgetary process. Aside from the now classical articles on Congressional oversight of administration by Arthur McMahon,[16] a splendid article on internal relationships within the House Appropriations Committee by Richard Fenno,[17] and several excellent books on aspects of military budgeting,[18] there is virtually nothing of

[16] Arthur MacMahon, "Congressional Oversight of Administration," LVIII *Political Science Quarterly* (June and September, 1943) pp. 161-190 and 380-414.

[17] Richard F. Fenno, Jr., "The House Appropriations Committee as a Political System: The Problem of Integration," LVI *The American Political Science Review* (June 1962) pp. 310-324.

[18] Frederick C. Mosher, *Program Budgeting: Theory and Practice, with Particular Reference to the U.S. Department of the Army* (Public Administration Service, 1954); Samuel Huntington, *The Common Defense* (New York, 1961) pp. 197-283; Warner Schilling, Paul Hammond, and Glenn Snyder, *Strategy, Politics, and Defense Budgets* (New York,

144   *Reforms*

substance about how or why budgetary decisions are actually made. Chapters 2 and 3 were devoted to filling in this gap in our knowledge of budgeting.

Our concentration in this volume on developing at least the rudiments of an adequate description of the national budgetary process is not meant to discourage concern with normative considerations or reform. On the contrary, budgeting is worth studying from both standpoints. Surely, it is not too much to suggest that a lot of reform be preceded by a little knowledge. Until we develop a more adequate description of budgeting, until we know something about the "existential situation" in which the participants find themselves under our political system, proposals for major reform must be based on woefully inadequate understanding. A proposal which alters established relationships, which does not permit an agency to show certain programs in the most favorable light, which does not tell influential Congressmen what they want to know, which changes prevailing expectations about the behavior of key participants, or which leads to different kinds of calculations, would have many consequences no one is even able to guess at today. Of course, small, incremental changes proceeding in a pragmatic fashion of trial and error could proceed as before without benefit of theory; but this is not the kind of change with which the literature on budgeting is generally concerned.

Suppose, however, that a fresh appraisal of the budgetary process were made taking as its point of departure the material that has been presented in Chapters 2 and 3 on the kinds of behavior that actually take place in budgeting. How well, then, would the existing process stand up under criticism, especially when compared to the alternative mechanisms that have been suggested to replace it? This is the question we shall examine in the final chapter.

1962). See also the earlier study by Elias Huzar, *The Purse and the Sword* (Ithaca, N. Y., 1950).

APPRAISALS

5

In DESCRIBING THE budgetary process we have identified a number of basic characteristics that have called forth a great deal of criticism. The aids to calculation have been decried as arbitrary and irrational. The specialized, incremental, fragmented, and sequential budgetary procedures have been faulted as leading to a lack of coordination and a neglect of consequences. The participants in budgeting have been attacked for concern with "special" rather than general interests. Their roles are considered to be excessively narrow rather than broad, and the strategies they follow are condemned as opportunistic if not immoral.

The alternative budgetary process envisaged by the critics is quite different from the one we now have. Instead of aids to calculation such as the incremental method, they prefer comprehensive and simultaneous evaluation of means and ends. Coordination should be made the explicit concern of a central hierarchy that should consider a wide range of alternative expenditures and investigate rather fully the consequences of each and the probability of their occurring. Furthermore, each participant should seek to protect the general interest rather than the particular interests directly within his jurisdiction. Strategies should be eschewed or, at least, based on the merits of the program rather than on making the best possible case.[1]

Our purpose in this chapter is to appraise the existing set of budgetary practices and the major suggested alternatives. I shall argue that the present budgetary process, though far from perfect, performs much better than has been thought, and is in many ways superior to the proposed alternatives. Far from doing away with budgetary reform, however, this conclusion opens the way for changes that are both more appropriate and more feasible.

COMPREHENSIVENESS

The inherent difficulty of many programs such as space exploration, the huge mass and magnitude of items encountered in such areas as defense, the technical knowledge required to understand such budgetary devices as work-load data, and the subtleties of comparing people's varied preferences in such areas as welfare programs, make complexity a central concern of the participants. Yet time is in short supply, man's ability to calculate is limited, and there are few theories and no a priori bases that would enable the participants to predict the consequences of alternative actions. For the men concerned with budgeting, finding some method of calculation that will

[1] The position of the critics is a composite judgment based on a reading of the literature, private conversations, and remarks made on several occasions when the author has lectured on the budgetary process. The literature referred to includes A. E. Buck, *Public Budgeting* (New York, 1929); (Hoover) Commission on the Organization of the Executive Branch of the Government, *Budget and Accounting* (Washington, D.C., 1949); Jesse Burkhead, *Government Budgeting* (New York, 1956); Arthur Smithies, *The Budgetary Process in the United States* (New York, 1955); and various articles. For a recent exposition of the comprehensive approach see Edward A. Kolodziej, "Congressional Responsibility for the Common Defense: The Money Problem," XVI *The Western Political Quarterly* (March 1963) pp. 149-160.

enable them to make decisions is no small task. So they take short cuts. They specialize. They use the past as a rough experimental guide to the present, and they use decisions made in increments to gather information on consequences. They make decisions repetitively and sequentially so that values neglected at one time and place may be considered at another. They fragment their areas of concern so they are not dealing with too much at any one time, and they rely on feedback for information on whether or not others have been hurt by their actions. And so on down the list of aids to calculation we have previously discussed. In addition, there are a great many personal work procedures which ordinarily are not written down but which involve drastic simplifications and short cuts.

Far from being unique, the kinds of apparently arbitrary aids to calculation employed in budgeting are universally followed in dealing with complex problems. Business organizations use "share of the market" as an operational guide to simplify their calculations.[2] Citizens use party preference, a favorite columnist, advice from a friend, to cut their information costs in making voting decisions.[3] We often take small steps (buying a suit at a time instead of all clothing at once) to see how things will turn out as a way of approximating in time a reasonable choice. Yet when these methods are brought out into the open in governmental decision making there is much muttering and shaking of heads. They are decried as being arbitrary, extraneous, foolish, irresponsible, and (worst of all) the epitome of irrationality.

One prescription for "rationally" solving problems of calculation is to engage in comprehensive and simultaneous means-ends analysis. But budget officials soon discover that ends are rarely agreed upon, that they keep changing, that possible con-

---

[2] See Richard Cyert and James March, *A Behavioral Theory of the Firm* (Englewood Cliffs, N. J., 1963).

[3] See Anthony Downs, *An Economic Theory of Democracy* (New York, 1957).

sequences of a single policy are too numerous to describe, and that knowledge of the chain of consequences for other policies is but dimly perceived for most conceivable alternatives. The result, as Charles Lindblom has demonstrated, is that although this comprehensive approach can be described it cannot be practiced because it puts too great a strain by far on man's limited ability to calculate.[4] What budget officials need are not injunctions to be rational but operational guides that will enable them to manage the requisite calculations. Commands like "decide according to the intrinsic merits," "consider everything relevant," "base your decision on complete understanding," are simply not helpful; they do not exclude anything; they do not point to operations that can be performed to arrive at a decision as do the aids to calculation.

In this context it can be seen that across-the-board cuts, the so-called meat-axe approach, have definite utilities for Congressmen and Budget Bureau people. If one supposes unlimited comprehension and knowledge, then across-the-board cuts have little to recommend them. But when no one really is in a position to predict the consequences of various alternatives or the probability of their occurring, or even to know what the facts are, this approach may enable the decision makers to test the accuracy of the agency's prognostications. A Congressman will tell you that he often finds that nothing terrible has happened; and when he does he can change things next year or permit the agency to change them as they come up. A percentage cut or increase, providing it is not too large, may be viewed as a marginal change enabling the participants to observe the consequences in a complex area and deal with them piecemeal as they emerge in the future. Obviously, a percentage cut may also enable a Congressman to gain credit for cuts without doing much work and without taking the

[4] "The Science of 'Muddling Through,'" XIX *Public Administration Review* (Spring 1959) pp. 79-88. See also Lindblom and Braybrooke, *A Strategy of Decision* (New York, 1963).

responsibility for making them in specific areas. Indeed, this practice is commonly regarded as uncraftsmanlike by other Congressmen because it suggests that recommendations are not based on very great understanding. But it does appear that the method may have a more persuasive justification as an aid to calculation than is usually credited to it.

All that is accomplished by injunctions to follow a comprehensive approach is the inculcation of guilt among good men who find that they can never come close to fulfilling this unreasonable expectation. Worse still, acceptance of an unreasonable goal inhibits discussion of the methods actually used. Thus responsible officials may feel compelled to maintain the acceptable fiction that they review (almost) everything, yet when they describe their actual behavior, it soon becomes apparent that they do not. As a case in point take former Budget Director Stans' injunction to follow the comprehensive approach: ". . . every item in a budget ought to be on trial for its life each year and matched against all the other claimants to our resources." But when Jackson questioned Stans about his practice in relation to the defense budget, he replied, ". . . We dealt with specific issues and specific programs. . . . When all of these specific issues and programs were resolved . . . one way or the other—the budget then was the result of all the considerations up to that point and there were no further issues to be resolved in respect to the total size of the budget."[5] It would be amazing if the President or the Budget Director had the time, let alone the capacity, to deal with more than six to ten major defense items at the outside. The vast gulf between the theories espoused by some budget officials and their practice stems, I believe, from their adherence to a norm deeply imbedded in our culture, which

[5] Committee on Government Operations, Subcommittee on National Policy Machinery, U.S. Senate, *Organizing for National Security; The Budget and the Policy Process*, 87th Congress, 1st Session, 1961, p. 1103.

holds that the very definition of rational decision is comprehensive and simultaneous examination of ends and means.

In a complaint typifying those made by advocates of comprehensive budgeting, Senator Mundt scores the existing process for its evident lack of simultaneous consideration of appropriations.

> I thought you [Stans] made a tremendously interesting point when you said that the Bureau of the Budget or congressional Appropriations Committees sometimes have a tendency to feel that they have done pretty well if they look at the budget for last year and use that as a floor. . . . There is some kind of Sir Galahad merit about not exceeding the previous year's budget, without examining whether there were previous expenses which did not have a right to recur.[6]

Failure to consider the contributions toward calculation of the existing budgetary process distorts the magnitude of the problem. We have seen that new programs and substantial increases and decreases in old programs do receive close attention. In addition, the political system brings subjects to public attention as interest groups, politicians, or bureaucrats, anxious to make an issue, demand an investigation. What escapes intensive scrutiny is not the whole but only certain parts, which carry on much as before. The fact that some activities do not receive intensive scrutiny is hardly sufficient reason to do everything over every year.

Insofar as a problem exists, it can be met by following an incremental approach making use of the division of labor in the government. Attention may be focused on those activities which do not change much from year to year, since these are the ones that are not thoroughly reviewed. Certainly, since they do not alter radically, a thorough going over approximately once in every four or five years ought to be sufficient.

[6] *Ibid.*, pp. 1106-1107. The author and a student, Arthur Hammond, are now engaged in a study of the attempt of the Department of Agriculture to carry out a zero-base budget.

Nor need any one organizaton do it all. Department Budget offices and the Budget Bureau may use a sampling technique so that together they review a few programs of this kind every year. The results could then be used to see if more activity was warranted the next year. The bureaus themselves, the House Appropriations Committee investigating staff, the General Accounting Office, might also select a small number of programs on a sampling basis. In this way one could meet a good part of the criticism while adding only a little to the burden of these governmental organizations.

The procedure advocated here should also help to reduce the temptation to engage in strategies capitalizing on the incremental nature of budgeting. These strategies are designed to show that a new program is really an extension of an old one or that large increases are not as great as they seem and, therefore, should avoid special scrutiny. (If the costs of programs are "hidden," Congress may be letting itself in for greater increases in appropriations than it realizes.) The Budget Bureau and the appropriations committee are on the lookout for these strategies and this has helped somewhat. Further progress has been made by requiring agencies to set out proposed expenditures over the life of the program. The expectation that a sampling procedure may bring to light these strategies should go further to reduce their incidence. Thus an incremental approach may be used to mitigate the evils arising out of its less desirable consequences.

Rather than turn everything upside down, it is often possible to modify or compensate for existing practices in a way that lessens the burden of calculation. One central budget office made a study of cost estimates and actual costs in field offices. It discovered that field personnel had excellent records in pointing out the work that would have to be done in order to meet program requirements and that they were reasonably accurate in estimating the amount and kinds of labor required. Where they fell down badly was in estimating the total cost, taking into account "hidden" factors such as pro-rated time of office personnel. The analysis of the central budget office permitted an incremental approach to the problem. In the reform, the estimates of field personnel for work required and labor costs were accepted as before by the budget office. It instituted new procedures, however, enabling it to estimate more accurately total costs by adding other factors to the figures supplied from the field. The goal of more accurate estimation was achieved by letting existing procedures go as far as they could and then correcting them.[7]

Improvements in methods of budgetary calculation are more likely to occur if the stigma attached to using some aids to calculation is removed. Then it may be possible to see whether some rules of thumb are not better than others. Instead of prestige attaching to the spurious claim to have considered everything, men might vie with one another to see whether they could not develop shorter cuts and better approximations to lessen the burden of calculation. As it is now, there is virtually no discussion of the rules of thumb currently in use because the practitioners know how rough their tools are and rightly fear that the necessity for using some such methods will not be appreciated.

COORDINATION

The fact that the budgetary process is not comprehensive has given rise to charges that it is uncoordinated. Indeed, the very terms that we have used to describe budgetary practices—specialized, incremental, fragmented, sequential, non-programmatic—imply that at any one time the budget is not effec-

[7] At times it is more efficient to work with the data at hand than to go to the expense of collecting new and better information. One agency discovered that by ordering a re-run of information already on IBM cards it could arrive at cost estimates that were tolerably close. By collecting new information, the reporting system could be improved to the point at which estimates would be more accurate. It was judged, however, that the additional accuracy would not be worth the added cost.

tively considered as a whole so as to systematically relate its component parts to one another. As long as the lack of coordination is the result of ignorance of other people's activities or the complexity of organization, there is a good chance of overcoming it by dedicated staff work or some formal mechanism to accomplish the intended result. But in many cases lack of coordination is a result of conflicting views about policy that are held by men and agencies that have independent bases of influence in society and in Congress. The only way to secure coordination in these cases is for one side to convince or coerce or bargain with the other. When it is understood that "coordination" is often just another word for "coercion," the full magnitude of the problem becomes apparent. For there is no one, the President and Congressional leaders included, who is charged with the task of dealing with the budget as a whole and who is capable of enforcing his preferences. (The question of whether it is possible to consider all or most of the relevant considerations is omitted here.) Vesting of formal power to effectively coordinate the budget would, as I have argued previously, be tantamount to a radical change in the national political system, requiring the abolition of the separation of powers and a federally controlled party system, among other things. What may be said about coordination, then, if we take the existing political system as not subject to drastic change?

By taking as our standard of coordination the establishment of a formal structure charged with the task and capable of executing it, we come up with an obvious answer: there is very little coordination excepting what the President can manage through the Budget Bureau. By accepting the possibility of informal coordination, of participants who take into account what others are doing, we can say there is a great deal of coordination that has escaped the notice of many observers.

Let us pose the following question: how does an appropriations subcommittee know when things are not working out in other areas affected by its actions? Are its decisions coordinated with budgetary decisions made by other subcommittees? Part of the answer is found in a comment by a committee member to the effect that "People can't be too badly off if they don't complain." The subcommittees do not consider themselves to be the only participants in budgeting. They expect, in accordance with sequential decision making, that subcommittees in the affected areas will take corrective action. When an agency shouts more loudly than usual, when an interest group mounts a campaign, when other Congressmen begin to complain, subcommittee members have a pretty good idea that something is wrong. If their perceptions of the array of political forces lead them astray, the appropriations subcommittees can be brought back into line by a rebellion within the full committee or by an adverse vote on the floor. For unless members have an exceedingly intense preference, they will try to come up with appropriations that will not be reversed on the floor. To do otherwise would be to risk losing the great prestige the committee enjoys. The subcommittee may be thought of as exercising discretion within a zone of indifference within which others are not aware or not sufficiently concerned to challenge them but beyond which others will begin to mobilize against them. In this way, a semblance of coordination is maintained. And as time passes the participants come to develop a tacit understanding as to the general level of most appropriations, a phenomenon we have previously designated by the notion of fair shares. No one has to check up on everyone; it is sufficient that occasional marked departures from commonly held notions of fair shares would generate opposition.

Widespread acceptance of this concept of fair shares may go a long way toward accounting for the degree of coordination (the extent to which participants take into account what others do) that does exist among expenditure totals. The total budget was rarely drastically out of line with expenditures before it was formalized in 1921, and even without control by a central authority today we do not usually get extraordinary increases or decreases in the absence of national emergencies. There has been much more subtle and informal coordination by tacit agreements and accepted limits than there has previously been thought to be.

To some the procedure by which the agencies (as well as the Appropriations Committees and the Budget Bureau to a lesser extent) try to gauge "what will go" may seem unfortunate. They feel that there must be a better justification for programs than the subjective interpretation of signals from the environment. Yet we live in a democracy in which a good part of the justification for programs is precisely that they are deemed desirable by others. What is overlooked is that these informal procedures are also powerful coordinating mechanisms. When one thinks of all the participants who are continuously engaged in interpreting the wishes of others, who try to feel the pulse of Congress, the President, interest groups, and special publics, it is clear that a great many adjustments are made in anticipation of what other participants are likely to do. This, it seems to me, is just another term for coordination.[8]

Instead of the enormous burden of calculating the consequences for others being placed on one man or organization, the fragmentation of influence assures that the task will be factored out to many participants. Those directly affected are expected to make their preferences felt so that they can be taken into account by others. The point is not that this system is perfect but rather that it does do some coordinating in a rough-and-ready way. One need not contemplate the

[8] If one insists that coordination be defined to include conscious control by a single individual or group, then the usage in this paragraph does not fit.

hopeless task of replacing the system; improvement is possible by an incremental approach, which asks where the system does not function well and seeks to remedy the worst difficulties.

NEGLECT

There can be no doubt that lack of comprehensiveness in budgeting means that in making a specific decision important values affected by that decision are neglected at that time. Hence the budgetary process is attacked for its apparent neglect of consequences. In countering this criticism, Charles Lindblom has put forth the proposition that consequences neglected by one participant may be considered by another or by the same participant working on another problem.[9] To the extent, therefore, that all significant interests tend to be represented in a fragmented political system, decision makers may reduce their information costs by neglecting many alternatives in the confidence that they will be picked up by others or by themselves at another time. Thus the budgetary process as a whole may be considered reasonable even though the actions of individual participants may not seem to be because they omit from their calculations consequences important for others. In response to this line of argument, the noted economist Abram Bergson has agreed that a realistic consideration of rationality should certainly include the costs of finding and using information on alternatives. But he "wonders . . . whether the official who neglected important aspects on the ground that they would be properly weighed in the decision-making process as a whole might not often be disappointed."[10]

We may begin to meet this objection by observing that many consequences are taken into account by someone in the

[9] See his "Decision-Making in Taxation and Expenditure," *Public Finances: Needs, Sources and Utilization,* National Bureau of Economic Research (Princeton, 1961) pp. 295-336.

[10] *Ibid.,* p. 333.

system. Moreover, the political process in a democracy has a built-in feature that assures that some presently neglected values will be considered. This mechanism exists because politicians and interest-group leaders are motivated, by their hope of retaining or winning office, to find needs that have not been met and proposing to fulfill them in return for votes. We need to concentrate, then, on those values which are likely to receive little or no consideration.

Some groups of people find that their preferences are neglected. Migrant laborers, for example, do not vote and are not organized. That the prizes in democratic politics go to the active and organized should come as no great surprise. The situation is not quite as bad as it might be, however, because the Department of Labor has to some extent constituted itself as a guardian of the interests of migrant laborers. By joining with private citizens who have some altruistic interest in this underprivileged group, the Labor Department has managed to do something for them. Thus one way of compensating for the defects of this system is to make a part of a bureaucracy the protector of a neglected interest. Naturally, this expedient is not as good as if the people affected possessed the resources to protect themselves. Those who claim that values are neglected but who are not willing to undertake the political work necessary to give them expression should not be shocked if they do not accomplish much.

Apart from this political activity, however, the demonstration that values of importance are being neglected may be taken as one of the tasks of social scentists. This task is often difficult. Consider the usual claim that the interests of future generations in the realm of natural resources are being sacrificed to the present. Extreme cases have certainly occurred in the past and the depletion of forests and recreation areas has been fought by sportsmen and conservation groups who have succeeded in establishing bureaucracies to protect these values. (This mobilization is itself not without its cost, since such a bureaucracy as the Forest Service comes to develop professional norms that are resistant to such improvements as controlled burning).[11] In many other instances, however, as Milliman has pointed out, conservation proposals may result in penalizing a poorer present in favor of a richer future. Standards of living have been rising and it is not always clear that the present should subsidize the future.[12]

Imagine (for purposes of discussion) that a clear and unequivocal demonstration could be made that certain values had been neglected. The proof might commend itself to men of good will and steps might be taken to remedy the situation. Yet the required action might carry with it disadvantages for others who would fight to protect themselves. The task would then be one of mobilizing the political support required to overcome their resistance, and part of this task would rest on the demonstration to others that important values had been neglected. Assuming the political system to be democratic, it is difficult to see how any changes, even of a radical kind, could do away with this political requirement. If the President were the only decision maker who counted, it would still be necessary to convince him that he could afford to follow the indicated policy. To maintain the contrary is to suggest that the politicians in a democracy need not be concerned with political costs.[13]

[11] Ashley L. Schiff, *Fire and Water: Scientific Heresy in the Forest Service* (Cambridge, Mass., 1962).

[12] J. W. Milliman, "Can People be Trusted with Natural Resources?" XXXVIII *Land Economics* (August 1962) pp. 199-218.

[13] By "political costs" I refer not only to loss of popularity with segments of the electorate, but also to loss of esteem and effectiveness with other participants in the political system, and to loss of ability to secure policies other than the one immediately under consideration. Those who continually urge the President to go all out—that is, use all his resources on a wide range of issues—rarely stop to consider that the price of success in one area of policy may be defeat in another. If he loses popularity with the electorate, as President Truman did, he may find that Congress turns down virtually his whole domestic program. If he cracks down on the steel industry, as President Kennedy did, he may find himself constrained to lean over backwards in the future to avoid unremitting hos-

This is not to say that improvements in calculating affected values, such as cost-benefit analysis, have no place. Assuming that the method will continue to be improved, and that one accepts the private market as the measure of economic value, it can certainly tell decision makers something about what they will be giving up if they follow a different policy. By using two methods—one based on regional and the other on national factors—an appraisal might be made of the economic costs of federalism. Cost-benefit analysis also has some possible political uses that might be stressed more than they have been. The technique gives the responsible official a good reason for turning down projects together with a public-interest explanation the Congressman can use with his constituents and the interest-group leader with his members. The burden of calculation may be reduced by following cost-benefit analysis for many projects and introducing other values only for a few. To expect, however, that the method itself (which distributes indulgences to some and deprivations to others) would not be subject to manipulation in the political process is to say that we shall be governed by formula and not by men.

Consider the situation in which an agency finds it desirable to achieve a geographical spread in its projects in order to establish a wider base of support. Assume (with good reason) that cost-benefit criteria will not permit projects to be established in some states because the value of the land or water is too low. One can say that this is just too bad and observe the agency seeking ways around the restriction by playing up benefits, playing down costs, or attacking the whole benefit cost concept as inapplicable. Another approach would be to recognize that federalism—meaning, realistically, the distribution of indulgences to state units—represents a political value

---

tility from the business community. Resources like patronage are strictly limited and use in one case prohibits use in another once the appointment has been made. Political benefits occur when an official gains in popularity, esteem, effectiveness, and resources that he can use in another case.

worth promoting to some extent and that gaining nation-wide support is important. From this viewpoint, a compromise solution would be to except one or two projects in each state or region from meeting the full requirement of the formula, though the projects with the highest benefit-cost ratio would have to be chosen. In return for sacrificing full adherence to the formula in a few instances, one would get enhanced support for it in many others.

Because the cost-benefit formula does not always jibe with political realities—that is, it omits political costs and benefits —we can expect it to be twisted out of shape from time to time. Yet cost-benefit analysis may still be important in getting rid of the worst projects. Avoiding the worst where you can't get the best is no small accomplishment.

Up to this point we have omitted an exceedingly important mechanism for overcoming the difficulties caused by the partial neglect of consequences in making individual budgetary decisions. Let us turn, therefore, to a discussion of the various roles adopted by participants in budgeting, roles that result in the protection of a multitude of different values by different participants.

ROLES

Roles (the expectations of behavior attached to institutional positions) are part of the division of labor. They may, therefore, be viewed as calculating mechanisms. In appraising them, however, it must be understood that no one role exists apart from others. The relationship between the whole complex of roles—the agency as advocate, the Budget Bureau as Presidential servant with a cutting bias, the House Appropriations Committee as guardian of the Treasury, the Senate Appropriations Committee as responsible appeals court— must be considered before the constitutent parts may be evaluated.

The roles fit in with one another and set up a stable pattern of mutual expectations, which do a great deal to reduce the burden of calculations for the participants. The agencies need not consider in great detail how their requests will affect the President's over-all program; they know that such criteria will be introduced in the Budget Bureau. The Appropriations Committees and the Budget Bureau know that the agencies are likely to put forth all the programs for which there is prospect of support and can concentrate on fitting them into the President's program or on paring them down. The Senate Committee operates on the assumption that if important items are left out through House action the agency will carry an appeal. If the agencies suddenly reversed roles and sold themselves short, the entire pattern of mutual expectations might be upset, leaving the participants without a firm anchor in a sea of complexity. This kind of situation sometimes appeared in Weather Bureau appropriations because the agency was exceedingly cautious in putting forth its claims. Hence the following type of questioning arose in House and Senate hearings:

> Rep. Thomas. You should have been a little more aggressive, should you not?
> Weather Bureau Official. I agree with you . . .
> Rep. Thomas. It is no fault of the committee [that the bureau ran out of essential funds]. It is no fault of the Bureau of the Budget.

> Senator Smith. Have you requested enough money to permit you to progress as fast as you can?
> Weather Bureau Official. Senator Smith, I wonder if there is any agency that ever gets enough money. There are always so many things you can do beyond the budget possibilities. Certainly we could use a great deal more . . .
> Senator Smith. My question was prompted because we cannot know what you could use unless you tell us. . . . If you do not ask for it, the point is, the responsibility is yours, is it not?

If the agency refuses the role of advocate, it increases the burden on the Congressmen; they not only have to choose among desirable items placed before them with some fervor, they also have to discover what these items might be. This is a task ordinarily far beyond their limited time, energy, information, and competence. Hence the insistence by Thomas and Smith that they should not be held responsible if the agency does not perform its expected role in the budgetary division of labor.

The roles also appear to be "natural" to the occupants of these institutional positions. A man who has spent many years working in, say, the natural resources area can be expected to believe that his programs are immensely worthy of support. (He may try to eliminate programs he deems unworthy but there are always others to take their place.) Indeed, he would hardly be worth having as a governmental employee if he did not feel this way in his position. One can only imagine what the reaction would be if such a person intimated that soil conservation, reforestation, or recreation might just possibly be all right but that he was more than ready to believe that many, many other things were equally or more important, and that his projects could easily be postponed or eliminated. By serving as advocate in the real world he sees to it that important values in his area are not neglected if he can help it.

Unless one is disposed to argue on political grounds that Presidents should be made less powerful, the existence of a Budget Bureau to overcome his limitations of time, energy, and knowledge seems desirable. And helping him as he wishes to be helped would seem to be the proper role for Bureau staff. Beyond the point of safeguarding the preferences of the Presidential constituency, the Bureau is compelled by agency advocacy to take on a cutting role. Even where the Bureau is disposed to increase a program over the previous year, the chances are that the agency is requesting even more and there is little choice but to wield the knife. The Bureau does on occasion work to help an agency get more funds in areas in which the political process seems negligent. It might be suggested that the Bureau do more of this and constitute itself a guardian of some interests not satisfactorily protected elsewhere, perhaps because appropriations committees find it attractive to cut in such places as administrative expenses and maintenance. How much of this the Bureau could afford to do might best be discovered by doing a little more.

The House Appropriations Committee's role of guarding the Treasury, with its emphasis on reducing requests, makes sense in the context of agency advocacy. If the Congressmen can be reasonably certain that the agency has put its best foot forward, then their decisions may be viewed as choices along the margins of the top percentage of expenditures advocated by the agencies. Guardianship provides the Congressmen with a stance that supplies reasonably clear instructions—cut the estimates—while keeping the area within which they must focus their attention—the largest increases—manageable in terms of their limited time and ability to calculate. Nor need the cuts be stereotyped. By varying the severity and the areas in which cuts are made, and by an occasional increase, committee members can keep administrators responsive. And it should be realized that the total sum of agency appropriations normally increases from year to year; it is the estimates, increased perhaps by the assumption of advocacy, which are cut.

Suppose we imagine that the House Appropriations Committee adopted the role of "attacking the Treasury" by consistently advocating increases in estimates. The orientations of other participants remaining the same, we would have to assume that the role of attacking the Treasury would put Congress in the position of advocating substantially greater expenditures. This event is unlikely, to say the least. A more likely consequence would be a change in roles by one of the other participants. Either the agencies would be compelled to accept artificially low estimates or the Budget Bureau would take over the role of guardianship, systematically reducing requests way below present practice. This, in turn, would depend on the President's willingness to accept a more negative role. One suspects that the game by which administrators make known their preferences to Congressmen would be played with a vengeance and that informal processes would operate to counteract the formal ones.

Barring an unexpected change in the agency role of advocacy, guardianship would seem to be a more appropriate and more viable role for appropriations committee members than one of attacking the Treasury. But "attack" and "guardianship" at least share one virtue; they both provide a firm orientation toward the budget that defines the roles of the participants and establishes a division of labor that reduces the burden of calculation.

An alternative role for the appropriations committee members would be one that could be described as "mixed." The Congressmen would be oriented toward neither cutting nor increasing but to doing both in about equal proportions. Each case would have to be considered on its own merits. To some extent, of course, this balance occurs under the prevailing system. The difference is one of degree but not less important for being such. For where they are in doubt or do not care to inquire in detail, the Congressmen may now follow their prevailing orientation—usually to cut at the margin—expecting to receive feedback if something drastic happens. Under a "mixed" role, however, an exhaustive inquiry into all or most items would be called for. The resulting increase in amounts of calculation required would be immense. And to the extent that other participants adopted a mixed role, the pattern of expectations upon which they are so dependent as a calculating device would no longer prove stable. The calculation of preferences, essential in a democratic system, would become far more burdensome since inquiries would have to be instituted to find out what the various groups wanted in specific cases.

Furthermore, the adoption of a mixed role would be likely to lead to a greater neglect of values (that is, events and objects desired by people) affected by decisions.[14] Unless the ability of each participant to calculate the consequences of his actions is much more impressive than the evidence suggests, he is bound to neglect more if he attempts to do more. Yet this is precisely what a mixed role would force him to do. Instead of concentrating on a limited range of values within his jurisdiction, as his present role requires, he would have to consider the widest possible range of values in order to make a mixed role work. In place of the reasonable certainty that each participant would do a good job of looking after the relatively narrow range of values entrusted to his care, we would have little certainty that any particular value would be protected because no one had been especially directed to look after it. Let us explore this question further as a fundamental problem in normative political theory.

PVPI VERSUS TVPI

Why, it may be asked, should the various participants take a partial view? Why should they not simply decide in accord-

[14] Alain Enthoven and Harry Rowen argue that ". . . One of the most important things any defense allocation mechanism should do is to help prevent gaps from appearing in our capability. . . . [I]t is valuable to have the separate Services 'looking for business,' trying to expand and take on new jobs. . . . Human limitations being what they are, there is good reason to believe that a decentralized competitive system, in which people have incentives to propose alternatives, will usually meet this test more effectively than a highly centralized system." The authors then go on to observe that the Army's tenacity in defending a place for ground forces was useful in helping mitigate an unfortunate tendency to believe that nuclear weapons provided all the capability the nation needed. "Defense Planning and Organization," *Public Finances, Needs, Sources and Utilizations*, National Bureau of Economic Research (Princeton, 1961) pp. 369-371.

ance with what the public interest requires? Actually, this is the principle the participants think they are following now; they all believe that their version of the public interest is correct. It is their differing institutional positions, professional training, and group values that lead to perspectives producing somewhat different interpretations of the public interest. Let us, then, rephrase the question to ask whether it is better for each participant to view the public interest as involved primarily in the achievement of his own goals (including the goals entrusted to him by virtue of his position), or whether he should view the goals of others as of prime or at least equal importance?

I am prepared to argue that the partial-view-of-the-public-interest approach is preferable to the total-view-of-the public-interest approach, which is so often urged as being superior. First, it is much simpler for each participant to calculate his own preferences than for each to try to calculate the preferences of all. It is difficult enough for a participant to calculate how the interests he is protecting might best be served without requiring that he perform the same calculation for many others who might also be affected. The "partial" approach has the virtue of enabling others to accept as an input in their calculations the determination of each participant as to his preferences, which is not possible under the total approach. The danger of omitting important values is much greater when participants neglect the values in their immediate care in favor of what seems to them a broader view. How can anyone know what is being neglected if everyone speaks for someone else and no one for himself? Can we expect participants to act to protect the interests of others (which they believe they should take into account but which are not theirs) as well as those who have these interests?

The partial approach is more efficient for resolving conflicts, a process that lies at the heart of democratic politics. Because the approach is partial, it does not require its practitioners to discover all or most possible conflicts and to work out answers to problems that may never materialize. It permits each participant to go his own way until he discovers that the activities of others interfere. Effort can then be devoted to overcoming the difficulties that do exist. The formation of alliances in a political system that requires them is facilitated by the expression and pursuit of demands by those in closest touch with the social reality from which they issue forth. Then it is not a matter of a kind of *noblesse oblige* that assures that rival demands are considered. It is, rather, that the articulators of these demands insist on being heard and have the political resources to compel a hearing. A partial adversary system in which the various interests compete for control of policy (under agreed-upon rules) seems more likely to result in reasonable decisions—that is, decisions that take account of the multiplicity of values involved—than one in which the best policy is assumed to be discoverable by a well-intentioned search for the public interest for all by everyone.

If it is granted that budgetary practices based on a partial view of the public interest are desirable, then it would appear necessary to accept the use of strategies designed to secure appropriation goals. It is not surprising, however, that critics find something basically underhanded, even undemocratic, in the maneuvering of "special interests" for strategic advantage. Would not a straightforward approach based on the "merits" of each program be preferable? Suppose we proceed to an appraisal of strategies in order to determine whether or not they are desirable in whole or in part.

STRATEGIES

Requiring an individual to commit suicide for the public good may at times have an acceptable rationale; suggesting that it become a common practice can hardly claim as much. I shall take it as understood, then, that asking participants in budgeting consistently to follow practices extremely disadvantageous to themselves and their associates is not reasonable. The participants must be able to maintain themselves in the existing environment. Some strategies may be preferable to others from a moral viewpoint or because they foster changes in response to changes in values and goals. Other strategies may be undesirable because they do not enable certain pressing difficulties to be met. But it would not be helpful to urge strategies which place individuals and programs in the worst possible light or which do not permit the achievement of some success in securing appropriations.

The notion that administrators go around telling each other (or believing in secret) that the purposes for which they request funds are not valid but that they want the money anyway in order to advance themselves and build empires is not worthy of consideration. It would be exceedingly difficult to keep people in an organization if they could not justify its purposes to themselves. Such an attitude would be bound to come to the attention of other participants, who would take appropriate action. It would be bad strategically as well as morally. Attempts to reduce a complex distributive process like budgeting to the terms of a western melodrama—the good men ride white horses and advance on their merits; the bad men wear black masks and rely on strategies—do away with the great problem of deciding upon expenditures advocated by officials who are sincere believers in their proposals, knowing that not all demands can be satisfied.

THE BEST CASE

Budgetary strategies may generally be characterized as proceeding from a standpoint in which requests for appropriations are drawn up in an attempt to make the best case for the agency at the best time. This behavior follows from the role of the agency as advocate. As a practical matter, we would expect any agency head worth his keep to respond to opportunities for increasing appropriations and warding off cuts. Who would want to work for a person who did not give his staff opportunities for achievement by emphasizing the importance of their activities at a time when the reaction is likely to be favorable? The contrary position—making the worst case at the worst time—is not likely to be greeted with enthusiasm.

This orientation need not (and in most cases does not) mean that the estimates are dishonest. The desirability of maintaining confidence over the years suggests, if nothing else, the inadvisability of the slippery statistic and the grossly inaccurate report. What it does mean is that in a world in which there are usually a variety of honest ways to present and compare programs, the approach that experience suggests is likely to make the best impression on the intended audience will be selected. An administrator may have what he considers a dozen good arguments for a program, some more impressive than others, but all valid in some sense. Naturally, he picks and chooses among these for the one with the most appeal at the time.

Take the case of the agency that has several possible bases for estimating how much it will need to spend on a program. It can use an average of the last five years' expenditures; it can use the previous year on the ground that it is closest in time; it can try to make a cost estimate based on an assumed level of services. Now all of these approaches have something to be said for them and all are subject to distortion, although no one can know for certain which will be the most accurate until after the predicted events have occurred. Why, then, should the agency choose the most disadvantageous prediction? In an uncertain world, prudence might dictate leaving an ample margin for error.

Seizing on the opportune moment for advancing the agency's budgetary goals has much to commend it. The nation is served by initiative in meeting the needs of the time. An element of flexibility is generated that helps ensure that opportunities for action will be taken. "Crisis" strategies belong in this category. What is the difference, we may ask, between using a crisis to increase appropriations and acting to meet the nation's requirements in an hour of need? Perhaps some uneasiness results from a fear that a crisis may be created out of whole cloth or exaggerated just to receive funds. The sanctions for deceit being so great we need not concern ourselves unduly with the purely fictional crisis. Exaggeration is the problem. There seems to be no way, however, of avoiding this difficulty other than by intelligent scrutiny of requests at a time when no one may be in a position to assess the magnitude of the danger. The special attention paid to new programs or large increases in old ones under an incremental approach gives some assurance that the proposal will receive considerable scrutiny. On balance, it seems desirable to accept the disabilities flowing from exaggeration in order to reap the benefits of quick response to emergent needs.

The desire to present the agency's requests in the best light can be used in a positive sense to improve the thinking of the operating units. The budget office can play an important role because, though it is in the agency, it is also somewhat outside by virtue of the necessity it faces of justifying actions to the outside world. By playing devil's advocate, by pointing out that justifications are not clear or persuasive, by saying that the program heads have to do better to convince the Budget Bureau or the Appropriations Committee, the Budget office may compel or encourage thinking from diverse perspectives. In this way, a wider range of interests and values receive consideration.

Program people sometimes think they have done enough if they defend their requests as desirable within the agency's own frame of reference. They may become upset, therefore, when the agency head or budget officer insists that this is not enough, that perspectives emanating from the Budget Bureau and Congress also have to be considered, even though the presentation is deemed adequate on its face. The higher one goes in the administrative hierarchy, the more important becomes the task of representing, negotiating, accommodating to the other participants. If this task is done effectively, the prestige of the top official within his agency rises. But in the process he may have to give away some of the things which his people want and which he agrees are justified. Unless one is prepared to argue that what other key participants—other agencies, interest groups, Presidents, Congressmen—want is immaterial, there seems to be no way out of this process of reconciliation of demands. Nor, so long as we accept the separation of powers and democracy, can this process be deemed anything but desirable.

Presenting the best possible case is an aid to calculation for the other participants. They know that if this path is followed they do not have to think about whether or not there are better justifications for the appropriations; they can assume that the best justifications have been made and concentrate on doing their part of the job. It may be that what we want is the best argument on the part of all the agencies so that the worth of the program will be clearly established as a starting point for consideration by others.

SUPPORT

Clientele and confidence strategies are desirable as well as inevitable in a democratic society. The feedback that clientele give to the participants is essential political information about who wants what programs, at what level, and with what degree of intensity. The establishment of confidence provides the trust necessary for living with complexity; the sanctions that follow from lack of confidence represent a great safeguard against duplicity. That morality is to some extent the handmaiden of necessity does not make it any less real or valuable.

Analysis of the principles by which constituencies are formed and cultivated may be used for good purposes. The reader may recall a previous illustration in which the Census Bureau was enabled to get support for a housing census by changing its program from a simple national survey into one in which metropolitan areas were covered, thus increasing greatly the number of interested Congressmen. As long as the essential purpose of the program is not perverted, fitting the activity to the need for widespread constituency support increases an important value in a democratic society—consent. Surely, a program like summer institutes for mathematics teachers is not rendered less desirable by being distributed in a good many constituencies.

The creative arrangement of clientele may be used to alleviate the worst consequences arising out of the need for support. An agency may have to give up some of what it wants in order to receive support for other programs. This bargaining element is woven into the fabric of a democratic system. If the situation becomes untenable, however, so that the agency faces virtual capture by the affected interests, a broader arrangement of constituencies may be in order. The Grazing Service suffered because of its rather complete dependence on stockmen and those who spoke for them in Congress. By merging the Service into an expanded Bureau of Land Management, an act accomplished with the aid of interests adversely affected under the previous arrangement, the new organization has reduced its dependence by being able to appeal to a broader constituency. The Soil Conservation Service, to cite another instance, can afford to incur the wrath of limestone producers, who object to conservation practices that do not use their product, because it gets support from the National Association of Soil Conservation Districts, an interest group it has done much to foster.

The use of strategies is one means by which an agency can try to protect values ordinarily neglected in the political system. Suppose an agency has a marketing program that benefits most people a few dollars a year. Although the total benefits for the whole program are large, it is difficult to gather support for it because no one person receives sufficient benefits to make it worthwhile for him to act. Such a program is a handy target when cuts are made because an active clientele that would protest is lacking. One way in which the agency can protect this less popular program is to adopt a strategy—cutting more popular programs to which funds are likely to be restored—which will leave the less popular program intact. Though the end appears to be justified, the means seem to be suspect. On the surface, a more honest position would seem to require reducing the least valuable program regardless of the consequences for the total budget. One difficulty is that the agency may not be able to rank its programs and may, therefore, see no reason why it should not make the cuts in the places most favorable for its purposes. If the programs with the greatest political popularity are also the least valuable, then no problem arises because the strategy and the moral standard coincide. Cuts will be proposed in the least valuable program. But if the least popular program politically is also least desirable comparatively speaking, and the least desirable is deemed to be valuable in itself, a difficult problem arises. Should we, in the name of honesty, require an agency to sacrifice a program it believes valuable in favor of a more valuable one that is likely to be supported anyway? One could at least argue that total value would be increased by retaining the less popular program, cutting the more popular one, and thus emerging with funds for both. The strategy, of course, is neutral: it could be used to protect poor programs.

DECEIT?

A naked recital of strategies is bound to suggest that a certain amount of trickery or duplicity is involved.[15] Some strategies that appear to be deceitful represent amoral adjustments to an environment that does not give the participants much choice. Consider the kind of duplicity that appears to be involved in the game wherein agency people make believe that they are supporting the President's Budget while actually encouraging Congressmen to ask questions that will permit them to talk about what they would really like to have. Is this behavior immoral or does the immorality belong to the Executive Office directive that tries to compel agency personnel to say things they do not believe in order to support the President? Congress has the power of the purse and it is difficult to argue that it should not have the kind of information—what the people in charge of the program think they ought to get—which may be most helpful in arriving at decisions. If one wants to get rid of Congress, then the problem solves itself. But if one accepts the separation of powers, then it may well be that there is no point in denying to Congress information it would like to have when it is manifestly in the interests of administrators to supply it. The biblical injunction against excessive temptation is appropriate here.

One way to eliminate the element of deceit is to do away with the cause by requiring the publication of what the agency originally asked for from the Budget Bureau. Agencies would still be bound by the President's Budget to the same extent they are now. They just would not have to engage in artful (or not so artful) dodging when the subject is mentioned at hearings. It may be judged that the fiction that the Presi-

---

[15] Lest anyone receive the mistaken impression that such practices are confined to the government, see the following reference on deceptive practices in industry: Frank Jasinsky, "Use and Misuse of Efficiency Controls," XXXIV *Harvard Business Review* (July and August, 1956) pp. 105-112.

dent's Budget is universally supported is worth maintaining in order to cut down the number of cases in which contrary information reaches Congress. This in itself is a strategic decision. Those who hold this view, however, should not then go on to complain that participants are acting deceitfully when all they are demonstrating is that the Emperor really does not have any clothes after all.

Strategies such as advertising and salesmanship belong in the same category. They are good if one likes the program that is being furthered, and bad if one does not. Scandalous propaganda by power-hungry bureaucrats quickly becomes information for the benefit of the American people depending on whether one approves or disapproves of a Polaris missile, an RS-70 bomber, Mission 66 Park, or even Smokey-the-Bear fire-prevention programs. The idea that the good programs somehow sell themselves runs contrary to experience, and not only in government.

Many of the same things can be said about the strategic wedge. If one approves of the program that was begun by keeping a foot in the budgetary door, then the strategy is an example of courageous foresight. If not, then the strategy is just a blatant raid on the treasury. When the emphasis is on reducing expenditures, a lot of wedging items may seem excessive. When the demand is for speedy action, the fact that a first step has been taken may appear most fortunate.

Taking advantage of the separation of powers and the division of labor in Congress may seem inordinately manipulative until one asks whether or not there is any reasonable alternative. As things stand now, an agency may suffer because it lacks support in one of the Houses of Congress, in the substantive or appropriations committees, in the Conference Committee, or in the Executive Office. The American political system provides many detours, not to say reverses and roadblocks. To ask the agency not to take advantage of an opportunity for using superior strength in one of these centers of power is to consign it to permanent impotence unless it is so fortunate as to be loved equally everywhere. A code of conduct that states that only the disadvantages of the system are acceptable is rather strange.

There are a few strategies that are clearly immoral. In 1957, for example, Secretary of Defense Wilson tried to end the Air Force practice of phased buying. By buying parts for a larger number of weapons, instead of the smaller number indicated in the appropriation request, the Air Force left the President and Congress little alternative but to pay for the remaining parts if any of the material was to be useful. After a public controversy, the Air Force agreed to mend its ways. Eternal vigilance being the price of liberty, such practices should be discouraged, and they are in part through the self-corrective mechanism of the loss of confidence. To the best of my knowledge, few agencies engage in similar strategies.

MERIT

Despite all that has been said, the very idea that strategies are employed may appear disturbing. Why cannot programs be presented on their merits and their merits alone?

The most obvious answer is that the question presupposes an agreement on what merit consists of when the real problem is that people do not agree. That is why we have politics. To lay down and enforce criteria of merit in budgeting would be, in effect, to deny the need for politics by deciding what the government shall do in advance.

Much of what is meant by merit turns out to be "meets my preferences" or "serves my interests" or "the interests of those with whom I identify." It would be most peculiar for a nation calling itself a democracy to announce that only the most meritorious policies were carried out despite the fact that they were not preferred by any significant group in the population.

The degree to which widespread preferences are met not only *is* but *ought* to be *part* of policies deemed meritorious.

We all know that people do not always realize what is good for them. They are occupied with many things and may not recognize the benefits flowing from certain policies. They may find it difficult to support policies that are meritorious but not directly related to individual constituencies. Here is where strategies come in. Where support is lacking, it may be mobilized; where attention is unfocused, it may be directed by advertising; where merits are not obvious, they may be presented in striking form. Ability to devise strategies to advance the recognition of merit is immensely more helpful than cries of indignation that political craftsmanship should be necessary.

Merit consists in part of the effectiveness with which programs are formulated and carried out. No one should doubt that this criterion is recognized in the budgetary process; estimates, justifications, and presentations are directed to this factor. Though effectiveness is indispensable—confidence would be lacking without it, for one thing; clientele would be dissatisfied, for another—agencies find that it does not take them far enough. An agency may be wonderfully effective in formulating and carrying out its programs and yet see its fortunes suffer because of the need to cut that year or to shift funds to some vital area. Defense appropriations are often a function of domestic concerns; stabilization policy may be constrained by military needs; the complexity of a project or the difficulty of demonstrating immediate results may militate against it. Consequently, the agency invariably finds that in some areas its good works and best efforts are not being rewarded. Prizes are simply not distributed for good deeds alone. The agency's mode of adapting to this circumstance is to use demonstration of good works as one among a number of strategies. Forbidding agencies to use strategies designed to give its good requests a better chance, because bad requests can also be dressed up, seems inadvisable as well as unlikely to succeed.

CONCLUSION

In appraising the budgetary process, we must deal with real men in the real world for whom the best they can get is to be preferred to the perfection they cannot achieve. Unwilling or unable to alter the basic features of the political system, they seek to make it work for them in budgeting rather than against them. Following Frank Knight, James Buchanan has observed "To argue that an existing order is 'imperfect' in comparison with an alternative order of affairs that turns out, upon careful inspection, to be unobtainable may not be different from arguing that the existing order is 'perfect.' "[16]

Participants in budgeting not only work within the specified constitutional rules, they also make active use of them. Problems of calculation are mitigated by the division of labor in the separation of powers; morality is enforced by substantial external checks as well as by inner motives; a wider range of preferences is taken into account by making the institutional participants responsible for somewhat different ones. A great deal of informal coordination takes place as participants adjust to their expectation of behavior by others. An incremental approach guards against radical departures most of the time, whereas agency advocacy and strategies designed to take advantage of emergent needs help ensure flexibility. A basic conclusion of this appraisal is that the existing budgetary process works much better than is commonly supposed.

There is, however, no special magic in the *status quo*. Inertia and ignorance as well as experience and wisdom may be responsible for the present state of affairs. Improvements of many kinds are undoubtedly possible and desirable. But the major suggested alternatives to the existing budgetary process such as comprehensive calculation and formal coordination turn out to be unfeasible, undesirable, or both. My view is

[16] James M. Buchanan, "Politics, Policy and the Pigovian Margins," XXIX *Economica* (February 1962) p. 19.

that the process should be taken as far as it will go and then should be corrected for its worst deficiencies. Future proposals for reform should advocate a more thoroughgoing incremental approach rather than a more comprehensive one. There should be greater use of aids to calculation rather than less. Agencies should not be told to give up advocacy but to make their best case even more persuasive.

To say that no strategies should be pursued is to imply that there are no purposes for which it is legitimate to plan (scheme, if you prefer) to secure funds.[17] Indeed, those who are serious about effectuating changes would do well to suggest that the strategies they prefer will prove more successful in securing funds than those currently being practiced. The proponents of change might consider ways and means of structuring the budgetary process so that their preferred strategies will turn out to be those which participants find it advantageous to pursue. I would take my stand with the authors of the *Federalist* (especially the superb fify-first number) who argue that the good may be most dependably secured by arranging things so "that the private interest of every individual may be a sentinel over the public rights."[18]

[17] It is instructive to observe that one of the outstanding proposals for budgetary reform was given a name with the strategic purpose of gathering support. According to Wilfred McNeil, who served on the Hoover Commission to reorganize the executive branch of the government, "It was Mr. [Herbert] Hoover who put the label on that plan, the word 'performance budget.' He himself said it [the reform] had to have some sales appeal, and the name 'performance' was selected." Committee on Government Operations, Subcommittee Hearings, U.S. House of Representatives, *Improving Federal Budgeting and Appropriations*, 85th Congress, 1st Session, 1957, p. 271.

[18] In discussing changes in accounting procedures, Wilfred McNeil states that "If we can get accounting and human nature to work together, we have got something, but if they are opposing we haven't solved the problem." He cited as an example a circumstance in which the Marine Corps had fairly good radio equipment but needed and wanted better radios. "From my standpoint," McNeil declared, "I could see why the people involved didn't want to cancel [large old contracts]. If they canceled under the annual appropriation system it [the item for procuring radios] was out, but the House and Senate Appropriations

The intimate connection between descriptive and normative statements is never more evident than when policy recommendations are made. For sensible policy depends as much on knowledge of the world as it is, as on knowledge of the world as it ought to be. Knowing more about what the budgetary process actually accomplishes, we are able to suggest more appropriate and less drastic suggestions for change. The more we know about how the process works, the better position we will be in to make recommendations to policy makers that make sense, and that do not fool either the giver or the recipients of this advice.

Committee that year changed their procurement funds to the continuing type. . . . The result was that there was about $300 million worth of materiel that was canceled to be replaced with orders for materiel that was up to date." Committee on Government Operations, Subcommittee Hearings, U.S. House of Representatives, *Budget and Accounting*, 84th Congress, 2nd Session, 1956.

PPB AND ZBB

6

If the old budgeting became anti-analytical because it arrested development at the level of inputs, the new budgeting became irrational by dwelling excessively on outputs. A fixation on what is put in has been replaced by a compulsion over what should be taken out. Objectives replace resources as *the* key to analysis. After decades of discussing effort instead of accomplishment — how hard teachers work but not how well students learn, how much money is spent on police but not how much crime is reduced — the urge to concentrate on results rather than resources is understandable. Unfortunately, the grip on one excess has been loosened only to embrace another; alas, the affair with resources has been replaced by the romance with objectives.

Policy analysis, in contrast to these two extremes, compares programs. Only programs combine the compromises between resources and objectives that make workable alternatives. Resources change objectives — a million dollars might make one think of different things to do than would a thousand — as much as the other way around. Each analysis, as well as every practical application, should teach us as much about what we prefer as about how much we put in. Ends and means are chosen simultaneously, and what life has joined, policy analysis must not rend asunder.

The idea that means alone should change, but never ends, is attractive. It suggests the lone hero, who keeps the faith — a vow to God, a promise to the people, a mandate from the movement. The price paid is rarely recognized; that there is invariably carnage along the way is less important than personal vindication. Rigidity becomes deified into righteousness. But righteousness is no substitute for right action; it is irresponsible to promise what cannot be delivered.

A policy alternative may be defined as a hypothesis: If certain things are done, then others will follow. A program tests this hypothesis in action. One way of thinking about objectives is that they are established before the hypothesis is tested and can be compared to consequences. But without resources there can be no objectives. A hypothesis includes "if" as well as "then"; if in a program specific amounts of resources are combined in certain ways by people possessing particular authority, then and only then does the policy hypothesis exist in a form that can be tested. A policy hypothesis includes both means and ends, not just one or the other.

Policy analysis does not consist in enunciating objectives as if no objective had to be sacrificed to achieve another. It is as easy and useless to make endless lists of objectives as to draw up and ignore New Year's resolutions. How much money for each objective? If the first one or two (an increase in Social Security, say, or a massive medical program) exhaust all available resources, it doesn't matter what the rest are, or in what order. How much for all? Analysts know that how far you go depends on what you've got to get there.

Analysis does not consist of showing that objectives have not been met; anybody can curse the fates. So what? Such evaluations do not help program managers who need to know which resources under their control they can manipulate to do better. Programs can only be countered by other programs. If a bad program is the best available, it may still be good compared to the alternatives. Bad, however, is not yet beautiful. Constraints exist to be overcome. At any one time, however, only the irresponsible promise the loosening of all restraints in a promised land of milk and honey, where no choice is necessary because there is no scarcity. Altering objectives to fit resources, therefore, is as much a part of good analysis as varying resources to accomplish objectives. That is why analysts advise not only on the allocation of resources but on the reformulation of objectives.

Although there has been some scrutiny of budgetary systems, they have never, so far as I know, been compared critically as modes of problem solving. It is assumed that their strength lies in assisting rational choice, their weaknesses in coping with the irrational features that political self-interest unfortunately brings to policymaking. My argument is different. These budgetary systems are defective because they constitute bad advice on what is (and how to get) good policy analysis. Analysis is about action as well as advice; therefore, analysis, judging information good only if organizations actually use it to do better, seeks to embed itself in organizational incentives. Analysis is historically grounded to use conflict creatively, for otherwise, by magnifying disagreement, it becomes its own worst problem. Analysis does not consider alternative objectives or alternative mixes of resources in isolation but rather together as alternative programs.

Before turning to PPB and ZBB, it is useful to say a few words about MBO (Management by Objectives) because it is the epitome of a method for improving choice based on analyzing objectives. The lesson of Management by Objectives is that what may begin as puffery (Look at our wonderful objectives!) often winds up as self-deception — ranking objectives equals analyzing problems.

MANAGEMENT BY OBJECTIVES

The idea behind Management by Objectives is that objectives should be specified and that management and workers should agree on the results by which workers are to be judged in accordance with these objectives. At each level objectives are formulated, discussed, agreed to, and passed up the hierarchy. Minor objectives are stacked like Chinese boxes within major ones. What could possibly be wrong with so appealing an idea? Managers should have objectives for their organizations, and workers should be held to account for achieving results. MBO, in a word, is a restatement of good management based on rational choice for effective decision making. The trouble is that the attempt to formalize procedures for choosing objectives without considering organizational dynamics leads to the opposite of what was intended: irrational choice and ineffective action.

The main product of MBO, as experience in the United States federal government suggests, is literally a series of objectives. Aside from the unnecessary paperwork, such exercises are self-defeating because they become mechanisms for avoiding rather than making choices. Long lists of objectives are useless because rarely do resources exist to carry out more than the first few. The experience of the various federal commissions on national priorities, for instance, is that there is no point in listing 846 or even 79 national objectives because almost all the money is gone after the first three or four are funded. If choosing objectives means abandoning choice, choosing objectives is a bad idea.

The larger the number of objectives, the greater the likelihood that some organizational activity will somehow contribute to at least one, the less the need to give up one thing for another. Public agencies prefer more objectives rather than fewer, so whatever consequences they cause are more likely to fit under one of them. Everyone knows that objectives of public agencies tend to be multiple, conflicting, and vague; multiple and conflicting because different people want different things with varying degrees of intensity, and vague because objectives can thus accommodate disagreement. Reconciling these conflicts is not made easier by telling bureaucrats that their strategic behavior — staking out their own objectives as a prelude to bargaining — has become sanctified as an object of virtue, indeed, as the essence of rationality itself.

The most elaborate evaluation of an MBO operation, "The Case of the Social and Rehabilitation Service," shows that MBO's chief effects are an increase in paperwork and in discussion of objectives and a decrease in time spent on programmatic activity. When asked what they would recommend as improvements beyond MBO, "Both regional and central administrators mention management accountability and responsibility . . . better teamwork . . . coordination . . . a need for clear mission goals and priorities . . . and the development of management information systems" — in other words, exactly what MBO was supposed to accomplish in the first place. Interviews with 159 top administrators reveal that MBO "is generally perceived by managers and supervisors as a system which reinforces such bureaucratic norms as centralized organizational control and decision-making, paperwork, efficiency emphasis and lack of participation." [1]

By putting all the emphasis on objectives, MBO subsumes critical problems of organizational design — how to relate people and activities so that errors become evident and are corrected — under the surface sentimentality of human relations jargon. What MBO does to program objectives, PPB does to organizational incentives.

[1] Jong S. Jun, "Management by Objectives in a Government Agency: The Case of the Social and Rehabilitation Service." Mimeographed. The Social and Rehabilitation Service Department of HEW (August 1973).

On August 25, 1965, President Johnson announced that he was asking the heads of all federal agencies to introduce "a very new and revolutionary system" of budgeting. Staffs of experts set up in each agency would define goals using "modern methods of program analysis." Then the "most effective and the least costly" way to accomplish these goals would be found.[2] The general idea is that budgetary decisions should be made by focusing on output categories like governmental goals, objectives, and end products instead of inputs like personnel, equipment, and maintenance. Once priorities among objectives were established, this budgetary procedure was supposed to determine the best expenditure mix in the annual budget to secure the largest future benefits. Hence it went by the name of Planning, Programming, and Budgeting Systems (PPB), or just program budgeting.

Although there are a few historical precursors of program budgeting,[3] its recent impetus came in the 1960s from the experience of the federal government. From there it spread with amazing speed to numerous American cities and states, foreign governments, and even international agencies. Clearly, from the standpoint of sheer effort and attention, PPB is the major budgetary phenomenon (perhaps cause célèbre would be more accurate) of our time. Hence it requires serious attention. First I shall consider three essential features of PPB — its objectivity, its centralization, and its political content. Then I shall briefly survey experience in implementing PPB and try to account for its difficulties.

[2] David Novick, editor, *Program Budgeting*, 2nd ed. (Cambridge, Mass., Harvard University Press, 1967), pp. v–vi.

[3] See Allen Schick, *Budget Innovation in the States* (Washington, D.C., The Brookings Institution, 1971); and David Novick, *Origin and History of Program Budgeting* (Santa Monica, California, RAND Corporation, October 1966).

Programs are not made in heaven. They must be manufactured by men, and no one can give instructions for making up programs. There are as many ways to conceive of programs as there are of organizing activity,[4] as the comments of the following writers eloquently testify:

> It is by no means obvious . . . whether a good program structure should be based on components of specific end objectives (e.g., the accomplishment of certain land reclamation targets), on the principle of cost separation (identifying as a program any activity the costs of which can be readily segregated), on the separation of means and ends (Is education a means or an end in a situation such as skill-retaining courses for workers displaced by automation?), or on some artificially designed pattern that draws from all these and other classification criteria.[5]

> Just what categories constitute the most useful programs and program elements is far from obvious. . . . If one puts all educational activities into a broad package of educational programs, he cannot simultaneously include school lunch programs or physical education activities in a Health Program, or include defense educational activities (such as the military academies) in the Defense Program. . . . In short, precisely how to achieve a rational and useful structure for a program budget is not yet evident.[6]

A first question one might ask is whether, given their nature, health activities merit a separate, independent status in a program budget. The question arises because these activities often are constituents of, or inputs into, other activities whose purpose or goal orientation is the dominating one. Outlays by the Department of Defense for hospital care, for example, though they assist in maintaining the health of one segment of the population, are undertaken on

[4] A look at the classic work by Luther Gulick and Lyndall Urwick, *Papers on the Science of Administration* (New York, 1937), reveals considerable similarity between their suggested bases of organization and ways of conceptualizing programs.

[5] Melvin Anshen in D. Novick, *op. cit.*, pp. 19–20.

[6] George A. Steiner in *ibid.*, p. 356.

behalf of national defense, and the latter is their justification.[7]

The difficulties with the program concept are illustrated in the space program. A first glance suggests that space projects are ideally suited for program budgeting because they are physical systems designed to accomplish different missions. Actually, there is a remarkable degree of interdependence between different missions and objectives — pride, scientific research, space exploration, military exploration and uses, etc. — so that it is difficult to apportion costs properly. Consider the problem of a rocket developed for one mission and useful for others. To apportion costs to each new mission is purely arbitrary; to allocate the cost to the first mission and regard the rocket as free for all subsequent missions is ludicrous. Making a separate program out of the rocket itself does violence to the concept of programs as end products. The difficulty is compounded because facilities that have multiple uses, like boosters and tracking networks, tend to be expensive compared to the items that are specific to a particular mission.[8] Simple concepts of programs evaporate upon inspection.

CENTRALIZATION

Who should exert power over which programs is a major question of government. How programs are structured is, therefore, a crucial political question. Political realities lie behind the failure to devise principles for defining programs. Asking if centralization is better than decentralization is equivalent to asking who will rule. As Melvin Anshen puts it, "The central issue is, of course, nothing less than the definition of the ultimate objectives of the Federal govern-

[7] Arthur Smithies in *ibid.*, p. 41.
[8] See the excellent chapter by Milton A. Margolis and Stephen M. Barro in *ibid.*, pp. 120–145.

ment as they are realized through operational decisions." The arrangement of the programs inevitably affects the specific actions taken to implement them. "Set in this framework," Anshen continues, "the designation of a schedule of programs may be described as building a bridge between a matter of political philosophy (what is government for?) and . . . assigning scarce resources among alternative governmental objectives." [9]

Proponents of program budgeting are markedly ambivalent about the necessity for reorganization of the federal government to centralize authority for wide-ranging programs in order to give PPB a chance to work. The problem is that responsibility for programs is scattered throughout the whole federal establishment and decentralized to state and local authorities as well. In the field of health, for example, expenditures are distributed among at least twelve agencies and six departments outside Health, Education, and Welfare. A far greater number of organizations are concerned with American activities abroad, with natural resources, and with education. The multiple jurisdictions and overlapping responsibilities do violence to the concept of comprehensive and consistent programs. It "causes one to doubt," Marvin Frankel writes, "whether there can exist in the administrative echelons the kind of overall perspective that would seem indispensable if Federal health resources are to be rationally allocated." [10] To G. A. Steiner it is evident that "the present 'chest of drawers' type of organization cannot for long be compatible with program budgeting." [11]

Program budgeting contains an extreme centralizing bias. Power is to be centralized in the Presidency (through the Office of Management and Budget) at the national level, in superdepartments rather than bureaus within the Executive

[9] Anshen, *op. cit.*, p. 18.
[10] Marvin Frankel in D. Novick, *op. cit.*, p. 237.
[11] Steiner, *op. cit.*, p. 248.

Branch, and in the federal government as a whole instead of state or local governments. Note how W. Z. Hirsh assumes the desirability of national dominance when he writes: "These methods of analysis can guide Federal officials in the responsibility of bringing local education decisions into closer harmony with national objectives." [12] G. A. Steiner observes that comprehensiveness may be affected by unrestricted federal grants-in-aid to the states because "such a plan would remove a substantial part of Federal expenditures from a program budgeting system of the Federal government." [13] Should there be reluctance on the part of state and local officials to employ the new tools, Anshen states "that the Federal government may employ familiar incentives to accelerate this progress." [14] Summing it up, Hirsch says, "It appears doubtful that a natural resources program budget would have much impact without a good deal of centralization." [15]

Within the great federal organizations designed to encompass the widest range of objectives, there would have to be strong executives. Cutting across the subunits of the organization, as is the case in the Department of Defense, the program budget could be put together only by the top executive. A more useful tool for increasing his power to control his subordinates would be difficult to imagine.

That all decisions ought to be made by the most central person in the most centralized body is a proposition difficult to justify on scientific grounds. In fact, it cannot be justified except as reflecting a distaste of politics — for the more centralized a system, the fewer the decision-makers and the less the need to bargain.

In the literature discussed earlier there appears several

---

[12] Werner Z. Hirsch in D. Novick, *op. cit.*, p. 370.
[13] Steiner, *op. cit.*, p. 347.
[14] Anshen, *op. cit.*, p. 365.
[15] Hirsch, *op. cit.*, p. 203.

times the proposition that "the program budget is a neutral tool. It has no politics." [16]

How could men make so foolish a statement? Perhaps they identify program budgeting with something good and beautiful, and politics with something bad and ugly. McKean and Anshen speak of politics in terms of "pressure and expedient adjustments," "haphazard acts . . . unresponsive to a planned analysis of the needs of efficient decision design." From the political structure they expect only "resistance and opposition, corresponding to the familiar human disposition to protect established seats of power and procedures made honorable by the mere facts of existence and custom." [17] In other places we hear of "vested interests," "wasteful duplication," "special interest groups," and the "Parkinson syndrome." [18] Somebody doesn't like politics.

POLITICS

Political rationality is the fundamental kind of reason, because it deals with the preservation and improvement of decision structures, and decision structures are the source of all decisions. Unless a decision structure exists, no reasoning and no decisions are possible. . . . There can be no conflict between political rationality and . . . technical, legal, social, or economic rationality, because the solution of political problems makes possible an attack on any other problem, while a serious political deficiency can prevent or undo all other problem solving. . . . Non-political decisions are reached by considering a problem in its own terms, and by evaluating proposals according to how well they solve the problem. The best available proposal should be accepted regardless of who makes it or who opposes it, and a faulty proposal should be rejected or improved no matter who makes it. Compromise is always irrational; the rational procedure is to determine which proposal is the

[16] Anshen, *op. cit.*, p. 370.
[17] R. McKean and M. Anshen, *op. cit.*, p. 289.
[18] *Ibid.*, p. 359.

best, and to accept it. In a political decision, on the other hand, action never is based on the merits of a proposal but always on who makes it and who opposes it. Action should be designed to avoid complete identification with any proposal and any point of view, no matter how good or how popular it might be. The best available proposal should never be accepted just because it is best; it should be deferred, objected to, discussed, until major opposition disappears. Compromise is always a rational procedure, even when the compromise is between a good and bad proposal.[19]

It will be useful to distinguish between policy politics (which policy will be adopted?), partisan politics (which political party will win office?), and system politics (how will decision structures be set up?). Program budgeting is manifestly concerned with policy politics, and not much with partisan politics, although it could have important consequences for issues that divide the nation's parties. My contention is that the thrust of program budgeting makes it an integral part of system politics.

It is hard to find men who take up the cause of political rationality, who plead the case for political man, and who are primarily concerned with the laws that enable the political machinery to keep working. One is driven to a philosopher like Paul Diesing to find the case for the political:

> . . . the political problem is always basic and prior to the others. . . . This means that any suggested course of action must be evaluated first by its effects on the political structure. A course of action which corrects economic or social deficiencies but increases political difficulties must be rejected, while an action which contributes to political improvement is desirable even if it is not entirely sound from an economic or social standpoint.[20]

[19] Paul Diesing, *Reason in Society* (Urbana, Ill., 1962) pp. 198, 203–204, 231–232.
[20] *Ibid.*, p. 228.

There is hardly a political scientist who would claim half as much.

A major task of the political system is to specify goals or objectives. It is impermissible to treat goals as if they were known in advance. "Goals" may well be the product of interaction among key participants rather than pronouncements of some deus ex machina or (to use Bentley's term) some "spook" which posits values in advance of our knowledge of them.

Once the political process becomes a focus of attention, it is evident that the principal participants may not be clear about their goals. What we call goals or objectives may, in large part, be operationally determined by the policies we can agree upon. In a political situation, then, the need for support assumes central importance. Not simply the economic but the political costs and benefits turn out to be crucial.

The literature of economics usually treats organizations and institutions as if they were costless entities. The standard procedure is to consider rival alternatives (in consideration of price policy or other criteria), calculate the differences in cost and achievement among them, and show that one is more or less efficient than another. This way of thinking is insufficient. If the costs include getting an agency to change its policies or procedures, then these organizational costs must also be taken into account.

PRACTICE

What happened when efforts were made to implement PPB? Did it change the traditional budgetary process? Did it alter substantive outcomes?

Marvin and Rouse conducted 400 interviews in a large number of agencies and found that even where PPB processes were well developed, their contribution to decision making was minor. "Detailed PPB processes have been developed in . . . [a] group of agencies; for example, Interior. With the exception of the work in an occasional bureau, the materials produced through these processes have not been used extensively by decisionmakers. . . ." [21] In another group of agencies, "well-developed analytic activities have contributed to decision making and did so long before the advent of PPB. . . . The result is that PPB's contribution in restructuring the decision-making process in these agencies has been marginal." [22]

Similar conclusions are found in another study prepared by a practitioner. Jack W. Carlson studied a group of twenty-six agencies and discovered that though program structures had been developed, "the formal structure has been only partially successful." [23] He concluded that the benefits derived from their preparation were mainly educational.[24]

Hard choices (trade-offs among activities devoted to similar ends) can be avoided either by proliferating categories so there is one for every major activity, or by severely limiting the number of categories so they are broad and vague. Both strategies were used in the Department of Agriculture. No important program cut across more than a single bureau; the new program elements essentially renamed old activities.[25]

And the first shall be last. Since 1961, Defense has been held up as the prime example of what PPB can do and how

[21] Keith E. Marvin and Andrew M. Rouse, "The Status of PPB in Federal Agencies: A Comparative Perspective," in R. Haveman and J. Margolis, editors, *Public Policy Expenditures and Policy Analysis* (Chicago, 1970), p. 448.

[22] *Ibid.*

[23] Jack W. Carlson, "The Status and Next Steps for Planning, Programming and Budgeting," in Haveman and Margolis, *op. cit.*, p. 374.

[24] *Ibid.*

[25] Aaron Wildavsky and Jeanne Nienaber, *The Budgeting and Evaluation of Federal Recreation Programs, or Money Doesn't Grow on Trees* (New York, 1973).

well it can succeed.[26] But PPB did not change budgetary decisions in DOD to any significant degree. Programming did not have the anticipated effect on budgeting. Rather, the yearly appropriations placed limitations on programs. John P. Crecine, who has conducted an intensive study of the subject, concluded that, "In spite of the many differences in necessary procedures under PPBS, the methods of arriving at dollar figures for the line items in the appropriations request, consistent with the fiscal constraints on the total . . . are not dissimilar from those utilized during the Truman-Eisenhower administrations." [27] The Department decides on what it will ask for in the same way as it did before PPB. Budget reviewers in DOD, when forecasting the cuts that are going to be made, base their decisions on past budget decisions. "Basically . . . *experience with the decision system* [the "base" in our terms] *is the prime ingredient in the budget review exercise*" (italics in original).[28]

PPB's application to DOD's final budget is insignificant, but within the Department it might be thought to have had an effect. However, this does not appear to have been the case, for two reasons: First, "PPB decisions are always made to conform to appropriations decisions made during the October–December budget crunch"; and second, "The current PPB system does not do what any foreseeable budget decision system has to do if it is to be the primary determinate of DOD resource allocation; it has to adapt to external, fiscal constraints." [29] PPB, apparently, is not only a "has been" in Defense but may well be a "never was."

PPB staffs often claim advances in the area of policy

[26] G. W. Shipp, "Program Budgeting in the Defense Department: A Small Change" (unpublished paper, University of California, Berkeley, 1966), p. 24.

[27] John P. Crecine, *Defense Budgeting: Constraints and Organizational Adaptations,* Discussion Paper No. 6, University of Michigan, Institute of Public Policy Studies (1969), p. 38.

[28] *Ibid.,* p. 49.

[29] *Ibid.,* pp. 54–55.

analysis. To support the claim they point to a number of so-called successful analytical studies. Had implementation really succeeded, of course, there would have been so many analytical studies that referring to one or two would have been a tremendous understatement. The rare analytical study which PPB officials hold out as proof for advancement is praised because it is unique, or as Schick calls it, a "museum piece . . . exuberantly displayed for outsiders but a 'hands off' practice bars their use in actual decisions." [30]

I have not been able to find a single example of successful implementation of PPB. As Harper, Kramer, and Rouse put it, "observers of the budgeting process agree that PPB has had limited influence on the major resource allocation decisions in domestic agencies of the federal government." [31] Even where implementation was seriously carried out and a large investment made, the primary goal — changing budgetary procedures and decisions — was never achieved.

Why? Did ugly old politics beat up nice young PPB? No doubt. But that is not the half of it. Practitioners of program budgeting were never able to define programs or attach costs to them, or make it worthwhile for organizations to figure out how to do so. What is worse, I shall argue, PPB deserved to die because it is an irrational mode of analysis that leads to suppression rather than correction of error.

POLICY

I have previously argued that program budgeting would run up against severe political difficulties. While most of these arguments have been conceded, I have been told that in a better world, without the vulgar intrusion of political factors (such as the consent of the governed), PPB would perform

[30] Schick, *op. cit.*, p. 104.

[31] Edwin L. Harper, Fred A. Kramer, and Andrew M. Rouse, "Implementation and the Use of PPB in Sixteen Federal Agencies," XXIX *Public Administration Review* (November/December 1969) p. 632.

its wonders as advertised. Now it is clear that for the narrow purpose of predicting why program budgeting will not work there is no need to mention political problems at all. It is sufficient to say that the wholesale introduction of PPB presented insuperable difficulties of calculation: *no one knows how to do program budgeting.* Another way of putting it is that many know what program budgeting should be in general, but no one knows what it should be in any particular case. Program budgeting cannot be stated in operational terms. The reason for the difficulty is that telling an agency to adopt program budgeting means telling it to find better policies, and there is no formula for doing that. One can (and should) talk about measuring effectiveness, estimating costs, and comparing alternatives, but that is a far cry from being able to take the creative leap of formulating a better policy.

On the basis of numerous discussions with would-be practitioners of program budgeting at the federal level, I can describe the usual pattern of its application. Instructions come down from the Bureau of the Budget (now the Office of Management and Budget): You must have a program budget. Agency personnel panic; they do not know how to do what they have been asked to do. So they produce a vast amount of inchoate data characterized by premature quantification of irrelevant items. Neither agency heads nor budget examiners can comprehend the material submitted to them. Its very bulk inhibits understanding. It is useless to the Director of the Budget in making his decisions. In an effort to be helpful, the program analysis unit says something like: "Nice try, fellows; we appreciate all that effort. But you have not quite got the idea of program budgeting yet. Remember, you must clarify goals, define objectives, relate these to quantitative indicators, and project costs into the future. Please send a new submission based on this understanding."

Another furious effort takes place. Huge amounts of overtime are put in. Under severe time pressure, even more data is accumulated. No one can say that agency personnel did not try hard. The new presentation makes a little more sense to some people and a little less to others. It just does not hang together as a presentation of agency policies. There are more encouraging words from the Budget Bureau and another sermon about specifying alternative ways of meeting agency objectives, though not, of course, taking the old objectives for granted. By this time agency personnel are desperate. "We would love to do it," they say, "but we cannot figure out the right way. You experts in the Budget Bureau should show us how to do it." Silence. The word from on high is that the Bureau of the Budget does not interfere with agency operations; it is the agency's task to set up its own budget. After a while, cynicism reigns supreme.

Although PPB dredges up data under numerous headings, it says next to nothing about the impact of one program on another. There is data but no information. Agency heads are at once oversupplied with numbers and undersupplied with propositions about the effects of any action they might undertake.

WHY PPB IS IRRATIONAL

To better understand the failure of program budgeting everywhere and at all times, it is helpful to imagine what would be required for its success. Most discussion has been confined to "sufficient" conditions. The critical assumption has been that it is easy to set up PPB but difficult to implement the system. The problems presumably lie, therefore, in rooted interests, recalcitrant politicians, and hidebound bureaucrats. It has been readily acknowledged, in addition, that the implementation of PPB has been hampered by lack of trained manpower, absence of essential data, and even inadequacies in the state of the art. The point is that all these putative defects can be remedied. Unreceptive politicians and bureaucrats can be got around or replaced. Training can be stepped up, better data can surely be collected, and knowledge of analysis will undoubtedly be improved. If these were the only difficulties, it would be difficult to explain why PPB has no successes whatsoever to its credit. For surely somewhere, sometime, the right conditions for PPB to prosper should have existed. Maybe they should have, but they didn't. Why not? To answer that question we have to be prepared to accept the possibility that PPB lacks "necessary" as well as sufficient conditions, that its disabilities occur not merely in program implementation but in policy design — that, in a word, its defects are defects in principle, not in execution. PPB does not work because it cannot work. Failure is built into its very nature because it requires ability to perform cognitive operations that are beyond present human (or mechanical) capacities.

Program budgeting is like the simultaneous equation of governmental intervention in society. If one can state objectives precisely, find quantitative measures for them, specify alternative ways of achieving them by different inputs of resources, and rank them according to desirability, one has solved the social problems for the period. One has only to bring the program budget up to date each year. Is it surprising that program budgeting does not perform this sort of miracle? Planning, Programming, and Budgeting Systems require a structure in which all policies related to common objectives are compared for cost and effectiveness. Not a single theory for a particular area of policy but, rather, a series of interrelated theories for all policies is required. If we barely sense the relation between inputs and outputs in any single area of policy, however, how likely are we to know what these relationships are across the widest realm of policy? As one area of ignorance interacts exponentially with other areas, we get not an arithmetic but a geometric increase in ignorance.[32]

There is no need to blink at the inevitable conclusion: PPB is not an embodiment of rationality; PPB is irrational. If the goal is to alter the allocation of resources in a more productive way, or to generate better analyses than those that are now used, PPB does not (because it cannot) produce these results. PPB is not cost effective. It produces costly rationales for inevitable failures.

But why do seemingly rational procedures produce irrational results? By sacrificing organizational incentives in the name of economic efficiency, program budgeting serves neither. The good organization is interested in discovering and correcting its own mistakes. The higher the cost of errors — not only in terms of money but also in personnel, programs, and prerogatives — the less the chance anything will be done about them. Organizations should be designed, therefore, to make errors visible and correctable, that is, noticeable and reversible, which in turn is to say, cheap and affordable.

Program budgeting increases rather than decreases the cost of correcting error. The great complaint about bureaucracies is their rigidity. As things stand, the object of organizational affection is the bureau as serviced by the usual line-item categories from which people, money, and facilities flow. Viewed from the standpoint of bureau interests, programs to some extent are negotiable; some can be increased and others decreased while keeping the agency on an even keel or, if necessary, adjusting it to less happy times, without calling into question its very existence. Line-item budgeting, precisely because its categories (personnel, maintenance, supplies) do not relate directly to programs, are easier to change. Budgeting by programs, precisely because money flows to objec-

---

[32] Aaron Wildavsky, "Policy Analysis is What Information Systems Are Not," IV *New York Affairs* (Spring 1977) No. 2, p. 16.

tives, makes it difficult to abandon objectives without abandoning the organization that gets its money for them.

Notice I do not say it is inadvisable for analysis to take place at the level of programs and policies. On the contrary, there is every reason to encourage analytical thrusts from different directions and dimensions of policy, provided only that no single one is encased in concrete and be considered the final way. It is better that non-programmatic categories be used in formal budget categories, thus permitting a diversity of analytical perspectives, than that a temporary analytic insight be made the permanent perspective through which money is funneled.[33]

If error is to be altered, it must be relatively easy to correct. But PPB makes it hard. Its "systems" are characterized by their proponents as highly differentiated and tightly linked. The rationale for program budgeting lies in its connectedness — like programs are grouped together. Program structures are meant to replace the confused concatenations of line-items with clearly differentiated, non-overlapping boundaries; only one set of programs to a structure. This means that a change in one element or structure must result in change reverberating throughout every element in the same system. Instead of alerting only neighboring units or central control units, which would make change feasible, all are, so to speak, wired together, so the choice is effectively all or none.

Imagine one of us deciding whether to buy a tie or a kerchief. A simple task, one might think. Suppose, however, that organizational rules require us to keep our entire wardrobe as a unit. If everything must be rearranged when one item is altered, the probability we will do anything is low. The more tightly linked the elements, and the more highly differentiated they are, the greater the probability of error (because the tolerances are so small), and the less the like-

[33] *Ibid.*, p. 17.

lihood error will be reported (because with change, every element has to be recalibrated with every other one that was previously adjusted). Why idealize an information system like PPB that causes many more mistakes than it can correct? Being caught between revolution (change in everything) and resignation (change in nothing) has little to recommend it.

At one time I knew only that program budgeting data was not used; now I believe I know why this superabundance of data was never converted into information: PPB did not provide information relevant to the user at any level. At the bureau level the questions addressed had to do with whether its existing programs should be abolished or replaced by others. This, to be sure, was a question bureaus not only did not want to answer positively but could not even respond to negatively because it was beyond bureau jurisdiction. To take programs from one bureau and place them in another is reserved for higher authorities — the Department, the President, and Congress. Since the advice was for "them" and not for "us," it was either doctored to appear impressive or ignored because nothing could be done about it. Secretaries needed information on how they might better allocate resources within their departments. Instead they got rationalizations of bureau enterprises.

In the past it has been said that PPB might have succeeded if it had produced better analyses. This, as structuralists say, is no accident.[34] By separating policy analysis from organizational power, PPB is simultaneously rendered unintelligent and impotent.

ZERO BASE BUDGETING

Zero Base Budgeting (ZBB) is the newest in a series of attempted budget reforms reacting against the seemingly anti-

[34] *Ibid.*, pp. 17–18.

analytic and fragmented approach of line-item budgeting. President Carter foresees that "by working together under a ZBB system, we can reduce costs and make the federal government more efficient and effective." [35] Carter includes among the benefits of ZBB avoiding overlap between programs, improving information, focusing on analysis and decision making, forcing managers to evaluate the cost effectiveness of their programs, allowing quick budget adjustments during the year, "and most important to me, broadly expanding management participation and training in the planning, budgeting and decision making process." [36]

Zero Base Budgeting was developed by Peter Pyhrr for use at Texas Instruments, an electronic firm, in 1969. In 1972 Governor Carter introduced the system into the state government in Georgia. Other states (as well as businesses) have subsequently experimented with ZBB. President Carter directed the heads of executive departments and agencies to implement ZBB in the fiscal year 1979 federal budget.

ZBB's major declared purpose is to examine simultaneously all programs from the ground up, to ferret out programs continuing through inertia which do not warrant being continued at all or should be continued only at a reduced level of expenditure. Its goal, Pyhrr maintains, is to:

> . . . force us to identify and analyze what we [are] going to do in total, set goals and objectives, make the necessary operating decisions, and evaluate changing responsibilities and work loads . . . as an integral part of the (budget) process.[37]

For the first time, detailed information about programs is to be available for department review in one place at one

[35] Joel Haveman, "Zero-Base Budgeting," IX *National Journal* (April 2, 1977) No. 14, p. 514.

[36] Jimmy Carter, "Jimmy Carter Tells Why He Will Use Zero-Base Budgeting," *Nation's Business* (January 1977) p. 26.

[37] Peter A. Pyhrr, *Zero-Base Budgeting: A Practical Management Tool for Evaluating Expenses* (New York, 1973), p. 10.

time. The process is to be made more effective by assuring that budgets are developed and reviewed in their entirety, not merely in terms of the justification for incremental increases. This focus requires a priority ranking of all programs and activities in increasing levels of performance and funding, starting from the ground up.

Program managers at each level are assumed to be in the best position to make decisions on priorities and trade-offs in the programs for which they are responsible. Managers are additionally responsible for defining the specific objectives and identifying the outputs of their programs. In a document called the "decision package," the basic tool of ZBB, this description of their program is combined with an analysis of the effects of conducting the program at alternative levels of funding. Typically these funding levels include a minimum below which the operation could not function, the current level above the minimum level, and a middle level between these two. Lower-echelon managers are placed in a position of great responsibility in this system, since they compute the marginal utility of changes in funding and assess the difference these changes would make. With respect to a discrete activity referred to as the "decision unit," a manager presents the activity's purpose, the consequences of not performing the activity, measures of its performance at various levels of operation, alternative courses of action at each level, and the costs and benefits of running the program at the current level.

The second stage of ZBB involves ranking the decision packages. Managers send the packages up the bureaucratic ladder to their direct superiors, who rank them according to the priority of that program within the agency. Subsequently, agency priorities are ranked within the overall department. Many different rankings are compiled as the decision packages gradually move toward the department head's desk. Superiors receive groups of ranked decision packages from those directly below them which they in turn rank, until there is one comprehensive ranking of all programs in the department. A cutoff line is drawn to delineate the expected amount of revenues for the year, or the level of "affordability." Packages that fall above the line receive funding while those below the line do not. This flexible cutoff line is reputed to facilitate accommodating late-year budget windfalls or deficits; the response to a change in expected revenues is merely to move the line and accept or reject several more decision packages.

After isolating the objectives of the program, managers are responsible for explaining the consequences of not funding certain activities. To determine these consequences, managers must thoroughly understand the effects their programs have upon other programs with which they do not normally deal in day-to-day operations. How are they to provide this information? No one knows. And, after figuring out the consequences of doing without particular activities, managers must also compute the efficiency of carrying them on at various levels below the current apportionment. They are asked, basically, "How well would this program function at another level?"; but this is a question to which there are an infinite number of possible answers. Managers must therefore decide which funding levels they wish to analyze.

In general, managers have been unable to assess programs' efficiency at that vague "other" level, and states have provided their managers with set increments at which they are to evaluate their programs. Consequently, managers are actually computing from a base above zero. Instead of trying to discover the minimum level at which to carry on a certain activity (a task posing insurmountable problems), they evaluate the program at an arbitrary low proportion of the current level, say 80 per cent. However, this method removes the assumption that there is any possibility of entirely canceling funding and obviates the necessity of determining the consequences of not performing the activity. Managers are now asked, "How would your program function at this specific level of funding?" Nevertheless, managers still require specific data relating announced objectives to program performance at alternative levels of funding.

Department heads face different considerations; they are in charge of the ranking procedure. If the objective of one package in the Department of Agriculture is to increase crop yields and the objective of another to encourage recreation, where is the basis for comparison? A common denominator between packages is necessary. Since one of the benefits of ZBB is to permit comparison between programs in order to weed out overlap and waste, it is especially important to be able to compare similar programs. Comparison is facilitated if common programs fall within the auspices of a single agency. Usually, however, objectives are distributed among several departments. Consequently, ZBB is often associated with governmental reorganization, or, in effect, consolidation. In Georgia Jimmy Carter simultaneously implemented ZBB and reorganized the state's agencies. As President he has announced similar intentions for the federal government.

Since resources affect objectives, is it possible that a department, when faced with a budget cut, would wish to revamp its programs entirely? No, for the only alternative the department has, after the decision packages have been sent up from below, is some ratio of its present operations, since departments faced with a cut in funds can allocate only through previous ranking of project packages. Consequently, even department heads, with their broader view, cannot alter the department's basic orientation. ZBB considers objectives to be immutable or dispensable but not variable. Objectives may be achieved or abandoned but, apparently, not modified, because the only variable is the level of resources — hence the name "Zero Base Budgeting." Department heads are expected to take a comprehensive view of their decision packages, ranked and competing with one another for funding, but they can only act in a marginal fashion.

Yet all programs may not receive funding and the department heads have to come up with some mixture of packages that will make the final ranking deserving of funding. Which programs will have to be administered at lower funding levels? This is the ultimate question facing department heads.

We see that the different management levels involved in ZBB are dependent upon vast amounts of data — for each level of funding from zero to zed, so to speak. But the different management levels also differ vastly in the type of information they use. Lower-level managers use data relating inputs to outputs of their own activities, while upper-level managers need information that cuts across their agencies by actually comparing programs sharing common objectives.

ZBB introduces the view that basic budget formulations should arise from low-level managers, whereas PPB generates initial requests from the very top, the department heads. Budget requests are sent upward in ZBB; in PPB the department heads send their formulation down so that agencies may conform to the overall program structures. Further, ZBB and PPB diverge in the manner in which programs are linked and evaluated. PPB aligns programs toward common objectives. ZBB does away with these program structures. Decision units must justify their own existence vertically, according to their own objectives, rather than horizontally by conforming to similar programs.

PRACTICE

The first semblance of ZBB was implemented in 1964 in the Department of Agriculture, where it was entirely unsuccessful. The Department used a comprehensive method that was supposed to justify all expenditures from zero but was unsupported by ZBB's analytic techniques. Members of the Department were interviewed to discover whether any decisions could in any way be attributed to the Zero Base Budget. Did the Agency or Department officials recommend different programs or different amounts for programs, or distribute funds among programs differently as a result of the Zero Base approach? Overwhelmingly, the answer was no.

Most statements were variants of "I don't think anyone would honestly tell you that they changed their budgets." Agency personnel continually reiterated their doubts that the Department was adequately staffed to digest such vast amounts of material. Asked for evidence of change, respondents usually replied that "the figures we put in have never been referred to as far as I know," or "it [Zero Base Budget data] was sent across the street [where the Department offices are located] and we never heard of it again." A couple of times an exceedingly small change was reported, though not without qualification. Although there was "no difference in the overall amounts requested or received from the department, analysis did lead to the transfer of $20,000 among programs. This analysis was, however, planned before the zero-base budget." An excess of expenditures for files in one agency was also mentioned. In one instance a Department official did say, "I am confident that decisions were made which would not have been made or even considered in the absence of a zero-base budget." But even he could give only one specific change — a reduction of $100,000 in an obsolete research program. The paucity of changes attributed to the Zero Base Budget is evident in the fact that this example was brought up repeatedly; many officials said they had heard of a change somewhere, but it always turned out to be this same one. Another Department official insisted that the Zero Base Budget procedure was not useful in "ferreting out all the sorts of dark and sinister things which shouldn't be done, which would turn up quickly anyhow." The general conclusion can be stated in the words of a person in a position to get a general view: "Some butterflies were caught, no elephants stopped." [38]

An interesting phenomenon was that Department officials thought ZBB was unnecessary for them but good for the bureaus, and people in the bureaus thought the reverse. Each level viewed ZBB as a message to the other: We're all right Jack, but you shape up! Information systems are not only methods of getting others to do what you want, they are communications saying "Don't bother. Modern science (PPB, ZBB, MBO, etc.) shows we've been inspected and proven pure."

The majority of the eleven states currently using ZBB in their budgeting procedures use some form of priority ranking for the programs, and most of the states make use of decision packages. In attempting to bridge the gap between upper- and lower-level managers, states have sacrificed the zero-based focus of ZBB. No states justify all programs from zero, and many have abandoned alternative funding levels. Instead, they submit budget proposals indicating the costs of the programs at set levels of operations. Arkansas, Illinois, and Texas selected 90 per cent of the base level of the program for the minimum level of operation. Above that comes the current budgeted amount, and then actually a 10 per cent increase over the base figure. Rather than being a Zero Base Budget, justifying from zero, these states have introduced a 90 per cent base budget.

Missouri, Idaho, and California are even further off zero base. Missouri and Idaho rank only proposed increases above the base. Similarly, California "focuses on proposed changes in the budget." [39] Ranking decision packages above the base

[38] Allen Schick and Robert Keith, "Zero-Base Budgeting in the States," Library of Congress Congressional Research Service (August 31, 1976) p. 28.
[39] *Ibid.*, p. 38.

seems indistinguishable from incremental budgeting. Tennessee has pursued another variant: each program must assess its performance at four preordained levels, which are approached in a unique manner. The levels are (1) continuation at current level of funding, (2) continuation at current level of service, (3) improvement to meet new legislative requirements and to replace lost federal aid, and (4) improvements based on departmental estimates of need.[40]

Few states have a long acquaintance with ZBB. For many, ZBB has only been used for one or two years. In these cases it is difficult to draw any definite conclusions. New Jersey encountered a number of difficulties (such as staff resistance and low-quality submissions), although it feels these problems can be overcome as its personnel become more accustomed to ZBB concepts and processes. Idaho reports that 75 per cent of its first-year reports were unsatisfactory.[41] This high failure rate was due largely to budgeters' inadequate understanding of the procedures. Other states complain, as well, of agency and staff resistance to the system, lack of understanding of basic concepts, and deficient quality of data. After two years in Georgia — one year when revenues markedly decreased and one when expenditures sharply increased — ZBB was abandoned and new submissions were requested.[42]

Even where states can definitely identify budgetary successes, it is not absolutely possible to attribute them to ZBB. Jimmy Carter claimed a 50 per cent savings in state administrative costs in Georgia resulting from the implemen-

[40] *Ibid.*, p. 14.

[41] *Ibid.*

[42] George S. Nimier and Roger H. Hermanson, "A Look at Zero-Base Budgeting — The Georgia Experience," *Atlanta Economic Review* (July-August 1976) pp. 5–12. In 1974 there was an increase in available funds and in 1975 a decrease.

tation of ZBB.[43] The only examples he has provided to indicate the success of ZBB have been the highway department saving 15 per cent of its budgetary costs by ceasing to mow the divider strips along highways and the mobilization of highway patrolmen who were replaced at desk jobs with handicapped people.[44] Georgia also underwent major government reorganization simultaneously with ZBB's implementation, so it is difficult to differentiate the successes attributable to agency redistribution or to ZBB.

Although there is unsubstantiated evidence for ZBB's ability to restrict spending, there is absolutely no support at all for ZBB's claims to evaluate programs and reallocate funding to those viewed as more efficient and desirable. In Texas, Roy Lee Hogan concludes, "Quite frankly, it is almost impossible to point to a decision and say that it was a better decision because of the utilization of the zero-base budgeting concept." [45] In Georgia, 100 per cent of the subjects surveyed indicated there had been no apparent shifting of financial resources between functions as a direct result of the new budgeting system.

> One of the major selling points of zero-base budgeting is its presumed ability to shift resources to those areas where they are most needed. It is evident that most survey participants believe that a shifting of resources has not occurred, much less a more efficient shifting of financial resources.[46]

Furthermore, in Georgia, during fiscal years 1973, 1974, and 1975, "not a single instance was found where a function

[43] Carter, *op. cit.*, p. 5.

[44] "Interview with Jimmy Carter," *Washington Post*, Vol. LXV (December 27, 1976), Sec. E., p. 22.

[45] Roy L. Hogan, "Zero-Base Budgeting: A Rationalistic Attempt to Improve the Texas Budget System" (Masters Thesis, University of Texas at Austin, 1975), p. 92.

[46] George S. Minmier, *An Evaluation of the ZBB System, Governmental Institutions*, Monograph 68, Georgia State University, p. 131.

received less funds than it had in the previous fiscal year budget." [47] Zero Base Budgeting, where are you?

Not only do states focus on only part of ZBB, the part which is used does not seem to produce identifiable results. Why is this? In Texas, again, Hogan indicates shortcomings that may lead ZBB's failure to fulfill its promises.

> Structuring information by program area often requires the accumulation of such data from several different agencies. To the author's knowledge, such questions were infrequently asked if they were ever asked at all. With regard to the ranking of programs and program levels against one another as they relate to the objectives and needs of the agency, this information was rarely displayed. . . .[48]

> Time constraints and other factors that were experienced during initial program structure design hindered the achievement of this objective on a statewide basis. For example, one-half of the examiners interviewed expressed the opinion that existing organizational structures were a major deterrent in the development of agency program structures. . . .[49]

> All nine examiners interviewed expressed the general opinion that the section dealing with the analysis of alternative methods of accomplishing program or activity did not prove useful to them in determining funding recommendations. . . . Such analysis was usually construed in such a manner so as to justify the present method of operation.[50]

ZBB has not been gloriously received in its few trials within the federal government. The Consumer Product Safety Commission (CPSC) and National Aeronautics and Space Administration (NASA) applied ZBB to their budgets in 1977 in response to the House Appropriations Committee's interest in ZBB's relevance to the federal government.

[47] *Ibid.*
[48] Hogan, *op. cit.*, p. 173.
[49] *Ibid.*, p. 105.
[50] *Ibid.*, p. 116.

Thaddeus Garrett, Jr., the Commissioner of CPSC, concluded about the experiment:

> ZBB is not a panacea. It may be impossible to institute a government-wide zero-based review procedure that will work. It could be so time consuming that it reduces rather than enhances the quality of the budget review.[51]

The CPSC's administration of ZBB resembled the states' attempts to design ZBB for their needs. The decision packages were not zero based but rather assessed programs at three different levels of operation: (1) a minimum level of 85 per cent to 90 per cent of the present appropriation, (2) the current level projected into 1978, (3) an improved level incorporating a 10 per cent to 15 per cent increase. However, Chairman Byington confessed "what we have submitted here was really the submission we gave in September, where we did some zero-base analysis on a gross basis, which became our current level document. Then we did the incrementals up and down." [52] Ultimately, the Commission's minimum levels equaled the current levels of funding, despite stern admonishments that minimum levels should be below current levels. CPSC was also unable to rank the final twenty-one decision packages, because it found that too many of the programs were actually interconnected, so it would be impossible to fund one at the expense of the others. Each program was necessary for the proper operation of the others. In a statement resembling pre-ZBB budgeting, the Commissioners declared they would not know what to do if they were faced with a cut of x per cent. NASA was also unable to rank its programs because of the difficulty of finding a basis for comparison between them. Apparently,

[51] Subcommittee of the Committee on Appropriations, U.S. House of Representatives, *Department of Housing and Urban Development — Independent Agencies Appropriations, Part 4: Consumer Product Safety Commission*, 95th Congress, 1st Session, 1977, p. 4.

[52] *Ibid.*

programs are either integral to one another or disconnected.

Like PPB, ZBB's reasons for failure appear to be built into its design. ZBB does not provide better information; better information is actually a prerequisite for ZBB's functioning. ZBB is dependent on the unqualified support of administrators. Such support has not been forthcoming; the managers complain of not thoroughly understanding the process and of inadequate help from their superiors. The ensuing problems are agency and staff resistance to ZBB, lack of understanding of basic concepts, no improvement in the quality of information, and no effect on the department's allocations.

INFORMATION

The difference in information requirements at the different levels of management in ZBB introduces the possibility of contradictions implicit within the system. These contradictions appear at two levels: (1) the data developed within the system is meant to be used for two different purposes; and (2) the department heads attempt to deal holistically with data which is, by its very nature, marginal. Lower-level managers possess an incremental view of their programs; their task is to analyze the effects of marginal changes in funding in order to find an optimum level, presumably below the current level. However, agency heads want an overview of the consolidated packages in order to compare them for overlap and waste. Lower-level managers compute whether Program X is efficient. Their superiors wish to determine whether Program X is better than Program Y. Each level needs different information which is not provided by a single source of data.

For lower-level managers knowledge of the past is necessary in order to assess the probable effects of alternative funding levels. Saying that output would drop 30 per cent with a 10 per cent funding cut is usually based on a historical relationship between funding and outputs. But history is irrelevant for department heads who are interested in the effectiveness of the alternative funding levels right now. At the bureau level, administrators are interested in which activities should be slowed down or speeded up, while at the department level, administrators are concerned with which activities should be replaced.

MOTIVATION

Since the data in ZBB is always produced by the unit below for use by the unit above, an important concern in evaluating the quality of information is the motivation behind the people who furnish it. When you ask, "Charlie, how much is this going to cost? You're the expert in the field," you are dependent upon Charlie's motives in answering the question accurately and truthfully. This leads to problems of discount and motivation. The discount problem is, "Does Charlie know — how expert is his expertise?" If he hasn't done this sort of thing before, anyone's guess may be as good as his. The motivation problem is that agencies soon learn that it is in their best interest at various times to estimate higher or lower than actual cost. If they want the program, they may say it costs less; when they ask for money, they may say it costs more. Since employees are often rewarded for their ability to meet or exceed targets, they have a further interest in biasing their estimates on the high side. How are we to know whether these people really know and whether indeed they are motivated to tell the truth as they know it?

John LaFaver concluded, after studying New Mexico's experiences with ZBB in 1973, that it is "not reasonable to expect an agency to routinely furnish information that might result in a lower appropriation — no matter what the justification might be." [53] Has experience born out his findings on negative motivations?

The critical defect of ZBB and PPB is not only inability to make the required calculations — who can combine all possible funding levels? — but the irrationality of doing so — who would want to? It is instructive to compare PPB, ZBB, and traditional budgeting as modes of rational choice.

ORGANIZATION

The tension between analysis, which seeks out error and promotes change, and organization, which seeks stability and promotes its existing activities, is inevitable. The bulk of analysis is rejected by the organizations for which it is intended.[54] Better information alone will not matter without incentives for organizations to use it. Struggling with organizational incentives, therefore, is a perennial (perhaps paramount) problem of policy analysis.

Ignoring the organizational levels, and the proper approaches to each, is the original sin of new budgetary systems. PPB fails because no organizational level gets information (1) that it is willing to use and (2) that is relevant to the resources at its disposal. MBO either obfuscates objectives, so higher levels will be unable to understand them, or overwhelms the upper echelons with objectives, so they cannot figure out which ones apply. After participating in a lengthy MBO exercise, as a result of which it was de-

---

[53] John D. LaFaver, "Zero-Base Budgeting in New Mexico," XLVII *State Government* (Spring 1974) p. 110.

[54] David H. Stimson and Ruth H. Stimson, *Operations Research in Hospitals, Diagnosis and Prognosis* (Chicago, Hospital Research and Education Trust, 1972), which evaluates several hundred analyses of hospital administration and suggests that a good 90 per cent were ignored or opposed by the sponsoring agency.

cided that the status quo was splendid, a business participant reported: "I suggest this is a conspiracy by the Board to prove the fruitlessness of deviation from established group practices." [55] MBO is better seen as a misguided effort to violate an analytic theorem — treating objectives apart from resources — than as a mode of analysis.

Clinging to last year's agreements is enormously economical of critical resources (particularly time and good interpersonal relations), which would be seriously depleted if all or most past agreements were reexamined yearly. If there is a mechanism for holding on to adequate solutions and sequentially proceeding to solve remaining problems — which focus on increases and decreases to the base — knowledge is more likely to result. Similarly, an agreement-producing process is more likely to work if past agreements can be retained while the system works on unresolved issues.

Only poor countries come close to Zero Base Budgeting, not because they wish to do so but because their uncertain financial position continually causes them to go back on old commitments. Because past disputes are part of present conflicts, their budgets lack predicictive value; little stated in them is likely to occur.[56] Ahistorical practices, which are a dire consequence of extreme instability and from which all who experience them devoutly desire to escape, should not be considered normative.

Analysis aims to bring information to bear on current decisions which do have future consequences. Taking these consequences into account — acting now to do better later — is what all analysis is about. Because prediction comes at a premium, however, analysis uses history — what has been tried in the past, how past patterns have led to present

[55] John Brandies, "Managing and Motivating by Objectives in Practice," IV *Management by Objectives* (1974) No. 1, p. 17.
[56] See Aaron Wildavsky, *The Politics of the Budgetary Process*, 2nd edition (Boston, 1974).

problems, where past obligations limit future commitments — as a source of both limits and possibilities.

A promise underlies public policy: if the actions we recommend are undertaken, good (intended) consequences rather than bad (unintended) ones will come about. Since causal connections are strict in designing public policy — if this is done by government, then that result will follow — failure to match promise with performance is likely to be high, as is reluctance to acknowledge error. Objectives are kept vague and multiple to expand the range within which observed behavior fits. Goal substitution takes place as the consequences actually caused by programs replace the objectives originally sought. Goal displacement becomes the norm as an organization seeks to make the variables it can control, its own efforts and processes, the objectives against which it is measured. This is how organizations come to justify error instead of creating knowledge. On all sides theoretical requirements are abandoned, by considering inputs or outputs alone, until there seems to be no error (and hence no truth), and it becomes impossible to learn from experience.

If our society lacks production functions — which is to say, policy relevant theory that purports to connect resources like teaching to objectives like reading — in most areas we wish to affect, how much more profound must be ignorance of the consequences of alternative programs across areas of policy and over time.[57] PPB and ZBB make demands on theory that cannot be met. They require knowledge of relationships between governmental action and social consequences over the broadest range of issues. Who is most misled by this — the proponents who sell these budget-

[57] See Aaron Wildavsky, "Policy as Its Own Cause," in *Speaking Truth to Power: The Art and Craft of Policy Analysis* (Boston, forthcoming).

ary systems or the politicians who buy them — is debatable. But if these systems represent the best in rational analysis, as many surely believe, and if this presumed rationality is doomed to failure, as it certainly is, then the sure loser is policy analysis, with its idea of applying intelligence to policy problems.

LEARNING

There is more than morbid curiosity in the study of Zero Base and program budgeting. Though one has died and the other should, their experiences teach about better budgeting by negative example. Whatever they do, the rule is, should not be done.

ZBB and PPB embody extreme (though different) forms of comprehensive calculation. (True, they can't practice what they preach; the effort either does them in or they lose any distinctive quality.) ZBB insists on making all possible vertical calculations, from zero to base, as it were, until the most efficient ways of achieving objectives are chosen. PPB covers at least all major horizontal relationships between related programs so the most cost-effective combination for achieving objectives is chosen. Ergo, the lesson is that budgeting should not be comprehensive. Since knowledge, time, and manpower are usually in short supply, most policy analysis is concerned with reducing rather than increasing the cost of calculations. Budgeting should not hinder that effort.

PPB is ahistorical in that it is interested in comparing programs in the here and now. The past is an anachronism, a leftover remnant of an outmoded era, and there is no evolution. ZBB doesn't so much ignore as set out to abolish history; the clock is always set at zero. Budgets apparently spring newborn like Minerva from the brow of Jove. The lesson is clear: budgets should be explicitly historical, comparing what is about to be done with what has recently happened. This evolutionary approach brings insight because policies have internal logics of their own — future policies are usually reactions to the defeats of past policies — that can best be appreciated from the inside.[58] In deciding whether policies are desirable, moreover, it is usually not possible to say that a problem has been solved since objectives are multiple and contradictory where they are not vague and resources including knowledge are usually insufficient. It is wiser, instead, to ask how policies of today (including the evils not yet mitigated) compare with those they superseded yesterday. A historical approach, therefore, not only conserves calculations by focusing on increments of change but also suggests the right kinds of calculations to make for purposes of evaluating public policy.

ZBB and PPB share an emphasis on the virtue of objectives. Program budgeting is about relating larger to smaller objectives among different programs, and Zero Base Budgeting promises to do the same within a single program. The policy implications of these methods of budgeting, which distinguish them from existing approaches, derive from their overwhelming concern with having and ranking objectives. Thinking about objectives is one thing, however, and making budget categories out of them is quite another. Of course, if one wants the objectives of today to be the objectives of tomorrow, if one wants no change in objectives, then building the budget around objectives is a brilliant idea. But if one wants flexibility in objectives (sometimes known as learning from experience), it must be possible to change them without simultaneously destroying the organization by withdrawing financial support.

The traditional line-item budget is, of course, uninterested in objectives. Budgeters may have objectives, but the budget itself is organized around activities or functions — personnel, maintenance, etc. One can change objectives, then,

[58] *Ibid.*

without challenging organizational survival. Traditional budgeting does not demand analysis of policy, but neither does it inhibit it.

Every criticism of traditional budgeting is undoubtedly correct. It is incremental rather than comprehensive; it does fragment decisions; it is heavily historical and looks backward more than forward; it is indifferent to objectives; and it is concerned about the care and feeding and control of organizations, their personnel, space, maintenance, and all that. Why, then, has traditional budgeting lasted so long? Because it has the virtue of its defects.

Traditional budgeting makes calculations easy precisely because it is not comprehensive. History provides a strong base on which to rest a case. The present is made part of the past, which may be known, instead of the future, which cannot be comprehended. Choices that might cause conflict are fragmented so that not all difficulties need be faced at one time. Because it is neutral in regard to policy, traditional budgeting is compatible with a variety of policies, all of which can be converted into line items. Traditional budgeting lasts, then, because it is simpler, easier, less stressful, and more flexible than modern alternatives like ZBB and PPB.

Needless to say, traditional budgeting also has the defects of its virtues. Though budgets look back, they may not look back far enough to understand how (or why) they got where they are. Comparing this year with last year may not mean much if the past was a mistake and the future likely to be a bigger one. Quick calculation may be worse than none if it is grossly in error. Policy neutrality may degenerate into disinterest in programs. So why has traditional budgeting lasted? So far no one has come up with another budgetary procedure that has the virtues of traditional budgeting but lacks its defects.

CONGRESS
7

THE DAY AFTER CONGRESS adopted spending and revenue limits for fiscal 1976, the *New York Times* predicted in a front-page article that Congressional budget reform "could drastically alter the way Congress transacts its business and rearrange its power structure as well." Has Congress established super Budget Committees that will decide national priorities and enforce their will upon the rest of the legislature, as the Cabinet does in Britain? Or is the new Congressional Budget Act a facade behind which business will go on as usual? Congress could use its new process merely to ratify what its committees have already done; or it actually could fulfill the promise of budget reform by relating individual expenditures to total spending and total spending to revenues.

REASONS FOR REFORM

Before we take a look at what is happening, it would be wise to consider why Congress wanted to reform its budget process. Legislators were unhappy with the collective consequences of their individual choices. They liked voting for spending but not for taxes. They got their way, in a manner of speaking, by riding roughshod over the appropriations committees, by tunneling beneath them through direct drafts on the Treasury ("backdoor spending"), or by getting around them entirely through tax expenditures (spending that allows certain people to reduce their taxes before these taxes get to the Treasury), or through loans and loan guarantees, which, except for defaults, do not count in the budget as direct spending. Individual members of Congress won but Congress as a whole lost; individual and collective rationality were at odds.

Presidential impoundments of funds, often with sub-rosa Congressional support, became common. Through them, members could vote for spending while the President took the blame for cutting. President Nixon, mounting a direct challenge to Congressional control of the purse, bent this practice so far that it broke in his hands.

As Congress grew more divided over the budget, the authorization–appropriations gap rose into the tens of billions. The legislative committees, whose members select themselves for their personal and constituency interests in particular areas of public policy, consistently authorized more spending than the appropriations subcommittees would support. The trend away from multi-year and toward annual authorizations was partly an effort by the legislative committees to lobby the appropriations committees for increased spending. The more Congressmen fought, the longer it took; the budget process became notorious for delay, delay which made it difficult for administrative agencies to carry out their responsibilities in an effective manner and difficult for state and local governments to fit federal grants into their plans in a timely fashion.

Then came Vietnam, which suggested Congress was negligent in its responsibilities for defense appropriations; Presidential impoundments, which suggested Congress was losing power domestically; and Watergate, which was all too suggestive of excess by the Chief Executive. Congressional power of the purse had to be strengthened. Taxing and spending are the center of Congressional power; if these powers decline, Congress declines as well. All these factors explain why Congress was willing to contemplate reform; they do not necessarily predict that the desires of individual legislators will give way to the collective interests of Congress in maintaining its institutional power.

CONGRESSIONAL REALITIES

Past proposals to reform Congressional budget review failed because they did not sufficiently take into account the realities of decision making in Congress. Whatever is recommended must be workable in a large, heterogeneous, and independent body that operates in an environment of fragmented and dispersed power. There is no sense in treating Congress as if it were, or could be led by, a small cohesive group easily able to agree or to impose its will on others. To avoid these traps, it may be helpful to state the characteristics of the Congressional environment in the form of criteria for evaluating alternative budgetary procedures.

Many committees, not one. A committee that makes a budget that is not then altered by other committees — a committee without rivals, a steering committee of the legislature — can be called a cabinet on the British model. In contrast, Congress is a pluralistic institution; it has many centers of power, depending on the time and the issue. To be effective Congress must exploit rather than fight its pluralistic nature, and a good way to exploit pluralism is to embrace specialization.

More specialization, not less. Without specialization there is no knowledge, and without knowledge there is no power. When executives wish to emasculate legislatures, they break up existing committees and prevent formation of new ones that are specialized enough to look into specific areas of policy and small enough to act with dispatch. Unless the legislature can keep up with the Executive, it will become an auditor after the fact rather than a budgeter in advance.

Simplification, not mystification. Rationality is supposed to mean effective action, not pretentious inaction. The rational person is not one who pretends to compare everything to everything else but rather one who manipulates the few variables under his control to good effect. If attention is focused on all or most possible relationships, it will be impossible to single out those most in need of change. However badly the Chief Executive confuses himself, he can always make a last-minute decision with a show of justification. If Congressmen confuse themselves, they will not be able to act at all. They need mechanisms to reduce the number of decisions to be considered at any one time; they need ways of structuring a series of votes so that these are both meaningful and manageable. Before a legislature can act wisely, it must be able to act. If Congressmen do not employ aids to calculation, they will be unable either to arrive at their own preferences or to settle their differences with others. Making calculations manageable lies at the heart of effective legislative decision making.

THE NEW RULES OF THE GAME

The Congressional Budget and Impoundment Control Act of 1974 (Public Law 93-344) states as its purpose that:

> The Congress declares that it is essential: to assure effective Congressional control over the budgetary process; to provide for the Congressional determination each year of the appropriate level of federal revenues and expenditures; to provide a system of impoundment control; to establish national budget priorities; and to provide for the furnishing of information by the Executive branch in a manner that will assist the Congress in discharging its duties.[1]

To accomplish these purposes the Act creates three new institutions: the House Budget Committee, the Senate Budget Committee, and the Congressional Budget Office. The Act also provides a new set of budgeting procedures, a timetable for budgetary actions, and a change in the fiscal year. Finally, it includes procedures to control Presidential impoundment.

The statutory authority for both the Senate and the House Budget Committees is the same. They are required to report at least two concurrent resolutions on the budget each year, to analyze the impact of existing and proposed programs on budgetary outlays, and to oversee the operations of the Congressional Budget Office.

The Senate Budget Committee has sixteen members, the House Budget Committee, twenty-five. The Senate Budget Committee is selected in the same way as other Senate committees (by the Democratic and Republican Conferences). The House Budget Committee is selected differently from other House committees. Of the twenty-five, five each must be drawn from the House Ways and Means Committee and the House Appropriations Committee and one from each party's leadership. The tenure of the members of the Senate Budget Committee is unlimited. No member of the House Budget Committee may serve for more than four years in any ten-year period. Traditional seniority rules of the House

---

[1] Public Law 93-344, "Congressional Budget and Impoundment Control Act of 1974," Section 2.

are suspended for their Budget Committee. In the Senate the Budget Committee is exempted from the reform that no member can serve on more than two major committees.[2]

The House Republicans allow their ranking members on Ways and Means and on Appropriations to choose the Republicans from those committees for the Budget Committee positions. The Republican Caucus chooses the other Committee positions. All the Republican members serve the same tenure. The Democrats had similar rules, except for the provision of staggering the tenure of the members to allow for continuity. The nominations of all Democratic members (except the representative of the leadership, who is picked by the leadership), including those who will represent Ways and Means and Appropriations, are made by the Democratic Steering and Policy Committee. The nominees must be ratified by a vote of the entire Caucus. The rules on staggering the membership have been changed to reflect greater control over the Committee by the leadership and Caucus. New members and standing members must be nominated at each new Congress by the Steering and Policy Committee. In December 1982, the Democratic Caucus changed the ratio of Democrats to Republicans to 20 to 10 and instructed the Steering and Policy Committee to appoint a member of the Rules Committee to the Budget Committee.[3] The Chairmanship of the Budget Committee is a self-nominating position open to any member of the Committee. The nominees must stand for a full Caucus vote for election to the Chair. This vote also must be carried out each new Congress.[4]

The third new institution is the Congressional Budget

---

[2] *Ibid.*, Section 101; Judy Gardner, "Economic Affairs," XXXIV *Congressional Quarterly Weekly* (November 27, 1976) p. 3233.

[3] *Federal Budget Report* (December 13, 1982) p. 2.

[4] XXXIV *Congressional Quarterly* (November 27, 1976) pp. 3229–3260; (December 18, 1976) pp. 3317–3348; XXXV *Congressional Quarterly* (January 1, 1977) pp. 1–32; (January 15, 1977) pp. 61–100.

Office, an analytical unit that is to provide a check on information from the Executive Branch. The Director of the CBO is appointed for a four-year term by the Speaker of the House and the President Pro Tem of the Senate on recommendations of the two Budget Committees. The CBO has three basic responsibilities: (1) monitoring the economy and estimating its impact on the budget, (2) improving the flow and quality of budgetary information, and (3) analyzing the costs and effects of alternative budgetary choices.[5]

THE PROCESS OUTLINED

The Act changed the beginning of the fiscal year from July 1 to October 1. The budget process is supposed to begin on November 10 with the submission by OMB of the Current Services Budget to the Joint Economic Committee. The Current Services Budget is defined by the Congressional Budget and Implementation Control Act as that budget determined as if:

> all programs and activities were carried on during such ensuing fiscal year at the same level as the fiscal year in progress and without policy changes in such programs and activities.[6]

It is what this year's budget would be next year if there were no policy changes. The Joint Economic Committee must report on the economic impact of the CSB and return it to the two Budget Committees. This report is the only role the JEC has in the budgetary process. The CSB is supposed to be a base from which Congress and its committees are to

---

[5] John Ellwood and James Thurber, "The New Congressional Budget Process: The House and Ways of House-Senate Differences," in Lawrence C. Dodd and Bruce I. Oppenheim, editors, *Congress Reconsidered* (New York, 1976).

[6] Public Law 93-344, Section 605. See also Ellwood and Thurber, *op. cit.*, p. 183.

work in the preparation of the budget for the next fiscal year. In reality only the Senate Budget Committee uses it in this fashion. The House Budget Committee uses the President's Budget as its base.

After the President's Budget is delivered, the two Budget Committees receive reports from the other committees in their respective houses. These reports contain views on budget authority, outlays, and revenues within the Committees' own jurisdictions.

The next period concerns work prepared for the two Budget Committees by the Congressional Budget Office. In these reports, budget figures and programs presented in the President's Budget are analyzed to allow the Committees to judge the merits of what the Executive Branch has prepared. The CBO also prepares economic reviews of alternative fiscal policies, including the President's, in order to make the Committees aware of the implications of their choices.

Each Budget Committee has a different way of deciding what it will report out as a Budget Resolution, which is due April 1 though the significance of the day has been lost on most people. In order to avoid a jurisdictional fight between the Budget and appropriating committees, the Act stipulated that targets and ceilings were to be set at high levels of aggregation; that is, for sixteen functional categories rather than the approximately 1,250 appropriation accounts. Each chamber of the legislature, however, is free to reach its results with as much or as little detail as it wishes. The House works at a low level of aggregation in order to emphasize its virtue of specialization. The Senate, on the other hand, works at a high level of aggregation with few specifics on each program within the sixteen broad categories.

The House also differs from the Senate in that the Chairman of the House Budget Committee uses a "Chairman's mark." This is a suggested budget resolution used as a starting point for committee debate at each markup. It is

specific and consists of the President's Budget level for each
function and any changes recommended by the Chairman.
The fact that the House Budget Committee uses a low level
of aggregation and a Chairman's mark at that level means
that the Budget Resolutions reported out of HBC can be
broken down to the appropriations account level. The Senate Budget Committee, on the other hand, adopts a given
spending level for the whole function. Before I describe the
report of this First Budget Resolution, let's look at the
resolution in more detail.

The First Concurrent Budget Resolution is a document
passed by both Houses to act as an agenda in the budgeting
process during the next five months. It contains all that
follows and more: the appropriate level of total budget outlays and of total new budget authority; an estimate of
budget outlays and an appropriate level of new budget authority for each major functional category, and for contingencies; the amount of the surplus or the deficit appropriate in light of economic conditions; the recommended level
of federal revenues and the amount by which they should
be increased or decreased; and the amount by which the
statutory limit on the public debt should be increased or
decreased.[7]

After debate in each House, there is a conference in which
the differences between the two Houses are hammered out.
The Conference Report and a Joint Statement of Managers
allocating targets is then adopted by both Houses. This
must be completed by May 15, before any authorizing or
spending legislation is passed. To take account of what has
actually gone on during the period since the First Concurrent Resolution, a Second Concurrent Budget Resolution
is proposed. It either reaffirms or revises the first in light of
those realities. Congress adjusts the First to the intent of

[7] Public Law 93-344, Section 301.

the Second Concurrent Budget Resolution. It does this only if the Second Concurrent Budget Resolution contains directions to one or more committees to determine and recommend changes in specified items. We shall return to this reconciliation process later.

THE CONTROL OF IMPOUNDMENT

Congress hopes to limit Presidential power by setting up two categories of impoundment: rescissions and deferrals. A deferral is an impoundment of funds not necessary to achieve Congressional intent. A rescission is an impoundment of funds in order to change Congressional intent. The President can defer the spending of appropriated funds until the end of the fiscal year, unless either House by a majority vote passes an impoundment resolution. The President can alter Congressional intent by not spending appropriated funds only if he submits a rescission bill that passes by a majority in both Houses within forty-five days. The Comptroller General has the authority to bring the President to court if he feels that the President is deferring funds that should be rescinded. The Comptroller General can also bring the President to court if he feels the President is not spending funds after a rejection of a rescission bill.

WHOSE BUDGETARY BASE?

Intended by Congress to serve as a base to simplify calculations for next year's budget, the Current Services Budget (CSB) submitted each November 15 by the Office of Management and Budget has been a failure, though, as I will explain, that may change. The CSB is not taken seriously by those preparing it at OMB and is not used in Congress. Efforts are currently under way to change its format and timing but, though procedural changes may be necessary, the basic difficulty is deeper: inability to agree on exactly what should constitute the base for analyzing next year's budget.

The Current Services Budget has been useless to OMB because OMB is waiting for one that is more to its liking, the President's Budget, which is submitted only two months later, in January. Hence OMB considered a CSB outdated practically as soon as it was prepared. The OMB would prefer, moreover, that the first look Congress has at an executive branch plan for the coming year be the President's formal Budget: the more Congressmen look at the President's Budget, the more of it they will incorporate in their own budget.

The treatment accorded the Current Services Budget by Congress does nothing to convince OMB that this is an important document. Congress' decision to send the CSB to the Joint Economic Committee (JEC) is equivalent to giving last rites: it is sending a useless document to a powerless body. This is the only Budget-Act duty of the JEC; since the JEC's power to review the CSB contains no legislative directive, OMB would prefer to spend its time on a document more important to the authoritative committees of Congress.

Part of the difficulty comes from the language of the Budget Act itself. The provision stipulating a Current Services Budget is subject to interpretation as to the requirements placed on the President. The Executive must submit a Budget for the ensuing fiscal year as if "all programs and activities were carried on during such ensuing fiscal year at the same level as the fiscal year in progress and without policy changes in such programs and activities." [8] But while the estimates are to be accompanied by economic and programmatic assumptions underlying the numbers, the current-

[8] *Ibid.*, Sections 344, 605.

services idea means different things to different people. In the science and energy areas, where many programs have relatively short lives and demonstration projects are continually finishing and being replaced by other demonstrations, the current services concept is ineffectual and confusing. Are new demonstrations that are expected to be begun during the coming year included in the CSB? Are programs that are winding down this year included at last year's level?

In the social areas the difficulty is no less vexing. Since economic assumptions are prominent in projecting levels of social-welfare expenditures, differences in these assumptions between the executive and legislative branches are certain to cause variations in expected program cost. The OMB's Current Services Budget does not contain alternative prognostications based on various economic assumptions.

When a similar enterprise was undertaken in Britain, numerous disputes occurred over the meaning of "current" and "services." [9] Is "current" restricted to what is happening now or to the improvements some said were supposed to take place? Does "service" signify the lower level that has (regretfully) been forthcoming or the higher one promised?

Despite these difficulties, the CSB is emerging in a new form. Now it is called the continuing resolution. When Congress cannot agree on the budget for an agency or program, so that an ordinary appropriations law is passed, it may, despite the stalemate, want the activity to continue. Therefore, one branch of the legislature or both may pass a resolution for the activity or agency to continue at last year's level. This is the CSB in all but name. Like the CSB, the continuing resolution raises the same questions of whether the base is what was spent last year, with or without price increases or quality improvement or other considerations.

[9] See Hugh Heclo and Aaron Wildavsky, *The Private Government of Public Money* (London, 1981), 2d ed., *inter alia.*

WHOSE BUDGET?

Opinions as to the effects of the Title X Impoundment Provisions of the Budget Act are mixed: "where one stands depends on where one sits." Some OMB officials feel castrated by the changes: OMB's power over programs has been severely restricted by Congress. Even outside OMB few are totally satisfied with present arrangements. Impoundment control was a necessary response to the excesses of the Nixon Administration. But some now find the solution to be more onerous than the problem it purported to solve.

When President Nixon, claiming a constitutional right to do so, proposed wholesale rescission of Congressionally appropriated funds in early 1973, he was directly challenging the most important power of the legislature. After all, Nixon explained, someone had to control the Budget and obviously Congress wasn't up to the task. This challenge — questioning the fiscal responsibility of the Democratic-controlled Congress — had to be answered. Some impoundment of funds was a mutually beneficial process in the past; Congress could pass programs and please its constituents, the President could quell "runaway spending" and please his. Nixon brought the system out into the open so that it became impossible to continue the charade. But in making the process public, Congress has also made it inflexible.

Impoundments today are subject to a series of complicated provisions. When a President wants to change the flow of money into a given project, he must court the approval of Congress. When a President proposes to reserve obligated budget authority, that is, not to spend (a rescission, Section 1012), he must submit a special message to both Houses of Congress specifying the amount of budget authority to be rescinded; the specific project or governmental function affected by the rescission; the reasons for his actions; the estimated fiscal, economic, and budgetary effect of the rescission; a statement of the circumstances; and the estimated effect of such rescission on a given program. Unless both Houses expressly approve the rescission bill within forty-five days of its submission to Congress, the money must be made available for obligation.

For deferrals (or delay) of funding (Section 1013), a similar message must be sent; the main difference is that the proposal automatically goes into effect unless either House passes an impoundment resolution disapproving the deferral. To reiterate: A rescission proposal must be approved by both Houses within forty-five days or it cannot take effect. Deferrals are allowed except when vetoed by either House.

The OMB finds the impoundment features of the Act to be a "paper mill." Officials there feel Congress, and especially the General Accounting Office (GAO), which is charged with overseeing the rescission and deferral processes, is saying, "we've caught you abusing your power, so now we'll take nothing you say seriously." They feel GAO implies some base intent by OMB to stifle the "will of the people" whenever impoundment messages are filed. All parties agree that the mechanisms generate lots of paperwork. There are those who believe the process can be simplified by drawing a distinction between "technical" and "policy" rescissions. Officials of OMB believe that Congress should trust the work going on at OMB and that only rescissions of a policy nature (and who is to say what that includes?) should require Congressional sanction. But the Johnson and Nixon years have left a lasting mark on relations between Congress and the Presidency, and trust is not something easily restored. The intricacies of impoundment are specifically set up to control the President. There is nothing in the Act that impels Congress to trust the executive branch. Yet as time passes, and rescissions and deferrals lose their ability to generate publicity as they did in Nixon's time, the process may become less heated and more subject to compromise.

In the past, the threat of impoundment was used by the administrative-branch program managers — shape up or be scuttled. Impounding, after all, is a sort of Sunset Law. Now most rescissions are neglected.[10] A negative attitude by Congress could mean more difficulty in the future in closing programs that have outlasted their effectiveness.

WHOSE INFORMATION?

Unlike the adversary relations engendered by GAO oversight of impoundment, the Administration has had amicable relations with the new boy in town, the Congressional Budget Office. In a short period of time, CBO has developed a budget-analysis division that rivals the capabilities of any government agency. Congress has never had or wanted an agency that would collect primary data for program cost estimation. An attempt to duplicate the informational capacity of the Administration would be a staggering investment. However, Congress does want an agency that can scrutinize the work of other sources. While most often using the primary materials coming out of other agencies, CBO is helping to improve the quality and objectivity of the executive branch. This competition in cost projection works on two levels. First, there are deficiencies in the quality of estimates. Agencies may often be content with poor techniques when newer and better tools come along. They may have outdated indices or irrelevant data sets that inhibit their "bits" of data from being put to use as relevant "information." The second difficulty is institutional bias. Before CBO, Congress' analytic ability was strictly limited; neither GAO's accounting divisions nor the Congressional Research Service could provide up-to-date analysis of economic forecasts or program costs.

[10] "Budget: 'Congress Shall . . . Pay the Debts.' " VIII *National Journal* (May 29, 1976) p. 743.

Before, the Council of Economic Advisors and OMB could monopolize numbers with little chance of having their interpretation challenged by Congress, but now CBO can check on them.

For the past several years, CBO has included an elaborate methodological piece on its economic assumptions in its five-year budget projections. Opening the methodology to public inspection, CBO puts OMB and CEA in a quandary. When either of the executive-branch agencies makes projections that differ from CBO's they are left open to potentially embarrassing questions. This is labeled by a CBO source as "healthy competition." In its first year, the rosy estimates of the Reagan Administration on the size of the deficit were countered by the more pessimistic CBO version, though it was not nearly pessimistic enough.

Consider a dispute over a program cost estimate done by HEW in support of their Basic Educational Opportunity Grant program. The HEW estimates submitted to Congress in an Appropriations hearing did not match previous Administration economic assumptions about income gains in the economy. These HEW estimates assumed that program participants' incomes would change differently than the average for the society. Spotting the discrepancy, CBO changed the agency position. Similarly, CBO analysis was able to convince Congress that the President's proposed budget receipts for outer continental shelf oil leases were overoptimistic.

Today Executive agencies are attempting to work out cost-estimate differentials with CBO before they are tested in Congress. For consideration of President Carter's welfare-reform package, for example, HEW solicited CBO's advice in designing the project's econometric model. Secretary Califano had been worried about the wide range of cost estimates which accompanied President Nixon's Family Assistance Plan in 1969 and which eventually helped scuttle it. Through executive-legislative cooperation in the use and design of the welfare model, if not the program itself, there would be a greater chance of debate on the relative merits of given programs at given costs, rather than a roundabout argument over whose numbers were more accurate.

The CBO is now considered the best source of budget numbers in Washington. This does not mean there is no debate on numbers. "The way the Hill works," as a legislative aide put it, "is to ask a lot of different agencies to do the same job, to see if they come out with the same answers." If they don't, interested legislators know where to probe.

The CBO produces scorekeeping reports enabling the House and Senate Budget Committees to monitor the rate at which appropriations are being approved so that it is possible to isolate spending proposals that would break the ceilings (assuming other appropriations keep on their current course). Naturally, scorekeeping does not guarantee Budget Committee action or its success but it does permit knowledgeable intervention.

The strenuous effort of CBO to edit its reports so that they are readable increases its potential audience. The community of policy analysts in Washington — private consultants, research corporations, Department and OMB officials, professors from all over — constitutes a retinue of people who know each other and are interested in the CBO's work. This community and its network have facilitated recruitment of an able professional staff and enhanced communication of ideas within it. Connecting these policy ideas to the interests of Congress is the problem.

The technical staff of the House Budget Committee sees CBO as an instrument to gather data supporting technical positions on a small scale. The more political staff of the Senate looks to CBO for broader policy analysis. Each year the CBO negotiates with the Budget Committees for a series of budget issue papers. True to form, the HBC looks for areas where CBO can concentrate on number crunching, while the Senate pressures CBO to analyze policy.

WHOSE BUDGET COMMITTEES?

Like all others who wish to be influential, the Budget Committees can afford to lose a few times but not too often, for if it becomes obvious that the Budget Committees are likely to lose, no one need pay attention to them. In order to avoid head-on clashes between Budget and Appropriations committees, the Act breaks down the budget by sixteen functions — health, income, security, veterans' benefits, etc. — instead of the more than twelve hundred individual items by which appropriations are actually voted upon by Congress. Should the Budget Committees confine themselves to totals in these sixteen functional areas or should they look into the items that make them up?

Following the tradition of the larger chamber in favor of specialization, the House Budget Committee builds up its functional targets by separating them into appropriations categories. Aside from being subject to the charge of duplication, this approach increases potential conflict with the Appropriations Committee and decreases conflict with Ways and Means and other committees that spend through tax legislation or direct drafts on the Treasury. Nevertheless, by avoiding direct confrontation and by generally supporting the Appropriations Committee, HBC has maintained good relations. For one thing, it avoids giving specific instructions to Appropriations, and for another, it supports Appropriations in its jurisdictional struggles against new backdoor-spending authority. The HBC's difficulties, to no one's surprise, have come from advocates of increased spending. In regard to a bill to extend the benefits of unemployment compensation, for example, the Ways and Means Committee required a waiver of a provision in the Budget Act forbidding passage of spending legislation before a budget resolution has been passed for the year in which spending is to occur. When HBC opposed the waiver, Representative Corman, in charge of the bill, let loose a blast:

I think the Budget Committee was trying to tell the Ways and Means Committee that it doesn't have much power any more. The whole game up here is power, and the staff of the Budget Committee would like to see the committee have a veto over all the other congressional committees.[11]

Or consider the case of highway spending, when both the Appropriations and the Budget Committees wanted to put a $2.2-billion cap on state spending. Although the Chairman of the Public Works and Transportation Subcommittee on Surface Transportation offered a successful amendment on the House floor to remove the ceiling, the Budget Committee tried to reinstate the ceiling in the final version in conference committee. No one would accuse Chairman Howard of undue restraint when he vented his feelings:

The Committee on the Budget, through its chairman and ranking minority member, has taken it upon itself to advise the House conferees to run up the white flag and surrender — or perhaps betray might be a more appropriate word — the expressed will of the House. In all my years in the House of Representatives, I cannot recall a more arrogant reach for power than this attempt to sell out our own conference stand and reverse the majority decision of the House.[12]

Controlling expenditure will not necessarily matter much unless revenue also is adjusted. Bringing resource allocation together with resource mobilization is, after all, the major purpose of the reform. This requires the cooperation (read, to some extent, subordination), of the revenue committees.

It is in the Senate that the clash between the Budget and Finance Committees has been most severe. Chairman Muskie of SBC was interested in the big picture. As he told the Senate, "The congressional budget process is not a line-item committee." [13] But expenditures going through the tax pro-

[11] VIII *National Journal* (September 25, 1976) pp. 1349–1350.
[12] *Ibid.*, p. 1350.
[13] *Ibid.*, pp. 1348–1349.

cess are so large, Muskie felt that to ignore them would be to nullify efforts at budget control. In colorful language, he raised and answered the rhetorical question:

> Are we supposed to meet each March to propose a congressional budget and then retire to the cloakroom until the fall, when it is too late to advise the Senate of the implications of its tax and spending decisions? And then pop back out like some unwelcome jack-in-the-box each fall to shout, "Surprise! You've blown the budget."? Hardly.[14]

Not to be outdone, Senator Russell Long, Chairman of the Committee on Finance, retorted, "The chairman of the Budget Committee cannot find anything small enough for the Finance Committee to decide anything about." [15] Back at the House, an HBC staff member expressed his dismay at such direct confrontation, saying, "We're aware that we'll get killed if we take on other committees head to head. All we have to work with is the good will of other committees." [16]

This was 1976. The following year witnessed an intensification of the dispute between the two Senate committees. Muskie maintained that the Budget Resolution not only contained a target but also the route by which certain revenues should be reached to maintain the relationship between revenue and expenditure. Senator Long insisted that there was only a grand total; otherwise, SBC would be writing tax legislation. This difference erupted over the important energy bill. "Whatever the merits of this bill as energy legislation," Muskie said, "it is irresponsible as fiscal action." [17] He claimed the bill would cost $4 billion in lost revenues. Long said, "We will take care of it" in conference. He wanted a free hand in horse-trading. Muskie, who had described the energy tax bill "not as a Christmas tree bill — it's too early

[14] *Ibid.*, p. 1347.
[15] *Ibid.*, p. 1348.
[16] *Ibid.*
[17] IX *National Journal* (November 5, 1977) p. 1733.

in the year for that — but as a 'Thanksgiving turkey,' " went on to warn that "from here on we can expect similar provisions in revenue laws that would make them completely outside the budget process." Long won.

Now that we are aware of the difficulties facing the Budget Committees, it should be easier to understand the results. Has the new budget process altered substantive outcomes? Not likely. It would be more accurate to say the Budget Committees have succeeded more in predicting outcomes than in influencing them. From the beginning, the Budget Committees saw they were entering an already established Congressional arena with prearranged power structures. Their early efforts have been to measure the way Congressional action would proceed. The recommendations for the First Concurrent Resolution on the budget each spring tend to be educated guesses about future Congressional action.

The budget reform is designed to help Congress relate obligations to income by setting targets for total expenditures. Senator Muskie says of legislators' voting for more spending and lower budget deficits simultaneously, "we just can't make the system work with that kind of a philosophy." [18] Yet Joel Havemann has reported several instances of Congressmen engaging in this sort of behavior on the grounds, as one put it, "That's the beauty of the budget process. You can vote for all your favorite programs, and then vote against the deficit." [19] What, then, has happened to Congressional efforts to engage in economic management?

[18] See Aaron Wildavsky, "Ask Not What Budgeting Does to Society but What Society Does to Budgeting," Introduction to the second edition of *National Journal Reprints* (Washington, D.C., 1977), p. 4.

[19] *Ibid*. See Mark S. Kamlet, David Mowery, and Gregory Fischer, "Modelling Budgetary Tradeoffs: An Analysis of Congressional Macrobudgetary Priorities, the Impact of the Congressional Budget Act, and The Reagan Counterrevolution," Paper prepared for the Midwest Political Science Association Meetings, Chicago, Illinois, April 22, 1983; and Louis Fisher, "In Dubious Battle? Congress and the Budget," 17 *The Brookings Bulletin* (Spring 1981), pp. 6–10.

One of the major aims of the budget reform was to more closely connect attempts to manage the economy with the expenditure process. And it does appear that members of the Budget Committee have taken the trouble to learn more about the relationship between levels of spending and the condition of the economy. One difficulty is that not much is known, and even that is being challenged. Huge deficits in 1982, for instance, coexisted with less inflation and lower interest rates. Another difficulty is that ability to apply whatever is known is strictly limited, as a brief survey of Presidential efforts will show.

Economic management (or fiscal policy, as it is called) requires a notion of an appropriate level of expenditures either to stimulate or depress economic activity. In that sense it is a top-down process. Those in government, of course, operate in a world they never made, which is only partially subject to their ministrations. Commitments of the past make up the largest part of the budget, and it is either legally or politically impossible to alter them drastically. Considerations of desirable defense and domestic expenditures compete of necessity with optimal fiscal policy, assuming anyone knows what that should be. Among the many constraints within which the makers of fiscal policy operate, the least understood are those imposed by time and by targeting.

There is a prospective fallacy that assumes, by a foreshortening of the future, that fiscal policy goes into effect at the time it is made. If it is the expenditures of fiscal policy we are talking about, that assumption cannot be correct. The most important time, usually, for bringing fiscal considerations to bear on budgetary totals is during the Spring Preview conducted by the Office of Management and Budget (OMB) in April. Suppose this is done in April 1984. Nowadays all this timing is way off, but we will pretend there is a schedule for relating economic forecasts to spending projections. In this make-believe way we can at least ascertain how this relationship is supposed to work. The fiscal policy total is considered along with other matters, and a budgetary target is established and passed down to the spending agencies by the OMB. For the moment, suppose that this total is not challenged by agencies nor revised by the President but goes directly into his Budget in the winter. Even if these contrary-to-fact conditions are met, Congress will not finish acting on appropriations bills until the fall of 1985. It will take spending agencies several months to act on this legislation, so that the impact of these expenditures will not begin to be felt until the winter of 1986. Thus, about two years elapse before the thoughts that went into fiscal policy are reflected in real budgetary behavior. By that time, to be sure, conditions may have markedly changed so that what seemed appropriate then is inappropriate now.

The two years can be shortened to eighteen months by postponing or modifying fiscal policy decisions until November or December. This alternative, however, sacrifices the benefit of considering fiscal policy in the ceilings initially set by the OMB. Renegotiating all the bargains of the prior six months in a few weeks in late November and December is an experience that most of the participants will try to avoid. By late fall, fiscal policy can be fiddled with but the entire orchestral arrangement, insofar as budgetary totals are concerned, is likely to have been settled earlier. Fall fiscal policy is much tighter than what was already an extremely constrained situation the previous spring.

There are more immediate ways of introducing fiscal policy into spending patterns but, resembling as they do the scatter-gun approach, they are as likely to miss their target and wound innocent bystanders as they are to hit it. I refer here to speeding up or slowing down the rate of expenditure to coincide with or to counter reported rhythms in the economy. Increases in spending that are temporary are hard to find. In any event, agencies normally cannot gear up quickly for substantially larger rates of spending, and their career administrators are reluctant to do so because of the traumatic effects of equally rapid reductions in personnel when the time comes to return to normal. In sum, it is easy to spend more but not immediately and not necessarily in the desired amount. Spending less, naturally, is harder. The result is likely to be an initial increase in spending as employees are given severance pay and contractors compensated for delay. In other words, the fine-tuning of spending is a splendid idea in the abstract, but it is far from practical in application.

The existence of unprecedented rates of inflation in the mid-1970s, followed by extraordinarily high interest rates in the late 1970s, coming together with multi-hundred-billion-dollar deficits in the early 1980s, topped off by the largest unemployment rate since the Great Depression, have highlighted Congressional responsibilities for economic management. But no Budget Committee can do this alone. Reducing the deficit, for instance, requires a package deal about taxation and domestic and defense spending that can be achieved only by concerted action among Congressional committees, backed up or led by the formal leadership. If this agreement is lacking, Congressmen will only end up fooling themselves. Funds for favored programs will be obtained by deferring significant amounts to supplemental appropriations, so as to ostensibly meet earlier spending targets. Or, by greatly reducing something essential, appropriations subcommittees can increase the amounts for other programs within the totals allotted by the Budget Committees, knowing the original reductions will have to be restored. Even demands for appropriations subcommittees to reduce funds a certain amount below legislative authorizations through the reconciliation process may be circumvented by setting the starting figures too high, so that the cuts are more apparent than real. Thus Congressional efforts at economic management have been stymied, both because of confusion over effective policy and inability (so far) to get together to enforce whatever set of actions is deemed desirable.

If it has proven easy for spending to soar and difficult to concert action so that spending can decline, does that mean that the budgetary process is biased toward higher spending? Is spending higher or lower than it would be in the absence of the reform? Is the reform neutral in that political majorities merely work their will through it? Or does it advantage or disadvantage spending advocates?

IS THERE A PRO-SPENDING BIAS IN THE BUDGETARY PROCESS?

Is the Congressional budgetary process as it now exists neutral in regard to claims for higher or lower spending? Let me put it this way: If the American people sent equal numbers of high and low spenders to Congress and to the White House, would the budgetary process pass through these opposing desires with equal force? Or would the nation end up with increasing or decreasing expenditures because existing institutions are biased one way or the other?

The Budget Act of 1974 expressed Congress' desire to enhance its own power of the purse by giving it the ability to visibly relate revenue and expenditure. Since the broad coalition supporting the Act was made up of both high and low spenders, however, the new process was not designed to favor either side. On the one hand, the mere existence of Budget Committees raised another possible impediment to higher spending; on the other hand, the need for these Committees to maintain collegial relations with the tax and spending committees as well as remain subject to the will of Congress, meant that they had to subordinate themselves to the widespread desires for higher spending. The evidence from Allen Schick's *Congress and Money* is conclusive:

> In almost a hundred interviews with Members of Congress and staffers, no one expressed the view that the allocations in budget resolution had been knowingly set below legislative expectations. "We got all that we needed," one committee staff director exulted. The chief clerk of an Appropriations subcommittee complained, however, that the target figure in the resolution was too high: "We were faced with pressure to spend up to the full budget allocation. It's almost as if the Budget Committee bent over backwards to give Appropriations all that it wanted and then some." [20]

In considering the related question of mandatory spending, required by law and not subject to the annual appropriations process, Schick makes a powerful plea to consider this a conscious choice, not "an inadvertence of the legislative process but a willful decision by Congress to favor non-budgetary values over budgetary control." [21] Since budgeting, like history, is selectivity, Congress makes its most important choices by choosing what not to consider. Uncontrollability is a biased form of control.

Public spending could be described as engaging in a game of reverse musical chairs — when the singing stops there are extra chairs to fill. The golden rule of agencies and program advocates is that each may do unto the other as the other does unto it so long as there is more for both. What must never happen to shatter the chain is for one sector to take resources from another. To "beggar thy neighbor" is *verboten*. Extraordinary programs, with special appeal, may go up so long as others do not go down. Even as defense spending in the 1970s declined as a proportion of total spending, defense retained the same constant dollar amount it had

[20] Allen Schick, *Congress and Money* (Washington, D.C., 1981) p. 313.
[21] *Ibid.*, p. 571.

since 1955. There is, in the language of evolution, selection "up" but not "out."

How are these happy accommodations possible? Because the public sector has been able to solve its internal problems both by absorbing the growth and decreasing the share of the private sector. Once that easy avenue has been blocked by limits on total spending, the necessity for resource subtraction, as well as resource addition, is brought home.

Up till now I have not specifically stated the most obvious and direct mode of expenditure limitation — acting intelligently on major items of expenditure. If you and I believe that expenditures are too high, the argument goes, we should say specifically which ones should be cut and by how much. If we want to cut expenditures, we must cut programs. Simply stated, these words have much to commend them; I know, for I used to say exactly that. But I have come to believe that analyzing individual items is misleading as a general guide to limiting expenditures.

Who, for instance, would take the lead in reducing expenditures? Each sector of policy is concerned with its own internal development. More money makes it easier to settle internal quarrels. Those who believe more is better for their department or their clientele come to this position naturally. Those who favor radical restructuring of programs soon discover that this is exceedingly difficult to do without sweetening the pie. The price of policy change is program expansion.[22] All internal incentives work to raise expenditures.

Suppose you and I agree to cut out preferred programs in the common interest. What good would that do unless everyone else does the same? If "our" loss is "their" gain, why should we play this game? The budgetary process is biased against limiting spending item by item.

---

[22] For examples, see Aaron Wildavsky, *Speaking Truth to Power* (Boston, 1979), Chapter 4, "Coordination Without a Coordinator."

Should there be an opposite opinion, reflecting a desire to slow down spending, it does not have an equal opportunity to manifest itself in the budget. In the past, it has been difficult for slow spenders to get together to enforce equal sacrifice so that the general rule becomes part and parcel of the calculus involved in individual spending decisions. To increase spending, no coordination is necessary; to decrease it, an enormous amount. Without spending ceilings that require choice among programs, budgeting by addition rather than subtraction will remain common practice.

In Denmark, Christensen informs us, governments have not abided by the limits they presumably imposed on themselves. Why not? Christensen explains

> . . . that for the public sector there is no such thing as resource scarcity. Even if resources may be scarce in the sense that demand for public expenditure always exceeds the resources available, a normal political response to this kind of resource scarcity has been to expand the total amount of resources available for public sector purposes. In other words, if resources are scarce in the public sector, they have to be made so politically. . . . Such processes should . . . make it politically possible to repudiate claims for supplementary appropriations which exceed the official limits for public sector growth. . . . Nothing like that happens. . . .[23]

Once it becomes commonly understood that limits are leaky, no one has sufficient incentive to abide by them.

The "substantial disaffection with the budgetary system used by the federal government," which Sanford Borins informs us had arisen in Canada by the mid-1970s, was undoubtedly based on the consideration that "without financial constraint, cabinet committees were thus characterized by unrepentant log-rolling." Policy initiatives were brought be-

[23] Jorgen Gronnegard Christensen, "Growth by Exception: or The Vain Attempt to Impose Resource Scarcity on the Danish Public Sector," II *Journal of Public Policy* (May 1982) p. 140.

fore a cabinet committee that recommended approval or disapproval "without much consideration of what its cost would be, or whether the money could better be spent on another project." [24] Policy analysis mattered little without resource limits.

On October 14, 1975, the federal government in Canada issued a white paper headed "Attack on Inflation," stating that "the trend of total spending by all governments should not rise more quickly than the trend of the gross national product." According to the civil servants in charge,

> This policy of restraint was applied to *total outlays* from the Consolidated Revenue Fund, including both budgetary and non-budgetary (loans, investments and advances) expenditures. The government made itself accountable for this new policy by announcing the target ceiling for total outlays in advance of the fiscal year. This created a very real political commitment and provided incentive for the government to take action to hold spending within the ceiling.[25]

The incentive consisted of the damage done to other programs and departments if any one vastly exceeded its prior amounts.[26]

[24] Sanford F. Borins, "Ottawa's Expenditure 'Envelopes': Workable Rationality at Last?" in G. Bruce Doern, editor, *How Ottawa Spends Your Tax Dollars: National Policy and Economic Development* (Toronto, 1982) p. 64.

[25] "Controlling Public Expenditure — The Canadian Experience," a paper prepared by civil servants for the Organisation for Economic Co-Operation and Development seminar on controlling public expenditure, Paris 28–30 May 1980, p. 2. See also G. Bruce Doern and Allen M. Maslove, editors, *The Public Evaluation of Government Spending* (Institute of Research on Public Policy, 1979) pp. 39–60; G. Bruce Doern, "Liberal Priorities 1982," in *How Ottawa Spends Your Tax Dollars*, p. 23; and R. Van Loon, "Stop the music: the current policy and expenditure management system in Ottawa," XXIV *Canadian Public Administration* (Summer 1981) 175–199.

[26] Aaron Wildavsky, "From Chaos Comes Opportunity: The Movement Toward Spending Limits in American and Canadian Budgeting," a paper prepared for a conference on "The Leading Public Policy Issues of the 1980s," Carleton University, Ottawa, Oct. 4–6, 1982.

The proponents of Senate Joint Resolution 58, the constitutional amendment designed to balance the budget and limit spending, are attempting to build such incentives into the American budgeting process so as to correct the bias they perceive at present in favor of spending. We shall turn to this amendment, as well as other proposals to alter the budgetary process, in Chapter 8.

LIMITS
8

THE CLASSIC sign of political dissensus is inability to agree on the budget. How we Americans used to snicker at the French (Third and Fourth Republic) practice of voting twelfths (one month's budget at a time, continuing at the prior year's rate) until, that is, we found ourselves making wholesale use of continuing resolutions. How we Americans used to deride the "banana republics" of the world for their "repetitive budgeting" under which the budget was reallocated many times during the year, until it became hardly recognizable, truly a thing of shreds and patches.[1] Yet resolutions that continue last year's funding for agencies, for want of ability to agree on this year's, are becoming a way of life in the United States.

An annual budget is a great accomplishment. Sending out signals on spending that remain predictable so that others can take them into account for a full twelve months is no mean achievement. If only we could count on that today!

[1] Naomi Caiden and Aaron Wildavsky, *Planning and Budgeting in Poor Countries* (New York, 1974).

In real life, a phenomenon that used to be confined to poor countries has now become standard practice in relatively rich nations as well. Whether the budget is formally reconfigured or not, its underlying premises, its financial assumptions and actual allocations, are subject to rapid change measured in months and weeks rather than years.

The decline of the annual budget has been accompanied by the virtual disappearance of balanced budgets. At the same time, the norm of comprehensiveness, requiring a single set of complete and comparable accounts for revenue and expenditure, is honored only in the breach. The disintegration of these traditional budgetary norms, accompanied by a substantial rise in spending, has led to widespread concern over the adequacy of governmental budgeting. These concerns have led to the introduction of a variety of proposals to reform again the process that had been altered in 1974. Here we consider proposed changes in the United States federal budgetary process from least to most radical.

INDEXING

In the past fifteen years, growth of federal spending has been encouraged by two seemingly automatic processes: revenues under a progressive income tax rise faster than inflation, while important transfer programs, such as Social Security, index benefits to the price level. The seemingly natural rise in revenues frees Congressmen from voting for tax increases to fund spending growth. Indeed, they can cut part of the tax bonus from this "bracket creep" and still raise spending. Indexing of benefits helps ensure that recipients maintain their share of total product. If the economy is growing through productivity increases, and if the beneficiary share of the population is stable, indexing spending does no more than keep them even. But when the economy stagnates, with prices rising faster than wages, or if the formula to which the index is tied overstates inflation, indexing benefits causes them to grow as a proportion of total product. Both stagnation and overstatement have occurred in recent years. Because indexing is the *status quo*, Congressmen, in order to restore the previous proportion, are forced to take aid away from beneficiaries. Were there no indexing, they could vote to increase benefits and be seen to do so without increasing them as much as indexing does currently. People don't like to feel something is being taken from them. The workings of both the progressive tax and of benefit indexing encourage spending by making tax increases seem less like confiscation while spending restraint seems more so.

Adjustments to the major benefit indexings are widely proposed but have made little headway. The 1981 tax bill did, however, establish tax "indexing," effective in 1985. The tax brackets are to be indexed to inflation. Thus if a taxpayer is paying 30 per cent on $30,000 in income, which with 10 per cent inflation becomes $33,000 the next year, he might have been pushed into a higher bracket, say 33 per cent, but under indexing he still pays 30 per cent. If this plan is actually implemented, the bracket creep that Jimmy Carter used in his attempt to balance the budget without cutting spending will no longer be available to policy makers. The balanced budget norm, or what is left of it, in combination with the restored difficulty of raising taxes, would then impede spending. If benefit indexing were also removed or reformed, it would be easier not to increase benefits. In fact, inflation would become a tax on beneficiaries but not on wage earners, because beneficiaries would receive dollars with less purchasing power. Instead of a pro-spending and taxing bias, consequently, the budget system would be biased in the opposite direction, toward a smaller size of government. Revenues would decline, because of the lack of bracket creep, but so too would spending because of the lack of cost-of-living increases. The budget would come closer to balance between revenue and expenditure but at a lower level.

The effects of various combinations of tax and spending indexing depend on economic variables, such as the rate of real growth or decline of the economy, and the rate of inflation. During a deflation (as unlikely as that may sound) indexing of benefits could favor restraint, because without indexing, cuts in nominal benefits levels would require visible action. As the price level declines, benefits go down without direct action. Because benefit indexing reflects widely held values (predictability and equity for recipients), and because growth even in entitlements is driven by demographics, eligibility requirements, and employment levels as well as by prices, we may well question whether the most anti-spending indexing reforms are likely to occur or to be sufficient in themselves to attain the goal of restraining spending.

RECONCILIATION AND RADICAL REFORM

Turning to statutory efforts (or even internal rule making), concern over deficits and over President Reagan's success in steamrolling cuts through Congress have led some Congressmen to think again about change in the budgetary process. By aggregating cuts and forcing a vote on them in total (the reconciliation procedure), President Reagan and the Republican legislative leadership simultaneously made large reductions attractive (because they amounted to something) and politically feasible (because mere billion-dollar cuts were harder to spot and because there were so many, Congressmen could, so to speak, "hide" amongst them). In the conclusion to this chapter, I will argue that "reconciliation" (an odd name for a hostile process) is here to stay. For the moment, a more radical reform deserves our scrutiny.

Those unfamiliar with budgetary nomenclature may see little of interest in the incipient debate in Washington over whether the Second or the First Budget Resolution should be binding. Between the two, however, may lie a revolution in Congressional procedure and in budgetary outcomes. Un-

der the Budget Reform Act of 1974, Congress should pass
a First Resolution relating revenue to expenditure by setting
a tentative total for spending. After Congress has acted on
the various programs that make up the total, the Second
Resolution adds them up so that they conform to a new
total. This is budgeting by addition; each program total is
added to the others and the "resultant" of these independent
actions is called the new total. Were Congress to reverse this
procedure by making the First Resolution binding, it would
have to force program items within preexisting totals. More
for one would mean less for another. Since the sums would
have to come out of their own programs, interest groups
and departments would have to be concerned that no one
got too much. Complaints could be handled by saying that
everyone was in the same boat (or Budget Resolution), and
by making it difficult to single out individual legislators as
the culprits. The growing feeling in Congress that it has lost
and should, therefore, regain control of the budget, would
receive an institutional manifestation in a binding First
Resolution.

Were the total too high, so that it accommodated almost
all desires, however, it would be worthless. To matter, it has
to cut into current preferences. But how high is too high?
As Congressmen cast about for a formula, I suspect they
will come up with something remarkably similar to tying
spending to the last year plus the increase in Gross National
Product. Last year's spending is some indicator of political
agreement on the level of spending and the growth (we
hope!) in the economy is some indicator of what is affordable.

In order to set a budget ceiling and to manage its internal
division among claimants, while retaining their willingness
to participate, however, it would be necessary for Congress
to accept considerably more central direction, albeit from
within the legislature. Would Congress have to become a

cabinet, run by a committee that would tolerate no rivals? Not quite, but neither could it remain the same. The governing coalition could change from year to year, but it would have to set total expenditure and stick to it. And that sounds remarkably like a cabinet government in a parliamentary system.

However this committee would be composed — Speaker and Whips, Caucus Chairmen, Heads of Budget, Finance, Ways and Means, Rules, or other Committees, partisan or nonpartisan — the odds against cohesion are considerable. But are they insuperable? That depends on whether Congress has to become a cabinet to generate and enforce a limit or whether it can enforce a spending limit even if a constitutional amendment is required to impose one.

Comparing statutory and constitutional approaches, the more severe constitutional alternative is easier on Congress. There is no requirement for central leadership; that is provided. What Congress has to do is what it is used to doing — divide up shares. It is self-imposed limits and their enforcement that would strain a fragmented political structure in which the fortunes of members do not rise or fall together. Since Congress need not agree on a limit, it could implement an amendment without basic changes in its structure.

Radical change could also come from constitutional amendments, some requiring a balanced budget, others limiting the permissible tax take or the amount that can be spent, usually a proportion of National Product. The leading contender limits spending to the prior year's amount times the proportionate increase or decrease in GNP. If GNP grows, say, by 3 per cent on a prior year's spending of $800 billion, the spending limit for the next year would be $824 billion.

There is a basic difference between an amendment to balance the budget and an amendment to limit total spending. Balance may be achieved through higher levels of taxation; it is compatible with larger government, providing the legislature is willing and able to raise the revenue. The limitation amendment put all the onus on spending; if National Product does not rise sufficiently to meet desired spending, it must be cut. The balanced budget–expenditure limitation amendment, as the current hybrid is called, makes balance permissible but spending limits mandatory.

IMBEDDING BUDGET BALANCE IN SPENDING LIMITS

The proposed balanced budget — Expenditure Limitation Constitutional Amendment, Senate Joint Resolution 58, House Resolution 350 — imbeds a spending limit within a balanced budget. The amendment does this by linking the change in total receipts between two fiscal years to the change in national income during the prior year.[2] If national income goes up x per cent, revenues and expenditures can increase only by the same proportion. All sides recognize that the amendment proposes important political changes. In a time when the mere mention of politics seems somehow underhanded, the proponents and opponents of this proposed budget amendment actually debated "high politics" — the structure of the American political system.

Let us begin this triple exercise in meta-politics — a political analysis of an effort to alter the politics of budgeting and taxation by restructuring the rules — by considering the current context out of which the balanced budget–tax limitation constitutional amendment (hereafter called the budget amendment or, simply, the amendment) has emerged.

Few people predicted that the Reagan Administration would succeed in cutting thirty-odd billion from the spending budget. Immediately the question arises of whether constitu-

---

[2] In its enabling legislation, Congress can choose among any of the standard estimates of national income, such as Gross National Product, National Income, or Gross Domestic Product. It is not the measure but consistency in its use that matters.

tional limitation is necessary in view of 1981's success, a success, at least, from the standpoint of those who favor lower spending. The explanation, given by some Reagan supporters, is that at long last a new Administration has arisen with the courage to tackle the spending interests; all it takes apparently is a combination of political support and political courage. The more analytically minded suggest a parallel scenario in which the strategic approach of the Reagan Administration differs from those of its predecessors. The disadvantages of cutting spending are all in the individual programs whereas the benefits come from reducing totals. In the past, legislators were faced with cutting this or that program with no certainty that a sufficient reduction in total would be achieved to be helpful for economic or social purposes. By aggregating cuts into the tens of billions under the "reconciliation" arrangement, the Reagan Administration overcame prior strategic weakness. In fact, this argument continues, with the first hurdle successfully leaped, it will become easier in the future to reduce taxes and spending.

If ordinary politics can do it, there is no need for a constitutional amendment. But I don't think that over a period of years this Reagan effort will be successful and I would like to explain why. For one thing, succeeding Administrations will not be able to mount the massive, concerted effort that was seen in 1981. Other matters will impinge on the political environment and it will not be easy to keep rallying the troops for what is ostensibly a final charge. Those who are hurt by spending cuts, as always, will mobilize more often and with greater persistence than those whose only stake is in limiting totals. Spenders, I believe, will tire out savers rather than vice versa.

In order to make even these modest reductions semipermanent, it would be necessary to keep winning electoral victories. No doubt if strong majorities committed to this purpose continue to be elected, there will continue to be lower than usual levels of spending. But if we set up a fairer test — mixed victories of higher- and lower-spending forces — will we discover as before that the outcome is continuously higher spending? The Senate debate over constitutional spending limits is helpful in answering this question, no matter what the answer turns out to be.

It is not often that Congress debates fundamental political theory. A strong statement of the pro-amendment position came from Senator Orrin G. Hatch (Republican, Utah):

> The premise of the amendment is that the representative, legislative process ought to have primary responsibility for day-to-day spending and taxing decisions. The further premise is that it cannot presently be entrusted to make those decisions in a responsive and responsible manner because of the existence of certain biases that . . . lead to higher levels of spending and higher levels of taxes. Once these biases can be overcome, it is not the business of the Constitution to dictate precise economic policies or precise spending and taxing decisions.
>
> These biases exist, in short, because of the fact that there are political advantages gained from supporting spending programs and a lack of political disadvantage gained from opposing them. The awareness and interest of the groups which benefit from a political program are great, leading to heavy lobbying and political pressures in behalf of such spending programs. On the other hand, the taxpayers who generally bear the costs of such programs lose relatively little from each particular program and lack similar political interest and leverage. Thus, spending advocates and taxpayers do not compete on an equal basis.
>
> The . . . amendment would reduce this bias toward spending by creating a countervailing political disadvantage for pro-spending votes that does not presently exist. For the first time, votes to increase spending would, under normal circumstances, have to be accompanied by votes to increase taxes or by votes to reduce other spending programs commensurately. Additional revenues that are presently available to elected officials, either through borrowing or through the automatic tax increases of inflation, and that make it

easy for members of Congress to avoid politically difficult votes, would no longer be available.[3]

The pro-spending bias Hatch finds in the political system is to be offset by new rules (Sections 1 and 2 of the amendment) creating an offsetting anti-spending bias.

Senator Hatch was by no means the only one to invoke basic political theory. Other Senators used their own experience to bolster the theory. This is the understanding reached by Senator Dennis De Concini (Democrat, Arizona):

> Everyone . . . is for a balanced budget. When those of us in the Senate are asked to translate that abstract proposition into concrete refusals to spend for specific programs, *my experience has been that this institution has failed* [emphasis supplied]. The purpose of my amendment is simply to increase the political pressure on the other side of the equation. . . . unless there is a legal mechanism to force the Congress to suffer the consequences of its own fiscal irresponsibility, it is unlikely this Nation will return to the era when the Federal revenues consistently matched Federal expenditures.[4]

His striking phrase — ". . . this institution has failed" — stands for a political failure, equivalent to the economists' market failure, which can be overcome only by rewriting the rules for political action.

The remedy in rewriting the rules is proposed by Senator Richard G. Lugar (Republican, Indiana), explicitly in terms of ". . . the structural realities of our system. . . ." [5]

[3] Opening Statement of Senator Orrin G. Hatch of Utah, Hearings on a Proposed Balanced Budget Constitutional Amendment, Subcommittee on the Constitution, Senate Judiciary Committee, March 11, 1981.

[4] Hearings before the Subcommittee on the Constitution of the Committee on the Judiciary, U.S. Senate, on Proposed Constitutional Amendment to Balance the Federal Budget, March 12, May 23, July 25, October 4 and 11 and November 1, 1979 (Serial No. 96–41), p. 153.

[5] *Ibid.*, p. 171.

Each day a congressional office must confront many well-organized interests demanding consideration for their programs. These programs are not unworthy ones, and the members of these groups are not evil men and women. The pressures to spend are simply not counterbalanced by pressures for restraint, which are very diffuse, with the result that Congress says "yes" to almost everyone.

Legislative rules frequently apply a procedural device to situations in which restraint is difficult, pressure intense, and in which the subject matter involves departure from an important norm. The device is the supermajority — the requirement of more than a mere 50 percent plus one vote and it is ideally suited to the most crucial single decision made by the Congress each year, the passage of the Federal budget.[6]

The kind of experience that would lead a legislator to call for restraint on his own behavior was described by Senator David Pryor (Democrat, Arkansas):

> Recently, a group of people from my own State of Arkansas, Mr. Chairman, came to see me in our Washington office. After several minutes of visiting they got out their shopping list and talked about this list of projects they wanted brought back home to their district. The grand total of their requests came to a sum well over $6 million. As they were leaving the office, the parting comment was, "Senator, there is one more item on our list. We want you to do all you can to balance the budget and cut down on Federal spending." [7]

Observing this sort of behavior among his Congressional colleagues as well, Pryor came to believe that ". . . we must add . . . an outside restraining force to the system." [8]

We can wrap up the political theory of the pro-amendment forces by referring to the committee report accompany-

6 *Ibid.*
7 *Ibid.*, p. 254.
8 *Ibid.*

ing Senate Joint Resolution 58, which argues that "there is a structural bias within our political system."

> In short, it is the [Senate Judiciary] Committee's view that our political process is defective insofar as it is skewed toward artificially high levels of spending, i.e., levels of spending that do not result from a genuine will and desire on the part of the people . . . because of the characteristics of the fiscal order that have developed in this country in recent decades. . . .
>
> Members of Congress do not have to reduce levels of spending for one program in order to accommodate increases in other programs because there is no effective limit as to how much Congress may spend in its budget. . . . The availability of deficit spending enables Members to avoid the hard political decision of having to choose *among* spending proposals and thereby creating for themselves some element of political disadvantage as well as political advantage.[9]

This Congressional ambivalence, to be sure, mirrors that of the voting public: most people support most spending programs but they also believe total spending is much too high.[10] The problem for a decision-making body is how to reconcile the two.

No one claims that unbalanced budgets are desirable in and of themselves. Instead, the argument against the amendment is made on two grounds: one is that the political budgetary process is neutral,[11] so that higher spending reflects

[9] Balanced Budget–Tax Limitation Constitutional Amendment, Report of the Committee on the Judiciary, United States Senate, on S.J.Res. 58 with Additional and Dissenting Views, July 10, 1981, 97th Congress, 1st Session (Report No. 97–151), pp. 4, 7, 42.

[10] See my *How To Limit Government Spending* (Los Angeles and Berkeley, 1980), and the sources cited therein.

[11] The neutrality position is well stated in Allen Schick's *Congress and Money* (Washington, D.C., 1980). The contrary position is taken in my review of Schick's excellent book in XIX *Society* (January/February 1982) pp. 86–89.

political will,[12] and the other is that any economic rule written into the Constitution must be too rigid because circumstances are bound to arise in which the rule proves counterproductive. First I shall take up the question of political neutrality and then go on to economic efficacy.

A direct challenge to the allegations of bias in the political process was made by Marshall Beil, speaking for the Committee on Federal Legislation of the New York City Bar, in opposition to the balanced budget amendment. Replying to a question by Senator Strom Thurmond (Republican, South Carolina) suggesting that the inability of Congress to control spending was one of those "discovered faults" (or structural defects) that James Madison had said justified amending the Constitution, Mr. Beil replied that

> There are no constitutional barriers or obstacles to Congress' control of federal spending. The Constitution already gives Congress plenary power in this area. Congress can balance the budget if a majority of Congress votes to do so. The "fault" you have identified, Senator, is in the political process, not the Constitution. There is no reason to tamper with the constitutional structure of the Federal government when Congress already has the power it needs to balance the budget by a simple majority vote.[13]

It's as simple as that: all that is required to lower spending is a majority vote.[14]

The implication is that higher rates of spending and taxing reflect the popular will, for otherwise it would be clear that democracy was not working. In the same manner, the "Open

[12] The counterargument was that there was already a law requiring a balanced budget (Public Law 95–435) that had been ignored, and no law could bind a future Congress. See the comments of Senator Harry F. Byrd, Jr., who introduced this provision, Hearings Before the Subcommittee on the Constitution, p. 26.

[13] *Ibid.*, p. 235.

[14] For the views of The Committee on Federal Legislation rejecting "Budget–Balancing by Constitutional Amendment," see pp. 239–249, Hearings Before the Subcommittee on the Constitution.

Letter Opposing a Constitutional Prohibition of Deficits in the Federal Budget," signed by more than five hundred economists, concluded that "The people of the United States have other and better means available to improve the wisdom of national policy: by electing national officials who are competent, responsible, and responsive to the will of the electorate." [15]

Confronting the contention of failure in the political process, Paul Samuelson, one of the three Nobel Prize winners in economics who signed the letter, wrote to the Senate Subcommittee on the Constitution, which held hearings on the balanced budget amendment, that

> Whenever it is the case that a bare or preponderant majority of the American people *permanently* conclude that the role of the public sector ought to be constrained in its fractional share of the total national income or in its trend rate of increase, our representative democracy is capable of translating that will of the people into effective action: the American republic is not defective in its present organizational structure to secure what are stated to be the goals of the amendment to balance the budget or the amendment to limit the share and growth trend of the public sector. *There is no inherent flaw in our checks and balances and division of responsibility among the legislative, executive and judicial branch of governments that makes inevitable a process of "logrolling" designed to swell the level of expenditures and taxes beyond that truly desired by the effective majority of the electorate.* Instead, the elaborated pure theory of public expenditure and of game theory more even-handedly shows that there are countertendencies favoring realization of *both less and more* government expenditures than the pluralistic electorate really desire.[16]

I am unaware of any attempt to use game theory or theories of public expenditure or any other theory to argue that the political process is impartial. Generally, social scientists say

[15] *Ibid.*, p. 540.
[16] *Ibid.*, p. 559.

that all forms of organization are forms of bias one way or another.[17]

The learned doctors were not the only ones to fear that, as Senator Gary Hart (Democrat, Colorado) put it, "The result [of a balanced budget amendment] would be economic disaster." [18] Current economic understanding is that while budget balance is sometimes desirable, in the words of the Director of the Congressional Budget Office, Alice Rivlin,

> When the economy is sliding into a severe recession, attempting to balance the Federal budget will almost certainly make the recession significantly worse. Deficits occur automatically in recession since declining incomes produce lower Federal revenues and spending for unemployment compensation rises. At such a moment, raising taxes or cutting spending in order to balance the budget would reduce aggregate demand further and throw additional people out of work.[19]

It is also widely believed, as Martin Gerbert, vice president of the International Union of the United Auto Workers, told the Subcommittee on the Constitution, that

> . . . if you have a requirement that you must always balance the budget, the immediate response is to raise taxes or to cut government expenditures in order to bring the budget back into balance. But the impact of increasing taxes is to suck money out of the economy. The impact of reducing expenditures is to reduce the flow of money into the economy. In both cases, the effect of the balance budget response is to aggravate the recession.[20]

Is S.J. 58 addressed to a long-run spending bias or is it a short-term economic policy or both? It is time to look at the proposed amendment itself.

---

[17] See Mary Douglas, "Cultural Bias," in *In The Active Voice* (London and Boston, 1982) pp. 183–254.
[18] Hearings Before the Subcommittee on the Constitution, p. 157.
[19] *Ibid.*, p. 261.
[20] *Ibid.*, p. 285.

The following sections tell the story:

Section 1. Prior to each fiscal year, the Congress shall adopt a statement of receipts and outlays for that year in which total outlays are no greater than total receipts. The Congress may amend such statement provided revised outlays are no greater than revised receipts. Whenever three-fifths of the whole number of both Houses shall deem it necessary, Congress in such statement may provide for a specific excess of outlays over receipts by a vote directed solely to that subject. The Congress and the President shall ensure that actual outlays do not exceed the outlays set forth in such statement.

Section 2. Total receipts for any fiscal year set forth in the statement adopted pursuant to this article shall not increase by a rate greater than the rate of increase in national income in the last calendar year ending before such fiscal year, unless a majority of the whole number of both Houses of Congress shall have passed a bill directed solely to approving specific additional receipts and such bill has become law.

Section 5. Total receipts shall include all receipts of the United States except those derived from borrowing and total outlays shall include all outlays of the United States except those for repayment of debt principal.[21]

But what story do they tell? The interaction between expenditure ceilings (limits on outlays) and a balanced budget (outlays must not exceed receipts) requires further elucidation. The language is straightforward but its consequences are roundabout.

For its proponents, a major purpose of the amendment is to remedy political biases in the existing process, one of which, in their opinion, is that spending may be voted without simultaneously having to accept the onus of voting increased taxation to cover it. No longer. In its second section, the amendment establishes a fiscal norm; ordinarily, Con-

---

[21] Report of the Committee on the Judiciary, pp. 1–2.

gress and the President are to limit revenue-spending increases to the percentage of increase in National Income that actually occurred in the prior fiscal year. To raise that proportionate spending level, Congress, by a majority vote of all its members, a vote larger than the usual majority of members present and voting, must pass a bill, which the President must sign, raising the revenue limit. Under a progressive tax system, however, economic growth generates about one-and-a-half times the amount of revenue for every percentage increase in personal income. Either the national debt must be paid off or taxes must be cut. A revenue-raising vote is made prior to, and a condition of, a spending vote. As the Report of the Senate Judiciary Committee asserts,

> Under its system of taxation, Federal tax receipts grow more rapidly than national income during either periods of real growth or periods of nominal growth caused by inflation. Stabilizing the share of that income available to the Federal government (as provided by section 2) would require Congress to enact annual tax cuts or to "index" the tax system, unless it was prepared to vote annually for tax increases that would increase the Federal government's share of the economy.[22]

The purported structural bias in favor of spending is offset by requiring a redistribution of revenues back to taxpayers, unless Congress votes to increase them every year. Thus the amendment effectively indexes tax brackets.

Suppose Congress does not want to raise taxes but rather to raise spending specifically so as to create a budget deficit? Leaving the question of enforcement aside for the moment, Section 1 of the proposed amendment requires a vote of three-fifths of the members of Congress to unbalance the budget. Congress can raise spending providing it raises revenues for the purpose, but it must have a three-fifths major-

---

[22] *Ibid.*, p. 43.

ity to run a deficit. The spending limit tying totals to the past movement of National Income is defended by the balanced budget requirement — revenues must match expenditures — and the balanced budget is defended by a three-fifths supermajority.

The key interpretive statement, expressing the essence of the amendment, comes from the Committee report: ". . . actual outlays cannot exceed statement outlays which cannot exceed statement receipts which cannot grow faster than the economy." [23]

Immediately questions and criticisms came crowding in. Since revenues and expenditures are both estimates, what happens if the plan for a balanced budget that Congress and the President are required to submit, the "Statement of Receipts and Outlays" mandated by the amendment, does not turn out as expected? Contrariwise, what is to stop Congress from deliberately putting in unrealistic estimates so that revenues fall far short of expenditures? Who is to enforce the amendment, and how?

All the amendment demands is that "The Congress and the President shall ensure that actual outlays do not exceed the outlays set forth in such [budget] statement." From this omission we learn that an excess or shortfall of revenues is not ruled out. If, to take the case that worries critics, an economic slowdown reduces revenues, Congress may amend its statement of outlays and receipts but it is not required to do so. Thus a reduction in expected revenues may cause a deficit for that year without running afoul of the letter or spirit of the amendment. Once a statement of outlays is approved, however, the amendment obliges the President and Congress to keep actual outlays (government spending that year) from exceeding the outlays specified in the statement of intentions. The word "actual" refers only to outlays.

[23] Report of the Committee on the Judiciary, p. 43.

In short, statement of a balanced budget expresses good intentions — the fiscal norm of budget balance — but enforcement is reserved for spending limits, not revenue-raising.

What we do not learn from the amendment itself is who will guard the guardians of the Treasury, since it appears they are to guard themselves. Irritating but fascinating: How can politics and politicians, which constitute the problem, be, by this amendment, made into its solution?

Faced with an intricate construction, which establishes budget balance as the norm but which does not mandate it, opponents of the amendment claim it is unworkable because it is both too easy to circumvent and too rigid to get around. Insisting on a balanced budget under all circumstances would make it too rigid, and allowing exceptions during emergencies would open up loopholes. Crises would be difficult to define. And so the drafters decided against using the notion of crisis or emergency (except for a state of war); instead Congress can raise expenditure or revenue with the right kind of majority without necessarily having to explain why. This approach has led to criticism on the grounds that supermajorities are undemocratic, allowing 41 per cent of Congress to dictate policy, and obstructionist, inhibiting response to changing circumstance. The proponents reply that it is the current budgetary political process that is rigid. According to Senator Lugar,

> We are presently on a course in which larger and larger portions of the budget are thought of as "uncontrollable," and therefore beyond the reach of serious scrutiny. This bizarre notion has vitality only because no binding limit on spending forces a reexamination of these spending programs or their automatic increases. A two-thirds requirement would liberate the budget process from the psychology of "uncontrollability". . . .[24]

[24] Hearings, *op. cit.*, pp. 174–175.

The amendment, Senator Simpson continues, "perfects our political process" [25] by demanding open votes and means that, in Senator Heflin's words, we need "not rely on hidden taxes such as inflation to drive up federal revenues and thus finance increased spending." [26] Is it inflexible to require a supermajority to unbalance the budget or is it inflexible to be controlled by "uncontrollable spending" or to be caught in the secret grip of bracket creep?

The argument of ineffectiveness is grounded in the view that the amendment will not work because it is too vague and because that vagueness will be used to defeat its purposes. An ancillary consequence is that unseemly disputes over the meaning of the amendment will discredit the very Constitution it is supposed to strengthen. Allen Schick tells it the way it is:

> Any constitutional restriction on deficits or expenditures must come to grips with the issue of what constitutes the budget of the United States Government. The question of what ought to go into the budget is by no means settled; current practices are a compound of written and unwritten rules, many of which were introduced by the executive branch without the explicit concurrence of Congress. [27]

The question of which items should be counted as belonging in the budget would be compounded, in his view, by disagreement over "what constitutes an outlay," since spending limits are imposed on outlays. He goes on to say that

> There is almost no law on the subject, and a jumble of conflicting practices and traditions complicates the quest for defensible criteria. Yet a spending limitation cannot be enforced without rules for deciding what is an outlay. The issue, at first glance, seems straightforward and without complication: an outlay occurs whenever the federal gov-

[25] *Ibid.*, p. 524.
[26] *Ibid.*, p. 529.
[27] *Ibid.*, p. 62.

ernment makes a payment of funds. The issue, however, is not whether a payment constitutes an outlay, but how outlays are computed for budgetary purposes. It is in the counting of outlays that difficulties abound.[28]

Another way of referring to this same lack of clarity is that the formal budget does not contain a comprehensive statement of spending.

Deciding what should be included is one problem; accurate estimation of future revenues and expenditures is another. Yet the amendment depends on achieving balance for future and not for past years.[29] How are both inclusion criteria and estimates to be decided? The amendment and the Committee report are quite clear on that subject: the Congress and the President will decide when they propose and adopt the required statement. As the Committee blandly comments,

> Because the amendment statement looks to the future, a future necessarily shrouded in some measure of uncertainty, reasonable men may disagree as to the proper amounts of receipts and outlays to be expected. As a practical matter, a Congressional majority will be the final arbiter among the estimates. At most, this majority can be charged with adopting better rather than worse estimates of receipts and outlays for the coming fiscal year.[30]

If Congress is the arbiter of estimates, what happens if it fails to act reasonably and who is to say what is reasonable? Without an amendment, people might or might not get upset and vote for new Congressmen, or suffer the consequences of the old ones' actions. But with an amendment, there is another possibility.

The major objection to the amendment (other than spending and tax limits themselves) is that it will make the judi-

[28] *Ibid.*, p. 65.
[29] *Ibid.*, pp. 62, 65, 67.
[30] Report of the Committee on the Judiciary, p. 45.

ciary the supreme arbiter of spending, a role for which it is wholly unsuited, thus bringing both Congress and the courts into disrepute. As Lane Kirkland, then secretary-treasurer of the AFL-CIO, expressed his concern:

> These proposed amendments would indirectly grant broad, sweeping new powers to the judicial branch. What if the Congress fails to provide for a balanced budget? Could the Members be sued, or jailed for contempt? Could a court determine how to achieve a balanced budget? Would the Supreme Court take over the Congress until it met its constitutional responsibility? Who would enforce such a provision?
>
> These are questions without answers, because even the sponsors have no idea as to how the courts would rule.[31]

In response, the majority of the Judiciary Committee supporting the amendment expressed a novel doctrine — the amendment would enforce itself. Though some members were leery of a lack of judicial self-restraint, they felt the courts would stay away so that they would not be stung by proximity to this hornet's nest. Private parties and individual legislators, the Committee report stated, would lack standing to sue. In order to leave interpretation in the political process, the Committee deliberately decided not to prohibit or encourage judicial review. Here are its own words on the meaning of silence about enforcement:

> it nevertheless is expected that the amendment will be largely self-enforcing and self-monitoring. First, Congress and the President each are expected to establish appropriate procedures for complying with the amendment; second, Congress and the President each are expected to monitor the actions of the other branch and, to the limits of their authority, enforce the provisions of the amendment against that branch; and, finally, the public is expected, and will be in a superior position, to monitor the actions of both of these branches of government and, where they fall short of

[31] Hearings, *op. cit.*, p. 190.

complying adequately with the provisions of the amendment, enforcing it through electoral means. Only as a final
resort, and only under the most compelling circumstances
(as, for example, when the practices of either the Congress
or the Executive undermine the ability of the amendment
to be self-enforcing), is there anticipated to be a significant
role for the judicial branch.[32]

What these "compelling circumstances" might be, short of
refusing to submit the required statement of a balanced
budget, or vote to override it, is difficult to imagine. In other
words, an amendment designed to correct a political fault is
to be left to be enforced by those committing it. Is this a
self-defeating idea or a self-reinforcing concept in which
politics depends on itself?

The amendment's sponsors give a political answer to a
political question:

Senate Joint Resolution 58 is designed to promote its own
enforcement through the political processes. By establishing
a focus upon two or three critical votes each year relating
to aggregate levels of taxation and deficits in place of the
present diffuse focus upon hundreds of individual spending
measures, Senate Joint Resolution 58 is designed to enable
the electorate to better identify those members of Congress
most responsible for higher levels of spending, taxing, and
deficits. To the extent that the amendment succeeds in
creating a more useful flow of political information to the
electorate, and this is a major objective of the amendment,
it will be enforced most effectively at the polls every other
November.[33]

Is this a believable response?

For the public to enforce the amendment, the public must
in fact be informed. Afficionados of the subject know about
the numerous end runs that are possible in any budgetary
process. These include imposing costs on the private sector

---

[32] Report of the Committee on the Judiciary, pp. 65–66.
[33] *Ibid.*, pp. 61–62.

through regulations; loans and loan guarantees (where only defaults are charged as expenditures); tax preferences; netting out the difference between the revenue produced by a service and the expenditure so that only the difference rather than the whole amount of spending counts toward the total; and much more.[34] A major criticism of spending limits is that, by damming up spending at one end, it would encourage greater recourse to end runs all over the place. I doubt this. The reason is not that there will be an absence of efforts to make end runs; we can count on plenty of attempts. The reason is that budgetary processes without spending limits (that is, almost all processes, so far as I know) are already full of end runs.

A false analogy is suggested between a pristine process uncontaminated by end runs and their sudden appearance after the imposition of spending limits. What we have now, without spending limits, is a proliferation of spending spigots of all kinds. It can hardly get much larger. With the United States at a level of some $700 billion in loan guarantees, for instance, it would take a lot to convince me that these would rise dramatically under a different process, if only because of the substantial negative effect on borrowers in the loan markets. Nor is it easy to use regulations and other devices to accomplish the kinds of social purposes that usually motivate spending. And should it be discovered that certain end runs, such as accounting changes, have a deep and deleterious effect, it is always possible to go after them.

When one wishes to make spending limits work, one takes the details of implementation as a challenge to win out in a trial of wits. When one wishes to show that the whole idea

---

[34] See my *How to Limit Government Spending* (Los Angeles and Berkeley, 1980), Chapter 6 on "End Runs," pp. 84–105. Rod Dobell, "Pressing the Envelope: The Significance of the New, Top-Down System of Expenditure Management in Ottawa," *Policy Options* (Nov./Dec. 1981) p. 17, deals with netting out.

of imposing limits is ridiculous, one makes implementation seem impossible or idiotic. Opponents of a spending-limit amendment, for instance, argue that since it would be virtually impossible to balance the budget immediately, the whole idea is cockeyed. Were they offered a bargain in which balance did not have to be achieved for five years, however, they would be unlikely to support the amendment.

If one were actually to believe there was a limit on resources, and that one could not afford to run over, everyone would invent devices for keeping track of spending (as is done with debt) and for absorbing unexpected increases. There would be, as there are in Canada, contingency funds. That this arrangement seems silly to some people is a measure of the deep-rootedness of budgeting by addition.

Though the imposition of spending limits may appear arbitrary and therefore anti-analytical, limits provide the essential basis for making analysis meaningful; namely, that the value of what is done is judged greater than what was given up to get it. No limits, no allocation, no need to use analysis. "It is in this sense," Rod Dobell writes, that Canadian spending limits "may lead individual Ministers and program managers, through pursuit of their own interests, also to pursue the social goal of a more efficient allocation of resources. . . ." [35] People may (and do) differ over the proper balance between the private and public sectors, but whatever the level of the limit, allocations within it should be more intelligent in that the decision makers would have a better idea of what they are getting for what they are giving.

RECONCILING INDIVIDUAL AND COLLECTIVE RATIONALITY

Canadian experience with spending limits enables us to pose several important questions about the institutional require-

[35] Dobell, p. 16.

ments of expenditure control. It had been assumed that spending ceilings were inappropriate in a parliamentary system because no one cabinet could bind another. Perhaps. Nevertheless, Canada shows that it is possible for several governments, coming from different parties, to act to continue the same process. Priorities may and do differ within broad programmatic areas but the size and structure of the spending ceilings are much the same.

The trailblazing Canadian effort may be used to argue on the opposite side of the street: spending limits can be imposed and enforced only in a parliamentary system run under a supercommittee that tolerates no rivals; namely, a cabinet. Obviously, a parliamentary system cannot be a sufficient condition for establishing and enforcing spending limits. It could hardly be argued, after immense experience to the contrary, that parliamentary regimes are somehow suited for controlling spending.

A capacity for control, if the desire is absent, is no guarantee of achievement. But is desire, absent capacity, sufficient? That depends on whether the imposition of a ceiling through a constitutional amendment will prove efficacious or whether party discipline in the legislature must be used to back it up. Which alternative would prove to be most efficacious, then, converting Congress into a cabinet or using a constitutional *deus ex machina* to supply the limit without altering traditional Congressional government? The United States is far likelier to pass a balanced budget–spending limit amendment than is Congress to act like a cabinet. If the amendment does not pass, however, there is still room for radical change.

The political rationale for a constitutional amendment should now be apparent: If a political bias toward big government is built into the spending and taxing processes, and if this "discovered fault" cannot be remedied by the normal workings of the political process, then the rules of the game may have to be changed so as to reconcile collective consequences with individual choice.

Though it is often said that the advantage of economic markets is that they make calculations manageable, such a statement, by itself, misses the mark. Central planners probably have the sheer quantitative capacity to mimic markets. Properly stated, what markets provide is calculating capacity tied to incentives for the participants to make efficient choices. This combination of economic calculation and political incentive is also the heart of the argument for spending limits. Once limits are put in place by constitutional amendment, each organizational participant in the spending process has the incentive to keep others from growing too fast, lest their programs pay the price. And since all participants now depend on economic growth for increases, because spending is tied to GNP, they have common cause to aid productivity.

Scanning the budgetary reforms of the past quarter century, we can now see that they are part of the problem rather than the solution. Performance budgeting accepts the task to be done, asking only how to perform it more efficiently. Program budgeting seeks out an optimal path among policies to achieve general objectives more effectively. Zero-base budgeting asks how these objectives might be achieved if the constraints of the past were removed. None of these reforms are concerned with totals, as in budgetary balance, or with limits on programs.

Where the budgetary reforms to which we are accustomed are concerned with the quality of spending, the new wave will emphasize quantity. Whereas old-line reforms sought to directly impose detailed methods for improving decisions, the new, streamlined models will work indirectly to increase incentives to value programs according to their best alternative use. Where PPB and ZBB and the rest were avowedly apolitical, drawing on economic or management science for legitimacy, spending limits will be openly political, resting on explicit choices about total spending and its major sub-divisions.

As for control of expenditure itself, experience will resolve itself down to this proposition: Limits on total spending do not guarantee budgetary control, but without limits on total spending there can be no control.

THE RISE OF RECONCILIATION

My personal preference is for constitutional spending limits. My judgment as a student of political feasibility, however, is that, though the balanced budget–spending limit amendment has gotten further faster than anyone thought possible a scant few years ago, its time has not yet come. A few years of multi-hundred-billion-dollar deficits may change that. But, though this amendment is having a hard time, the budgetary process may nevertheless evolve in its direction.

It is the way of evolution that it need not be consciously intended. The various participants react to emerging conditions and, willy-nilly, find themselves moving in a direction no one intended. The current chaotic economy, I think, will lead Congressmen and Presidents, big- and little-government adherents, to support reconciliation. Whether it will come in the form of a single vote on the entire budget as a package, or in several votes, the important thing is that bundles of items will be tied together so that they must be voted up or down together, not item by item. By the time the present budget crisis is over (to be replaced, no doubt, by others), reconciliation may have become a way of life. Experience under it may reveal untapped potential; Congressional coherence, by increasing ability to resist external forces, may make members influential. Relations within the legislature would grow in importance compared to those outside. *Congressional Government*, the title with which Woodrow Wilson rebuked Congress, may become more of a reality. For from years of reconciliation could come a binding First Budget Resolution, which in turn could spawn a leadership capable of making it work. From budgetary acorns (consider the history of parliaments), the oak of more coherent Congressional government may grow.

A GUIDE TO BUDGET TERMS AND CONCEPTS

APPORTIONMENT: Under this authority, the director distributes appropriations and other budgetary resources by time periods (usually quarterly) or by particular projects or activities. The apportionment system is intended to achieve an effective and orderly use of available funds. It is a violation of law for an agency to incur obligations or make expenditures in excess of the apportioned amounts.

APPROPRIATION: An act of Congress that allows federal agencies to incur obligations and to make payments out of the Treasury for specified purposes. This is the most common form of budget authority.

AUTHORIZATION: Basic substantive legislation enacted by the Congress that sets up a federal program or agency either indefinitely or for a specified period of time. Such legislation is a prerequisite for the subsequent enactment of budget authority and may set limits on the amount that can be appropriated.

BACKDOOR AUTHORITY: Legislative authority to obligate funds provided outside the normal appropriation process. The most

This Guide has been prepared with and adapted from the guide used in the third edition of this work and those in two other basic texts on the budget process: Stanley E. Collender's *The Guide to the Federal Budget: Fiscal 1983 Edition*, and Allen Schick's *Congress and Money*. One may also consult U.S. General Accounting Office, *A Glossary of Terms Used in the Federal Budget Process*, 3d ed., Report No. PAD–81–27 (Washington, D.C.: Government Printing Office, March 1981).

common forms of backdoor authority are borrowing authority and contract authority. In other cases, a permanent appropriation is provided that becomes available without current action by the Congress.

BACKDOOR SPENDING: Backdoor authority as well as mandatory spending legislation; that is, legislation that mandates the payment of benefits or entitlements, such as increases in veterans' compensation or pensions. Such mandatory legislation requires the subsequent enactment of appropriations.

BALANCES OF BUDGET AUTHORITY: The amount of budget authority which is unspent at the end of the fiscal year and which is still available for conversion into outlays in the future. Such amounts are called "unexpended" or "undisbursed" balances. Balances of budget authority result from the fact that not all budget authority enacted in a fiscal year is obligated and paid out in that same year.

BORROWING AUTHORITY: A form of budget authority that permits a federal agency (other than the Treasury and Federal Financing Bank) to borrow funds from the public or another federal fund or account and to incur obligations and make payments for specified purposes out of that borrowed money. Borrowing authority differs from an appropriation, which permits a federal agency to incur obligations and make payments directly from the Treasury. Borrowing authority is a type of backdoor spending. See Backdoor authority or Backdoor spending.

BUDGET AMENDMENT: A proposal, submitted by the President after his formal budget transmittal, which increases or decreases the amount of budget authority previously requested in the budget. Amendments are transmitted prior to completion of appropriation action by both Houses of Congress.

BUDGETARY RESERVES: Portions of budget authority set aside under authority of the Antideficiency Act (31 United States Code 665), as amended by the Impoundment Control Act of 1974, for contingencies or to effect savings whenever savings are made possible by or through changes in requirements or greater efficiency of operations. Section 1002 of the Impoundment Control Act of 1974 restricts the establishment of budgetary reserves and requires that all reserves be reported to the Congress. See Deferral.

BUDGET AUTHORITY: Authority provided by law that permits government agencies to incur obligations, requiring either immediate or future payment of money. The amount authorized by the Congress to become available for obligation in a given fiscal year is called budget authority for that year.

There are three basic kinds of budget authority — appropriations, contract authority, and authority to spend debt receipts.

BUDGET DEFICIT: For any given year, an excess of budget outlays over budget receipts. The amount of the deficit is the difference between outlays and receipts. Deficits are financed primarily by borrowing from the public.

BUDGET SURPLUS: For any given year, an excess of budget receipts over outlays. The amount of the surplus is the difference between receipts and outlays.

BUDGET UPDATE: A statement summarizing amendments to or revisions in budget authority requested, estimated outlays, and estimated receipts for a fiscal year that has not been completed. The President may submit updates at any time but is required by the Congressional Budget Act of 1974 to transmit such statements to the Congress by April 10 and July 15 of each year.

CONCURRENT RESOLUTION ON THE BUDGET: Legislation passed by both houses of Congress that establishes, reaffirms, or revises the Congressional budget for a fiscal year. The First Concurrent Resolution, which is expected to pass by May 15, is the Congressional budget in its earliest form and establishes targets for the aggregate levels of budget authority, outlays, revenues, and deficit or surplus; the appropriate level of the public debt; and an estimate of the budget authority and outlays for each of the nineteen budget functions. The Second Concurrent Resolution, which is expected to pass by September 15, revises or reaffirms the aggregate and functional targets of the First Resolution and changes the aggregates into an absolute "ceiling" on spending and minimum "floor" on revenues. If needed, subsequent budget resolutions for a fiscal year may be adopted at any time after the passage of the Second Resolution. A concurrent budget resolution does not require the President's signature to become law.

CONGRESSIONAL BUDGET: The budget established by Congress in a concurrent resolution on the budget.

CONSTANT DOLLARS: The dollar value of goods and services adjusted for inflation. Constant dollars are determined by dividing current dollars by an appropriate price index, a process generally known as "deflating." Constant dollars are used to discount increases or decreases in prices when comparing transactions over a period of time. When using constant dollars, any differences will reflect changes in the volume of the goods and services.

CONTINUING RESOLUTION: Legislation enacted by the Congress to provide budget authority for specific ongoing activities in cases where the regular fiscal year appropriation for such activities has not been enacted by the beginning of the fiscal year. The continuing resolution usually specifies a maximum rate at which the agency may incur obligations, based on the rate of the prior year, the President's budget request, or an appropriation bill passed by either or both Houses of Congress.

CONTRACT AUTHORITY: A type of budget authority that permits an agency to incur specific obligations in advance of an appropriation. Contract authority does not provide the money to pay the obligation; therefore, it must be followed by an "appropriation to liquidate" (pay) any obligations incurred.

CONTROLLABILITY: The ability of Congress and the President to increase or decrease outlays in the year in question, generally the current or budget year. "Relatively uncontrollable" refers to spending that the government cannot increase or decrease without changing existing substantive law. Such spending is usually the result of open-ended programs and fixed costs (for example, Social Security, veterans' benefits) and payments coming due under commitments made earlier.

CROSSWALK: A procedure for translating budget information from one form to another — for example, from a budget resolution to an authorization or appropriations bill.

CURRENT DOLLARS: The dollar value of a good or service in terms of the prices at the time the good or service was sold.

CURRENT POLICY: An estimate, provided by the Congressional Budget Office, of the budget authority and outlays needed for a program or agency to continue to operate this year at the same level as in the past year, adjusted for inflation, including anticipated changes in the number of beneficiaries and changes already enacted in law.

CURRENT SERVICES BUDGET: Information required by the Congressional Budget and Impoundment Control Act of 1974 (P.L. 93-344), to be transmitted by the President to the Congress, by November 10 of each year. The current services budget is required to show the estimated outlays and proposed appropriations that would be necessary to continue existing programs at their current operating levels (without policy changes) in the ensuing fiscal year, together with the economic and programmatic assumptions underlying them.

DEFERRAL: Any executive branch action or inaction — including the establishment of reserves under the Antideficiency Act — that delays the availability of funds. Pursuant to the Congressional Budget and Impoundment Control Act (P.L. 93-344, Title X), the President is required to report each deferral to the Congress in a special message published in the *Federal Register.*

ENTITLEMENT: Legislation that requires the payment of benefits to all persons or governments that meet the eligibility requirements established in the law. Examples of entitlement programs are Social Security, Medicare, and veterans' pensions. See also Backdoor authority and Controllability.

EXPENDITURES: Actual spending, generally interchangeable with outlays.

FISCAL POLICY: Federal policies on taxes, spending, and debt management, intended to promote the nation's goals, particularly with respect to employment, Gross National Product, inflation, and balance of payments. The budget process is a major vehicle for determining and implementing fiscal policy.

FISCAL YEAR: Since fiscal year 1977, it has been defined as the year running from October 1 to September 30 and designated by the calendar year in which it ends. Before FY 1977, it was the year running from July 1 to June 30 and designated by the calendar year in which it ended.

FORWARD FUNDING: Budget authority provided in an appropriations act that allows funds to be committed to a specific purpose (obligated) this year for programs that will be implemented next year. Forward funding can be made by the federal government prior to the start of the school year and local school officials can plan their budgets.

FULL-EMPLOYMENT BUDGET: The estimated receipts, outlays, and surplus or deficit that would occur if the economy were continually operating at full capacity (conventionally defined as a 4 per cent unemployment rate for the civilian labor force).

FULL FUNDING: Providing the budget authority to cover the total cost of a program or project at the time it first is approved. This differs from partial or incremental funding, where budget authority is provided for only those obligations of the program or project which are likely to be incurred in a given fiscal year.

FUNCTIONAL CLASSIFICATION: A means of presenting budgetary data in terms of the major purposes being served. Each program or activity is placed in the single category (for example, national defense, health, agriculture) that best represents its major purpose, regardless of the spending agency or department.

GOVERNMENT-SPONSORED ENTERPRISES: Enterprises that are established and chartered by the federal government to perform specific functions under the supervision of a government agency. As private corporations, these enterprises are excluded from the budget. Examples of government-sponsored enterprises are the Federal Home Loan Bank Board and the Federal National Mortgage Association.

GRANT: A cash award given by the federal government to a state or local government or other recipient for a specified purpose. This differs from a grant-in-aid, which is a grant limited solely to a state or local government. The two major forms of federal grants are "block" and "categorical." Block grants are awarded primarily to general-purpose governments, are distributed to them according to the formulas established in the law, and can be used for any locally determined activities that fall within the functional purpose of the grant as stated in the law. Categorical grants can be used only for a specific purpose and usually are limited to narrowly defined activities.

GRANTS-IN-AID: For the purposes of the budget, grants-in-aid consist of federal outlays used to support, promote, or encourage specific state- and local-government activities.

IMPOUNDMENT: A term used to characterize any executive-branch action that precludes the obligation of funds appropriated by the Congress. See Deferral and Rescission.

IMPOUNDMENT RESOLUTION: A resolution of the House of Representatives or the Senate disapproving a deferral of budget authority set forth in a special message ordinarily transmitted by the President under Section 1013 of the Impoundment Control Act of 1974. Passage of an impoundment resolution by either House of Congress has the effect of overturning the deferral and requires that such budget authority be made available for obligation.

LAPSED FUNDS: Budget authority that, by law, ceases to be available for obligation.

LOAN GUARANTEE: An agreement by which the government pledges to pay part or all of the principal and interest of a loan to the lender or holder of a security if the borrower defaults. If it becomes necessary for the government to pay part or all of the loan principal or interest, the payment is an outlay. If not, then the loan guarantee does not affect federal spending and appears in the budget only as budget authority.

MANDATORY SPENDING LEGISLATION: See Backdoor spending.

MIDYEAR REVIEW OF THE BUDGET: An updated version of the President's January budget proposal, prepared by the Office of Management and Budget and required to be submitted to Congress by July 15. The midyear review includes revised projections on the economy and its likely effect on the President's program, any policy changes proposed by the President since January, and the latest information on the previous year's spending and revenue totals.

MULTIPLE-YEAR APPROPRIATION: An appropriation that is available for a specified number of years.

NO-YEAR APPROPRIATION: An appropriation made available for obligation until the objectives have been attained (for example, appropriations for major construction, procurement, research and development). Accordingly, no time limit is set on the availability of the funds for obligation.

OBJECT CLASSIFICATION: A means of analyzing the obligations incurred by the federal government in terms of the nature of the goods or services purchased (for example, personnel compensation, supplies and materials, equipment, and so on), regardless of the agency involved or purpose of the programs for which they are used.

OBLIGATED BALANCE: The amount of a budget authority committed for a specified purpose but not yet actually spent.

OBLIGATIONAL AUTHORITY: The total available to an agency in a given fiscal year. Obligational authority is the sum of the budget authority newly provided in a fiscal year, the balance of budget authority from prior years that has not yet been obligated, and amounts authorized to be credited to a specific fund or account during that year, including transfers between accounts.

OBLIGATIONS: Contracts or other binding commitments made by federal agencies to pay out money for products, services, or other purposes — as distinct from actual payments. Obligations incurred may not be larger than available budget authority.

OFF-BUDGET AGENCIES: Federally owned and controllable agencies whose transactions have been excluded from the budget totals under provisions of law (for example, Rural Telephone Bank, Postal Service, Federal Financing Bank). The fiscal activities of these agencies are not reflected in either budget outlays or the budget surplus or deficit, and the appropriation requests for their off-budget activities are not included in the totals of budget authority.

OFFICE OF MANAGEMENT AND BUDGET (OMB): The division of the Executive Office of the President that assists the President in the discharge of his or her budgetary and management responsibilities.

OFFSETTING COLLECTIONS: Moneys received by the government as a result of business types of transactions with the public (sale of goods and services) or as a result of a payment from one government account to another. Such collections are netted in determining budget outlays. Intragovernmental transactions are payments from governmental accounts to budgetary receipt accounts. Since they are payments from the government to itself, they are offset against outlays rather than being counted as budget receipts.

ONE-YEAR APPROPRIATION: An appropriation made available for obligation for one year.

OPEN-ENDED PROGRAMS: Programs for which the law places no limit on the amount of obligations that may be incurred. They are programs for which eligibility standards are established by law, and outlays are determined by the number of eligible persons who apply for benefits. Thus, for example, veterans' benefits programs and Medicaid are open-ended programs.

OUTLAYS: The actual amount of dollars spent for a particular activity. The total results from both new budget authority provided this year and unexpended balances of budget authority provided in previous years. It is the level of outlays compared to the level of revenues that determines whether the budget is in surplus or deficit.

PERMANENT AUTHORITY: See Budget authority.

PRESIDENT'S BUDGET: The proposal sent by the President to Congress in January each year as required by the Budget and Accounting Act of 1921, as amended. The President's budget consists of five documents: The Budget of the United States Government; The Budget of the United States Government, Appendix; Special Analyses; The Budget of the United States Government in Brief; and Major Themes and Additional Budget Details.

PROGRAM: An organized set of activities directed toward a common purpose or goal, undertaken or proposed by an agency to carry out its responsibilities.

PUBLIC DEBT: The total of all direct borrowings of the United States Treasury, as opposed to borrowings of other federal agencies.

RECONCILIATION: The process used by Congress to force its committees to comply with the totals set in a budget resolution. As designed in the 1974 Budget Act, it was to be applied to the Second Budget Resolution. Since 1980, it has been applied to the First Resolution. Language is included in the resolution directing one or more committees to make changes in current law that will help Congress meet its targets. Only dollar amounts for a given committee are specified. The committees in each House report their recommendations to its budget committee, which can package them all into a single bill and bring it to the floor. If the committees are recalcitrant, the budget committees, under certain circumstances, can themselves specify the changes. Taxes and appropriations, as well as authorizations, may be reconciled. The result of the process is an Omnibus Act (or Acts), potentially (as in 1981) affecting policy and spending in a great many areas.

REPROGRAMMING: Utilization of funds in an appropriation account for purposes other than those contemplated at the time of appropriation. Reprogramming is generally accomplished pursuant to consultation between the federal agencies and the appropriate Congressional committees.

RESCISSION: Enacted legislation that cancels (rescinds) budget authority previously granted by the Congress that otherwise would remain unused and available for obligation. Pursuant to the Congressional Budget and Impoundment Control Act (P.L. 93-344, Title X), the President is required to transmit a special message to the Congress whenever he proposes rescission of budget authority. These special messages are also required to be published in the *Federal Register*.

SCOREKEEPING: A procedure used by the Congressional Budget Office for up-to-date tabulations and reports of Congressional budget actions on bills and resolutions providing new budget authority and outlays and changing revenues and the public debt limit for a fiscal year. Such reports include, but are not limited to, status reports on the effects of these Congressional actions to date and of potential Congressional actions, and comparisons of these actions to targets and ceilings set by Congress in the budget resolutions. Periodic scorekeeping reports are required by Section 308(b) of the Congressional Budget Act of 1974.

SPENDING AUTHORITY: See Backdoor authority.

SPENDING COMMITTEES: The standing committees of the House and Senate with jurisdiction over legislation that permits the obligation of funds. For most programs, the House and Senate Appropriations Committees are the spending committees. For other programs, the authorization legislation permits the obligation of funds without an appropriation, and so the authorization committees have the spending power. The revenue-raising committees (House Ways and Means and Senate Finance) at times also can be considered to be spending committees because of tax expenditures.

SUPPLEMENTAL APPROPRIATIONS: Appropriations made by the Congress, after an initial appropriation, to cover expenditures beyond original estimates.

TAX EXPENDITURE: Tax revenue losses attributable to laws of the United States that provide tax exclusions, tax deductions, preferential tax rates, or tax deferrals.

TOTAL OBLIGATIONAL AUTHORITY (TOA): See Obligational authority.

TRANSITION QUARTER (TQ): The three-month period between the end of fiscal 1976 and the beginning of fiscal 1977 (July 1 to September 30, 1976) resulting from the change from a July 1 through June 30 federal fiscal year to an October 1 through September 30 fiscal year.

TRUST FUNDS: Funds collected and used by the federal government for specified purposes in accordance with the terms of a trust agreement or statute (for example, Social Security and unemployment trust funds). Receipts held in trust are not available for the general purposes of the government. Trust fund receipts that are not anticipated to be used in the immediate future are generally invested in government securities and earn interest.

UNDISTRIBUTED OFFSETTING RECEIPTS: Money collected by the federal government from payments to trust funds by government agencies for their employees' retirement, interest paid to trust funds on their investments in government securities, and proprietary receipts from rents and royalties on the Outer Continental Shelf. These receipts are not distributed to the function that best describes their substantive role, but are included as a separate function.

UNEXPENDED BALANCE: The amount of budget authority previously granted to an agency but still unspent and available for future spending. The unexpended balance is equal to the sum of the obligated and unobligated balances.

UNIFIED BUDGET: The budget of the federal government. In the Federal Budget, the receipts and outlays for federal funds and trust funds are combined, and the various interfund transactions that occur between them are deducted before arriving at the totals.

UNOBLIGATED BALANCE: See Balances of budget authority.

BIBLIOGRAPHY

Abellera, James W. and Roger P. Labrie, "The FY 1982–1986 Defense Program: Issues and Trends," 3, *American Enterprise Institute Foreign Policy and Defense Review.*

Anton, Thomas J., *The Politics of State Expenditure in Illinois* (Urbana, 1966).

————, Jerry P. Cawley and Devin L. Kramer, *Moving Money: An Empirical Analysis of Federal Expenditure Patterns* (Cambridge, Mass., 1980).

Arnow, Kathryn Smul, *The Department of Commerce Field Offices*, The Inter-University Case Program, ICP Case Series, No. 21, February 1954.

Banfield, Edward C., "Congress and the Budget: a Planner's Criticism," XLIII *The American Political Science Review* (December 1949) pp. 1217–1227.

Beck, Morris, *Government Spending: Trends and Issues* (New York, 1981).

Behn, Robert D., "President Reagan Cuts the 1982 Budget: How Big a Victory?" Paper presented at the National Conference of the American Society for Public Administration, Honolulu, Hawaii, March 22, 1982.

————, "The Receding Mirage of the Balanced Budget," *The Public Interest*, no. 67 (Spring 1982) pp. 118–130.

Berman, Larry, *The Office of Management and Budget and the Presidency* (Princeton, N.J., 1979).

Biehl, Dieter, "Budget Equilibrium in the Long and the Short Run," in Horst Claus Recktenwald, editor, *Tendances à Long Terme du Secteur Public* (Paris, 1976).

Bird, Richard, *Financing Canadian Government: A Quantitative Overview* (Toronto, 1979).

Borcherding, Thomas, "A Hundred Years of Public Spending, 1870–1970," in Thomas Borcherding, editor, *Budgets and Bureaucrats: The Sources of Government Growth* (Durham, N.C., 1977).

———, *Budgets and Bureaucrats: The Sources of Government Growth* (Durham, N.C., 1977).

———, "The Growth of U.S. Public Spending: Another Look," Simon Fraser University, School of Business Administration and Economics, Burnaby, British Columbia, Canada, Discussion Paper 82-02-2 (1977).

Borg, Sten G., and Francis G. Castles, "The Influence of the Political Right on Public Income Maintenance Expenditure and Equality," XXIX *Political Studies* (December 1981) pp. 604–621.

Boskin, Michael J., and Aaron Wildavsky, editors, *The Federal Government: Economics and Politics* (San Francisco, Calif., 1982).

Braybrooke, David, and Charles E. Lindblom, *A Strategy of Decision* (New York, 1963).

Break, George F., "Government Spending Trends in the Postwar Period," in Michael J. Boskin and Aaron Wildavsky, editors, *The Federal Government: Economics and Politics* (San Francisco, 1982).

Breit, William, "Starving the Leviathan: Balanced Budget Prescriptions Before Keynes," in *Fiscal Responsibility in Constitutional Democracy*, James M. Buchanan and Richard E. Wagner, editors (Leiden and Boston, 1978).

Brown, David S., "The Staff Man Looks in the Mirror," XXIII *Public Administration Review* (June 1963) pp. 67–73.

Brown, William H., and Charles E. Gilbert, *Planning Municipal Investment: A Case Study of Philadelphia* (Philadelphia, 1961).

Browning, Rufus P., "Innovative and Non-Innovative Decision Processes in Government Budgeting (Mimeo., 1963).

Bruner, Jerome S., Jacqueline Goodnow, and George Austin, *A Study of Thinking* (New York, 1956).

Buchanan, James M., "Politics, Policy and the Pigovian Margins," XXIX *Economica* (February 1962) pp. 17–28.

———, *Democracy in Deficit: The Political Legacy of Keynes* (New York, 1977).

———, and Richard E. Wagner, *Fiscal Responsibility in Constitutional Democracy* (Leiden and Boston, 1978).

Buck, Arthur E., *The Budget in Governments of Today* (New York, 1934).

———, *Municipal Finance* (New York, 1926).

———, *Public Budgeting* (New York, 1929).

Burkhead, Jesse, *Government Budgeting* (New York, 1956).

Caiden, Naomi, and Aaron Wildavsky, *Planning and Budgeting in Poor Countries* (New York, 1974).

Cameron, David R., "On the Limits of the Public Economy," 459 *The Annals of the American Academy of Political and Social Science* (January 1982) pp. 46–62.

Campbell, John Creighton, *Contemporary Japanese Budget Politics* (Los Angeles and Berkeley, 1977).

Carlson, Jack W., "The Status and Next Steps for Planning, Programming, and Budgeting," in *Public Policy Expenditures and Policy Analysis*, Robert Haveman and Julius Margolis, editors (Chicago, 1970) pp. 367–412.

Cleveland, Frederick A., "Evolution of the Budget Idea in the United States," LXII *Annals of the American Academy of Political and Social Science* (November 1915) pp. 15–35.

———, and Arthur E. Buck, *The Budget and Responsible Government* (New York, 1920).

Collender, Stanley E., *The Guide to the Federal Budget: Fiscal 1983 Edition* (Washington, D.C., 1982).

Colm, G. and M. Helzner, "The Structure of Governmental Revenue and Expenditure in the United States" (*L'Importance et la Structure des Recettes et des Dépenses Publiques*), International Institute of Public Finance (Brussels, 1960).

Commission on Economy and Efficiency, *The Need for a National Budget*, 62d Congress, 2d Session, 1912, House Document No. 854.

Committee on Appropriations, Subcommittee on Agriculture Appropriations, U.S. House of Representatives, *Hearings on Agriculture Department Appropriations Bill for 1947*, 79th Congress, 2d Session, 1946.

Committee on the Budget, U.S. Senate, *Tax Expenditures: Relationships to Spending Programs and Background Materials* (Washington, D.C., March 17, 1982).

Committee on Government Operations, Subcommittee on National Policy Machinery, U.S. Senate, *Organizing for National Security; The Budget and the Policy Process*, 87th Congress, 1st Session, 1961.

————, Subcommittee Hearings, U.S. House of Representatives, *Improving Federal Budgeting and Appropriations*, 85th Congress, 1st Session, 1957.

————, Subcommittee Hearings, U.S. House of Representatives, *Budget and Accounting*, 84th Congress, 2d Session, 1956.

Committee on the Judiciary, U.S. Senate, "Hearings before the Subcommittee on the Constitution of the Committee on the Judiciary, U.S. Senate, on Proposed Constitutional Amendment to Balance the Federal Budget," March 12, May 23, July 25, October 4 and 11, and November 1, 1979 (Serial No. 96–41).

————, U.S. Senate, "Report of the Committee on the Judiciary on S.J.Res. 58 with Additional and Dissenting Views," July 10, 1981 (No. 97–151).

Committee on Rules, U.S. House of Representatives, *To Create a Joint Committee on the Budget*, 82d Congress, 2d Session, 1952.

Congressional Budget Office, *Federal Credit Activities* (Washington, D.C., 1982).

————, *Reducing the Federal Budget: Strategies and Examples, Fiscal Years 1982–1986* (Washington, D.C., 1981).

————, *Reducing the Federal Deficit: Strategies and Options* (Washington, D.C., 1982).

————, *Tax Expenditures* (Washington, D.C., 1981).

Coughlin, Richard M., *Ideology, Public Opinion, and Welfare Policy*, Research Series, No. 42 (Berkeley, Calif., University of California, Berkeley: Institute of International Studies, 1980).

Crecine, John P., "Coordination of Federal Fiscal and Budgetary Policy Processes," Selected Proceedings, American Political Science Association, 1977, University Microfilms.

————, *Defense Budgeting: Constraints and Organizational Adaptation*, Discussion Paper No. 6, University of Michigan, Institute of Public Policy Studies (1969) p. 38.

————, *Governmental Problem Solving: A Computer Simulation of Municipal Budgeting* (Chicago, 1969).

————, "The Role of OMB in Executive Branch Budgetary Decision Making," in John P. Crecine, editor, *Research in Public Policy and Management* (Greenwich, Conn., 1981).

————, and Gregory Fischer, "On Resource Allocation Processes in the U.S. Department of Defense," Discussion Paper, University of Michigan, Institute of Public Policy Studies (October 1971).

Crocker, Royce, "Federal Government Spending and Public Opinion," I *Public Budgeting and Finance* (August 1981) pp. 25–35.

Cyert, Richard, and James March, *A Behavioral Theory of the Firm* (Englewood Cliffs, N.J., 1963).

Dahl, Robert A., and Charles E. Lindblom, "Variation in Public Expenditure," in *Income Stabilization for a Developing Democracy*, Max F. Millikan, editor (New Haven, 1953), pp. 347–396.

Danziger, James N., *Making Budgets: Public Resource Allocation* (Beverly Hills, Calif., 1978).

Davis, Otto A., M. A. H. Dempster, and Aaron Wildavsky, "A Theory of the Budgetary Process," LX *The American Political Science Review* (September 1966) pp. 529–547.

————, "On the Process of Budgeting II: An Empirical Study of Congressional Appropriations," in *Studies in Budgeting*, Byrne, Charnes, Cooper, Davis, Gilford, editors (Amsterdam and London, 1971) pp. 292–375.

————, "Toward a Predictive Theory of the Federal Budgetary Process," IV *The British Journal of Political Science* (1974) pp. 419–452.

Dempster, M. A. H., and Aaron Wildavsky, "On Change: Or, There Is No Magic Size for an Increment," XXVII *Political Studies* (September 1979) pp. 371–389.

Derthick, Martha, *Uncontrollable Spending for Social Services Grants* (Washington, D.C., 1975).

Dexter, Lewis A., "The Representative and His District," XVI *Human Organization* (Spring 1957) pp. 2–13.

Diesing, Paul, *Reason in Society* (Urbana, 1962) pp. 198, 203–204, 231–232.

Dobell, Rod, "Pressing the Envelope: The Significance of the New, Top-Down System of Expenditure Management in Ottawa," *Policy Options* (Nov./Dec. 1981) pp. 13–18.

Dodd, Lawrence C. and Bruce I. Oppenheimer, editors, *Congress Reconsidered* (New York, 1977).

Downs, Anthony, *An Economic Theory of Democracy* (New York, 1957).

———, "Why the Government Budget Is Too Small in a Democracy," XII *World Politics* (July 1960) pp. 541–563.

Eismeier, Theodore J., "The Political Economy of Tax Expenditure Budgeting," (Typescript, 1981).

Elwood, John William, editor, *Reductions in U.S. Domestic Spending: How They Affect State and Local Governments* (London and New Brunswick, N.J., 1982).

Enthoven, Alain, and Harry S. Rowen, "Defense Planning and Organization" in *Public Finances: Needs, Sources and Utilizations, National Bureau of Economic Research* (Princeton, 1961) pp. 365–420.

Fenno, Richard F., Jr., *Congressmen and Committees* (Boston, 1973).

———, *Home Style: House Members in Their Districts* (Boston and Toronto, 1978).

———, "The House Appropriations Committee as a Political System: The Problem of Integration," LVI *The American Political Science Review* (June 1962) pp. 310–324.

———, *The Power of the Purse: Appropriations Politics in Congress* (Boston, 1966).

Fiorina, Morris, *Congress—Keystone of the Washington Establishment* (New Haven, Conn., 1977).

Fisher, Louis, "Congress, the Executive, and the Budget," 411 *Annuals of the American Academy of Political and Social Sciences* (1974) pp. 102–113.

———, "Impoundment of Funds: Uses and Abuses," XXIII *University of Buffalo Law Review* (Fall 1973) pp. 141–200.

————, "In Dubious Battle? Congress and the Budget," 17 *The Brookings Bulletin* (Spring 1981) pp. 6–10.

————, "Presidential Spending Discretion and Congressional Controls," XXXVII *Law and Contemporary Problems* (Winter 1972) pp. 135–172.

————, *Presidential Spending Power* (Princeton, N.J., 1975).

————, "Reprogramming of Funds by the Defense Department," *Journal of Politics* (February 1974).

————, "The Congressional Budget Act: Does It Have a Spending Bias?" Paper prepared for the Carl Albert Congressional Research and Studies Center Conference on the Congressional Budget Process, University of Oklahoma, February 1982.

Fitzpatrick, Edward A., *Budget Making in a Democracy* (New York, 1918).

Flora, Peter, and Arnold J. Heidenheimer, editors, *The Development of the Welfare State in Europe and America* (New Brunswick, N.J., 1981).

Forsythe, Dall W., *Taxation and Political Change in the Young Nation, 1781 and 1833* (New York, 1977).

Froman, Lewis A., Jr., "Why the Senate Is More Liberal Than the House," in his *Congressmen and Their Constituencies* (New York, 1963) pp. 69–97.

Gabis, Stanley T., *Mental Health and Financial Management: Some Dilemmas of Program Budgeting*, Public Administration Program, Department of Political Science Research Report, No. 3 (East Lansing, Mich., 1960).

Gilmour, Robert, "Central Legislative Clearance: A Revised Perspective," XXXI *Public Administration Review* (March/April 1971) pp. 150–158.

Golembiewski, Robert T., and Jack Rubin, editors, *Public Budgeting and Finance: Readings in Theory and Practice*, 2d ed. (Itasca, Ill., 1975).

Greider, William, "The Education of David Stockman," *The Atlantic Monthly* (December 1981) pp. 27–54.

Gulick, Luther, and Lyndall Urwick, *Papers on the Science of Administration* (New York, 1937).

Hammond, Thomas H., and Jack H. Knott, *A Zero-Based Look at Zero-Base Budgeting; Or, Why Its Failures in State Gov-

ernment Are Being Duplicated in Washington (New Brunswick, N.J., 1979).

Harper, Edwin L., Fred A. Kramer, and Andrew M. Rouse,
"Implementation and the Use of PPB in Sixteen Federal
Agencies," XXIX *Public Administration Review* (November/
December 1969).

Hartman, Robert W., "Budget Controllability and Planning,"
in Barry M. Blechman, Edmund M. Gramlich, and Robert
W. Hartman, editors, *Setting National Priorities: The 1976
Budget* (Washington, D.C., 1975).

———, "Congress and Budget-Making," *Political Science Quarterly* (Fall 1982) pp. 381–402.

———, "Federal Employee Compensation and the Budget," in
Michael J. Boskin and Aaron Wildavsky, editors, *The Federal
Budget: Economics and Politics* (San Francisco, 1982).

———, "Making Budget Decisions," in Joseph A. Pechman,
editor, *Setting National Priorities: The 1983 Budget* (Washington, D.C., 1982).

———, and Robert D. Reischauer, "A Defense of Current Federal Budgetary Procedures," Paper prepared for Conference
on Constraining Federal Taxing and Spending, Hoover Institution, October 21–23, 1981.

Havemann, Joel, *Congress and the Budget* (Bloomington, Ind.,
1978).

Heclo, Hugh, "OMB and the Presidency," *The Public Interest*
No. 38 (Winter 1975) pp. 80–98.

———, and Aaron Wildavsky, *The Private Government of Public Money: Community and Policy Inside British Political
Administration* (London and Berkeley, 1974).

Hitch, Charles J., "Management of the Defense Dollar," XI *The
Federal Accountant* (June 1962) pp. 33–44.

———, and Roland N. McKean, *The Economics of Defense in
the Nuclear Age* (Cambridge, Mass., 1960).

Hood, Ronald C., "Reorganizing the Council of Economic Advisers," LXIX *Political Science Quarterly* (September 1954)
pp. 413–437.

Hoover Commission on the Organization of the Executive

Branch of the Government, *Budgeting and Accounting* (Washington, D.C., 1949).

Horn, Stephen, *Unused Power: The Work of the Senate Committee on Appropriations* (Washington, D.C., 1970).

Huntington, Samuel P., *The Common Defense* (New York, 1961).

Huzar, Elias, *The Purse and the Sword* (Ithaca, N.Y., 1950).

Inter-University Case Program, "The Impounding of Funds by the Bureau of the Budget," ICP Case Series: No. 28, November 1955.

Ippolito, Dennis S., *Congressional Spending: A Twentieth Century Fund Report* (Ithaca, N.Y., and London, 1981).

——, *The Budget and National Politics* (San Francisco, 1978).

Jasinsky, Frank, "Use and Misuse of Efficiency Controls," XXXIV *Harvard Business Review* (July, August 1956) pp. 105–112.

Jones, Charles O., "Representation in Congress: The Case of the House Agricultural Committee," LV *The American Political Science Review* (June 1961) pp. 358–367.

Jump, W. A., "Budgetary and Financial Administration in an Operating Department of the Federal Government," (Mimeo.) Paper delivered at the conference of the Governmental Research Association, September 8, 1939.

Kahn, Herman, *On Thermonuclear War* (Princeton, 1960).

Kamlet, M. S., and D. C. Mowery, "The Budgetary Base in Federal Resource Allocation," 24 *American Journal of Political Science* (1980) pp. 804–821.

Kammerer, Gladys M., *Program Budgeting: An Aid to Understanding* (Gainesville, Fla., 1959), Public Administration Clearing Service of the University of Florida, Civic Information Series No. 38.

Keith, Robert A., "Budget Reconciliation in 1981," I *Public Budgeting and Finance* (Winter 1981) pp. 37–47.

Key, V. O., Jr., "The Lack of a Budgetary Theory," XXXIV *The American Political Science Review* (December 1940) pp. 1137–1144.

Kimmel, Lewis H., *Federal Budget and Fiscal Policy, 1789–1958* (Washington, D.C., 1959).

Kolodzicj, Edward A., "Congressional Responsibility for the Common Defense: The Money Problem," XVI *The Western Political Quarterly* (March 1963) pp. 149–160.

Korb, Lawrence, "The Budget Process in the Department of Defense 1947–77: The Strengths and Weaknesses of Three Systems," XXXVII *Public Administration Review* (July/August 1977) pp. 334–336.

Kristensen, Ole P., "The Logic of Bureaucratic Decision-Making as a Cause of Governmental Growth," 8 *European Journal of Political Research* (1980) pp. 249–264.

———, "The Role of Organized Interests in Decisions with Implications for Public Spending," Paper prepared for presentation at the ECPR Workshop on Interest Groups and Governments, Florence, Italy, March 25–30, 1980.

Larkey, P. D., C. Stolp, and M. Winer, "Theorizing About the Growth of Government: A Research Assessment," I *Journal of Public Policy* (1981) pp. 157–220.

Lawton, Frederick J., "Legislative-Executive Relationships in Budgeting as Viewed by the Executive," XIII *Public Administration Review* (Summer 1953) pp. 169–176.

Leiserson, Avery, "Coordination of Federal Budgetary and Appropriations Procedures Under the Legislative Reorganization Act of 1946," I *National Tax Journal* (June 1948) pp. 118–126.

LeLoup, Lance T., *Budgetary Politics: Dollars, Deficits, Decisions* (Brunswick, Ohio, 1977).

———, "Discretion in National Budgeting: Controlling the Controllables," 4 *Policy Analysis* (Fall 1978) pp. 455–476.

———, and William B. Moreland, "Agency Strategies and Executive Review: The Hidden Politics of Budgeting," 38 *Public Administration Review* (May/June 1978) pp. 232–239.

———, *The Fiscal Congress: Legislative Control of the Budget* (Westport, Conn., 1980).

Leonard, Herman B., and Elizabeth H. Rhyne, "Federal Credit and the 'Shadow Budget,'" *The Public Interest*, No. 65 (Fall 1981) pp. 40–58.

Levine, Charles H., and Paul L. Posner, "The Centralizing Effects of Austerity on the Intergovernmental System," 96 *Political Science Quarterly* (Spring 1981) pp. 67–85.

———, and I. Rubin, editors, *Fiscal Stress and Public Policy* (Beverly Hills and London, 1980).

Lewis, Verne B., "Toward a Theory of Budgeting," XII *Public Administration Review* (Winter 1952) pp. 42–54.

[Rear Admiral] Leydon, John K., "Review of *The Politics of the Budgetary Process*," *U.S. Naval Institute Proceedings* (February 1966) p. 115.

Lindblom, Charles E., "Decision-Making in Taxation and Expenditure," in *Public Finances: Needs, Sources and Utilization*, National Bureau of Economic Research (Princeton, 1961) pp. 295–336.

———, "Policy Analysis," XLVIII *American Economic Review* (June 1958) pp. 298–312.

———, "The Science of 'Muddling Through,'" XIX *Public Administration Review* (Spring 1959) pp. 79–88.

Long, Norton, "Power and Administration," IX *Public Administration Review* (Autumn 1949) pp. 257–264.

Lord, Guy, *The French Budgetary Process* (Berkeley, 1973).

Lynch, Thomas, editor, *Contemporary Public Budgeting* (New Brunswick, N.J., 1981).

Maas, Arthur, "In Accord with the Program of the President?" Carl Friedrich and Kenneth Galbraith, editors, IV *Public Policy* (Cambridge, Mass., 1954) pp. 77–93.

MacMahon, Arthur, "Congressional Oversight of Administration," LVIII *Political Science Quarterly* (June and September, 1943) pp. 161–190 and 380–414.

Mann, Thomas E., and Norman J. Ornstein, editors, *The New Congress* (Washington, D.C., 1981).

Marvick, L. Dwaine, *Congressional Appropriation Politics: A Study of Institutional Conditions for Expressing Supply Intent* (Ph.D. Dissertation, Columbia University, 1952).

Marvin, Keith E., and Andrew M. Rouse, "The Status of PPB in Federal Agencies: A Comparative Perspective," in *Public Policy Expenditures and Policy Analysis*, Robert Haveman and Julius Margolis, editors (Chicago, 1970) pp. 444–460.

Marx, Fritz Morstein, "The Bureau of the Budget: Its Evolution and Present Role, I and II," XXXIX *The American Political Science Review* (August and October 1945) pp. 653–684 and 869–898.

Masters, Nicholas, "Committee Assignments in the House of Representatives," LV *The American Political Science Review* (June 1961) pp. 345–357.

Mayhew, David, *Congress: The Electoral Connection* (New Haven, Conn., 1974).

Meltsner, Arnold J., "Budget Control Through Political Action," in Michael J. Boskin and Aaron Wildavsky, editors, *The Federal Budget: Economics and Politics* (San Francisco, 1982).

———, *The Politics of City Revenue* (Berkeley and Los Angeles, 1971).

Merewitz, Leonard, and Stephen H. Sosnick, *The Budget's New Clothes: A Critique of Planning-Programming-Budgeting and Benefit-Cost Analysis*, Series on Public Analysis (Chicago, 1971).

Milliman, J. W., "Can People Be Trusted with National Resources?" XXXVIII *Land Economics* (August 1962) pp. 199–218.

Mosher, Frederick C., *Program Budgeting: Theory and Practice, with Particular Reference to the U.S. Department of the Army*, Public Administration Service (Chicago, 1954).

———, and Orville F. Poland, *The Cost of Governments in The United States: Facts, Trends, Myths* (Mimeo., August 1963).

———, and John Harr, *Programming Systems and Foreign Affairs Leadership: An Attempted Innovation* (New York, 1970), pp. 68–69.

Mueller, Eva, "Public Attitudes Toward Fiscal Programs," LXXVII *The Quarterly Journal of Economics* (May 1963) pp. 210–235.

Musgrave, Richard A., "Leviathan Cometh — Or Does He?" in Helen F. Ladd and T. Nicholas Tideman, editors, *Tax and Expenditure Limitations* (Washington, D.C., 1981) pp. 77–120.

————, "Themes of Fiscal Crises: An Essay in Fiscal Sociology," in Henry J. Aaron and Michael J. Boskin, editors, *The Economics of Taxation* (Washington, D.C., 1980) pp. 361–390.

————, and J. M. Culbertson, "The Growth of Public Expenditures in the United States, 1890–1948," VI *National Tax Journal* (June 1953) pp. 97–115.

Nelson, Dalmas H., "The Omnibus Appropriations Act of 1950," XV *Journal of Politics* (May 1953) pp. 274–288.

Neustadt, Richard E., "Presidency and Legislation: The Growth of Central Clearance," XLVIII *The American Political Science Review* (September 1954) pp. 641–671.

————, "Presidency and Legislation: Planning the President's Program," XLIX *American Political Science Review* (December 1955) pp. 980–1021.

Nienaber, Jeanne, and Aaron Wildavsky, *The Budgeting and Evaluation of Federal Recreation Programs, or, Money Doesn't Grow on Trees* (New York, 1973) pp. 116–142.

Niskanen, William A., *Bureaucracy and Representative Government* (Chicago, 1971).

————, "Bureaucrats and Politicians," XVIII *Journal of Law and Economics* (December 1975) pp. 617–644.

————, "Deficits, Government Spending and Inflation: What Is the Evidence?" 4 *Journal of Monetary Economics* (August 1978) pp. 591–602.

————, *Structural Reform of the Federal Budget Process* (Washington, D.C., 1973).

Nourse, Edwin G., *Economics in the Public Service: Administrative Aspects of the Employment Act* (New York, 1953).

Novick, David, *Origin and History of Program Budgeting* (Santa Monica, Calif., October 1966).

————, editor, *Program Budgeting* (Cambridge, Mass., 1965) p. vi.

Oates, Wallace E., "The Changing Structure of Intergovernmental Fiscal Relations," in Horst Claus Recktenwald, editor, *Tendances à Long Terme du Secteur Public* (Paris, 1976).

————, editor, *The Political Economy of Fiscal Federalism* (Lexington, Mass., 1977).

Organisation for Economic Co-Operation and Development, Studies in Resource Allocation: "Public Expenditure on Education" (1976); "Public Expenditure on Health" (1977); "Public Expenditure on Income Maintenance Programs" (1976); "Public Expenditure Trends" (1978) (Paris: OECD).

————, *The Welfare State in Crisis* (Paris, 1981).

Panetta, Leon E., "Reconciliation: A Congressional Tool for Spending Restraint," in Alvin Rabushka and William Craig Stubblebine, editors, *Constraining Federal Taxing and Spending* (Stanford, Calif., 1982).

Paulson, Robert I., "Poverty, Uncertainty, and Goal Dissensus: The Causes of Underspending in the Model Cities Program" (Paper submitted to Aaron Wildavsky's seminar, "Budgets as Political Instruments." Political Science Department, University of California, Berkeley, Spring 1973).

Peacock, Alan T., and Jack Wiseman, "Approaches to the Analysis of Government Expenditure Growth," 7 *Public Finance Quarterly* (January 1979) pp. 3–23.

————, and Jack Wiseman, *The Growth of Public Expenditures in the United Kingdom* (Princeton, 1961).

Pechman, Joseph A., editor, *Setting National Priorities: The 1983 Budget* (Washington, D.C., 1982).

————, editor, *Setting National Priorities: The 1982 Budget* (Washington, D.C., 1981).

————, editor, *Setting National Priorities: The 1981 Budget* (Washington, D.C., 1980).

————, editor, *Setting National Priorities: The 1980 Budget* (Washington, D.C., 1979).

————, editor, *Setting National Priorities: The 1979 Budget* (Washington, D.C., 1978).

————, editor, *The 1978 Budget: Setting National Priorities* (Washington, D.C., 1977).

Penner, Rudolph G., "Forecasting Budget Totals: Why Can't We Get It Right?" in Michael J. Boskin and Aaron Wildavsky, editors, *The Federal Budget: Economics and Politics* (San Francisco, Calif., 1982) pp. 89–110.

Pfiffner, James P., *The President, the Budget, and Congress:*

Impoundment and the 1974 Budget Act (Boulder, Colo., 1979).

Phillips, John, "The Hadacol of the Budget Makers," IV *National Tax Journal* (September 1951) pp. 255–268.

Pierce, Lawrence, *The Politics of Fiscal Policy Formation* (Englewood Cliffs, N.J., 1971).

Polsby, Nelson W., *Congress and the Presidency*, 3d ed. (Englewood Cliffs, N.J., 1976).

Pondy, Louis R., "A Mathematical Model of Budgeting" (Mimeo., Carnegie Institute of Technology, January 24, 1962).

Pressman, Jeffrey, and Aaron Wildavsky, *Implementation*, 2d ed. (Berkeley and Los Angeles, 1979; 3d ed. forthcoming 1983).

Prest, A. R., and R. Turvey, "Cost-Benefit Analysis: A Survey," LXXV *The Economic Journal* (December 1965) pp. 683–735.

Pyhrr, Peter A., *Zero-Base Budgeting: A Practical Management Tool for Evaluating Expenses* (New York, 1973).

Rabushka, Alvin, "Fiscal Responsibility: Will Anything Less Than a Constitutional Amendment Do?" in Michael J. Boskin and Aaron Wildavsky, editors, *The Federal Budget: Economics and Politics* (San Francisco, Calif., 1982) pp. 333–354.

———, and Pauline Ryan, *The Tax Revolt* (Stanford, Calif., 1982).

———, and William Craig Stubblebine, editors, *Constraining Federal Taxing and Spending* (Stanford, Calif., 1982).

Raskin, Marcus G., et al., editors, *The Federal Budget and Social Reconstruction: The People and the States* (New Brunswick, N.J., 1978).

Rawson, Robert H., "The Formulation of the Federal Budget," I *Public Policy* (Cambridge, Mass., 1941), C. J. Friedrich and E. S. Mason, editors, pp. 78–135.

Recktenwald, Horst Claus, editor, *Tendances à Long Terme du Secteur Public/Secular Trends of the Public Sector* (Paris, 1976).

Riggs, Fred, "Prismatic Society and Financial Administration," V *Administrative Science Quarterly* (June 1960) pp. 1–46.

Rose, Richard, and Edward Page, "Chronic Instability in Fiscal Systems," Studies in Public Policy, No. 104, Centre for the Study of Public Policy, University of Strathclyde (Glasgow, Scotland, 1982).

———, and B. Guy Peters, *Can Government Go Bankrupt?* (New York, 1978).

———, and B. Guy Peters, "The Juggernaut of Incrementalism," Studies in Public Policy, No. 24, Centre for the Study of Public Policy, University of Strathclyde (Glasgow, Scotland, 1978).

Sayre, Wallace S. and Herbert Kaufman, *Governing New York City* (New York, 1960).

Schelling, T. C., *The Strategy of Conflict* (Cambridge, Mass., 1960).

Schick, Allen, *Budget Innovation in the States* (Washington, D.C., 1971).

———, "Budgetary Adaptations to Resource Scarcity," in C. H. Levine and I. Rubin, editors, *Fiscal Stress and Public Policy* (Beverly Hills and London, 1980) pp. 113–134.

———, *Congress and Money: Budgeting, Spending and Taxing* (Washington, D.C., 1980).

———, "Controlling the Budget by Statute: An Imperfect but Workable Process," in Alvin Rabushka and William Craig Stubblebine, editors, *Constraining Federal Taxing and Spending* (Stanford, Calif., 1982).

———, How the Budget Was Won and Lost," in Norman J. Ornstein, editor, *President and Congress: Assessing Reagan's First Year* (Washington, D.C., 1981).

———, "Off-Budget Expenditure: An Economic and Political Framework," Paper prepared for the OECD, Technical Co-operation Service, Co-Operative Action Programme, Joint Activity on Public Management Improvement (August 1981).

———, "The Budget Bureau That Was: Thoughts on the Rise, Decline, and Future of a Presidential Agency," XXXV *Law and Contemporary Problems* (Summer 1970), pp. 519–539.

———, "The Road to PPB: The Stages of Budget Reform,"

XXVI *Public Administration Review* (December 1966) pp. 243–258.

———, "The Three-Ring Budget Process: The Appropriations, Tax, and Budget Committees in Congress," in Thomas E. Mann and Norman J. Ornstein, editors, *The New Congress* (Washington and London, 1981).

Schiff, Ashley L., *Fire and Water: Scientific Heresy in the Forest Service* (Cambridge, Mass., 1962).

Schilling, Warner R., Paul V. Hammond, and Glenn H. Snyder, *Strategy, Politics and Defense Budgets* (New York, 1962).

Schultze, Charles L., *The Politics and Economics of Public Spending* (Washington, D.C., 1968).

———, Edward L. Fried, Alice M. Rivlin, and Nancy H. Teeters, *Setting National Priorities: The 1973 Budget* (Washington, D.C., 1972), p. 11.

———, *Setting National Priorities: The 1974 Budget* (Washington, D.C., 1973), p. 8.

Schumpeter, Joseph A., "The Crises of the Tax State," *International Economic Papers*, No. 4 (Macmillan, 1954), pp. 5–38.

Seligman, Lester, "Presidential Leadership: The Inner Circle and Institutionalization," XVIII *Journal of Politics* (August 1956), pp. 410–426.

Sharkansky, Ira, *The Politics of Taxing and Spending* (Indianapolis, Ind., 1969).

Shepsle, Kenneth A., "The Failure of Congressional Budgeting," Center for the Study of American Business, Washington University, Publication No. 46 (March 1982).

Shipp, G. W., "Program Budgeting in the Defense Department: A Small Change." (Unpublished paper, Political Science Department, University of California, Berkeley, 1966).

Simon, Herbert A., *Administrative Behavior*, 2d ed. (New York, 1957).

———, *Models of Man* (New York, 1957).

———, Donald Smithburg, and Victor Thompson, *Public Administration* (New York, 1950).

Sinclair, Barbara, "Coping with Uncertainty: Building Coalitions in the House and the Senate," in Thomas E. Mann and Norman J. Ornstein, editors, *The New Congress* (Washington, D.C., 1981) pp. 178–220.

Smithies, Arthur, *The Budgetary Process in the United States* (New York, 1955).

Staats, Elmer B., "Evaluating Program Effectiveness" in *Selected Papers on Public Administration*, D. L. Bowen and L. K. Caldwell, editors, Institute of Training for Public Service, Department of Government, Indiana University (Bloomington, Ind., 1960).

Stein, Herbert, "The Decline of the Budget-Balancing Doctrine, or: How the Good Guys Finally Lost," in James M. Buchanan and Richard E. Wagner, editors, *Fiscal Responsibility in Constitutional Democracy* (Leiden and Boston, 1978).

Stourm, René, *The Budget*, translated by Thaddeus Plazinski (New York, 1917).

Straussman, Jeffrey D., "Spending More and Enjoying It Less," *Comparative Politics* (January 1981) pp. 235–251.

Sundelson, Jacob Wilner, *Budgetary Methods in National and State Governments* (Albany, N.Y., 1938).

Symposium on Budget Theory, X *Public Administration Review* (Winter 1950) pp. 20–31.

Symposium, "Performance Budgeting: Has the Theory Worked?" XX *Public Administration Review* (Spring 1960) pp. 63–85.

Tarschys, Daniel, "The Growth of Public Expenditures: Nine Modes of Explanation," 10 *Scandinavian Political Studies* (1975) pp. 9–31.

————, "Curbing Public Expenditures: A Survey of Current Trends," Paper prepared for the Joint Activity on Public Management Improvement of the OECD (Technical Co-operation Service) April 1982.

Tufte, Edward R., *Political Control of the Economy* (Princeton, N.J., 1978).

Van Gunsteren, Herman R., *The Quest for Control* (New York, 1976).

Waldo, Dwight, *The Administrative State* (New York, 1948).

Walker, Robert, "William A. Jump: The Staff Officer As a Personality," XIV *Public Administrative Review* (Autumn 1954) pp. 233–246.

Wallace, Robert Ash, "Congressional Control of the Budget," III *Midwest Journal of Political Science* (May 1959) pp. 151–167.

Webber, Carolyn, and Aaron Wildavsky, *A History of Taxation and Expenditure in the Western World* (Typescript, 1983).

Weisbrod, Burton A., *The Economics of Public Health: Measuring the Economic Impact of Diseases* (Philadelphia, 1961).

Wildavsky, Aaron, "The Annual Expenditure Increment," XXXIII *The Public Interest* (Fall 1973) pp. 84–108.

———, *Budgeting* (Boston, 1975).

———, "A Budget For All Seasons? Why the Traditional Budget Lasts," 6 *Public Administration Review* (November/December 1978) pp. 501–509.

———, "Budgets as Compromises Among Social Orders," in Michael J. Boskin and Aaron Wildavsky, editors, *The Federal Budget: Economics and Politics* (San Francisco, 1982) pp. 21–38.

———, *Dixon-Yates: A Study in Power Politics* (New Haven, 1962).

———, *How To Limit Government Spending* (Los Angeles and Berkeley, 1980).

———, "The Party of Government, the Party of Opposition, and the Party of Balance: An American View of the Consequences of the 1980 Election," in Austin Ranney, editor, *The American Elections of 1980* (Washington, D.C., 1981) pp. 329–350.

———, "The Political Economy of Efficiency: Cost-Benefit Analysis, Systems Analysis, and Program Budgeting," XXVI *Public Administration Review* (December 1966) pp. 292–310.

———, "Political Implications of Budgetary Reform," XXI *Public Administration Review* (Autumn, 1961) pp. 183–190.

———, "Rescuing Policy Analysis from PPBS," XXIX *Public Administration Review* (March/April 1969) pp. 189–202.

———, Review of Allen Schick, *Congress and Money: Budget-*

ing, Spending and Taxing, in 19 *Society* (January/February 1982) pp. 86–89.

———, "The Self-Evaluating Organization," XXXII *Public Administration Review* (September/October 1972) pp. 509–520.

———, "The Three-Party System — 1980 and After," *The Public Interest,* No. 64 (Summer 1981) pp. 47–57.

———, "TVA and Power Politics," LV *The American Political Science Review* (September 1961) pp. 576–590.

———, and Arthur Hammond, "Comprehensive Versus Incremental Budgeting in the Department of Agriculture," X *Administrative Science Quarterly* (December 1965) pp. 321–346.

Wilensky, Harold, "Leftism, Catholicism, and Democratic Corporatism," in Peter Flora and Arnold J. Heidenheimer, editors, *The Development of the Welfare State in Europe and America* (New Brunswick, N.J., 1981) pp. 345–382.

Willoughby, William Franklin, "The Budget," *Encyclopedia of the Social Sciences,* Vol. III (New York, 1930), pp. 38–44.

———, *The Movement for Budgetary Reform in the States* (New York, 1918).

———, *The National Budget System* (Baltimore, 1927).

———, *The Problem of a National Budget* (New York, 1918).

Wilmerding, Lucius, Jr., *The Spending Power* (New Haven, 1943).

Wyden, Peter, "The Man Who Frightens Bureaucrats," *Saturday Evening Post* (January 31, 1959) pp. 27, 87–89.

INDEX